PUBLIC RELATIONS RESEARCH

PUBLIC

RELATIONS

RESEARCH

E. W. Brody and
Gerald C. Stone

New York
Westport, Connecticut
London

Library of Congress Cataloging-in-Publication Data

Brody, E. W.
    Public relations research / by E. W. Brody and Gerald C. Stone.
        p.   cm.
    Bibliography: p.
    Includes index.
    ISBN 0-275-92870-5 (alk. paper)
    ISBN 0-275-92871-3 (pbk. : alk. paper)
    1. Public relations—Research.   I. Stone, Gerald (Gerald C.)
II. Title.
    HM263.B673   1989
    659.2—dc19   88-29270

Library of Congress Catalog Card Number: 88-29270
ISBN: 0-275-92870-5
        0-275-92871-3 (pbk.)

First published in 1989

Praeger Publishers, One Madison Avenue, New York, NY 10010
A division of Greenwood Press, Inc.

Printed in the United States of America

The paper used in this book complies with the
Permanent Paper Standard issued by the National
Information Standards Organization (Z39.48–1984).

10   9   8   7   6   5   4   3   2   1

For
Sandy Brody
and
Donna Stone

Contents

PART TWO: FORMAL RESEARCH METHODS

1   Research Redefined

The word *research* once was simply defined as diligent and systematic inquiry or investigation into a subject to discover or revise facts, theories, applications, and so on. The definition originated in the physical sciences but soon was applied generically to virtually any subject. It may remain applicable today in the physical sciences and the academic world, but has progressively become subject to question in the social sciences, which include public relations.

Research techniques used in the social sciences differ significantly from those applied in the physical world. The latter are conducted under controlled conditions, usually in laboratories, where chemists, physicists, and biologists are able to isolate their experiments from external influences. Temperature, humidity, atmosphere, and a host of other factors that may influence results can be precisely controlled. Even the influence of gravity has been eliminated in experiments conducted aboard space shuttles.

Public relations practitioners and other social scientists function in very different settings. They study human behavior and their subjects are exposed to changing environmental conditions. Neither researchers nor their subjects can be isolated from the stimuli that influence human behavior. Individuals might conceivably be isolated for days or weeks but the rigorous laboratory requirements of the physical sciences would still go unmet. Those involved would remain influenced by their original, diverse environments. In addition, their post-test behaviors would be influenced by the environments to which they must return.

Since environmental factors cannot be excluded in public relations research, the process requires a different approach than the one applied in the social sciences. Rather than attempting to exclude environmental variables, practitioners must integrate them into the research process. The task is difficult but not impossible. It requires identifying and understanding the function of diverse environmental influences within the context of specific public relations problems.

As numbers of multiple-income households increase, for example, needs of their members will change as well. Care for the elderly and the very young will become a major concern. Stress and anxiety will tend to increase in occupational as well as residential settings. Thus employers might experience reduced pressure for greater compensation. Concurrently, however, they should expect greater absenteeism and tardiness problems.

As research in public relations must necessarily involve greater breadth and depth than in the physical sciences, practitioners must develop and maintain substantial bodies of knowledge concerning the environments with which they deal.

THE SOCIAL ENVIRONMENT

Environmental factors are major variables in social research. They have become increasingly significant in recent years as a result of accelerating social change. Consider, for example, such readily measurable data as household income levels in the United States. Statistics indicating relatively little short-term change in this sector are readily available from the Bureau of the Census and other sources. Taken in a vacuum, they are highly misleading. Although the data show household incomes have remained relatively stable in recent years, they do not indicate that a household income increasingly consists of several individual incomes.

Nor do the household income data reveal that the number of women employed in the United States increased at an unprecedented rate during the 1970s and 1980s, primarily because of two factors. One was the dissolution of legal and social barriers. Equal employment opportunity has enabled women to enter increasing numbers of professions and occupations from which they had previously been barred. The second factor was economic. The purchasing power of wage earners' dollars was declining in relative and absolute terms. Numbers of rich and poor were increasing while the middle class by almost any definition was shrinking. Women were entering the work force as much out of economic need as to capitalize on newly created opportunities.

Misleading Data

Data indicating relative stability in household income during this period thus tend to conceal substantial socioeconomic change. The nature and extent of the change are significant in several contexts. Wage earners' efforts to preserve household purchasing power were changing the environments in which their children were being reared. The consequences of these changes in part remain to be seen because long-term differences in human behavioral patterns resulting from environmental change develop over extended periods. Other changes, however, were immediately noticeable.

Organizations employing large numbers of females found absenteeism and tardiness rates increasing. Their operating costs increased as the federal government and several states required them to grant parental leave to men as well as women for adoption as well as birth.

Personal service industries ranging from restaurants to house cleaning services grew in size and number as multiple-wage earner households increased. The problems of "latch key children" induced development of "crisis" telephone services dedicated to their needs. Families became less stable and alternative lifestyles became more accepted in the United States. By the late 1980s, the "typical" household consisting of male wage earner, housewife, and children no longer was predominant.

Origins of Change

These changes and others were not exclusively a product of the decline of the middle class. Each was and is influenced by other factors. Their collective significance in public relations and other social sciences is a function of their complexity and interrelationships. They are so interwoven that they defy the sort of laboratory analysis that has traditionally characterized research. More important, they are generated by accelerating social change whose magnitude demands redefinition of the word.

Contemporary social scientists are faced with very different conditions than their colleagues in the physical sciences. Bodies of knowledge necessary for research in the physical sciences, which changed more rapidly in earlier decades, are now relatively stable. Academic journals and meetings are adequate for the interchange of information necessary to enable researchers to stay abreast of the "state of the art."

Conditions in the social sciences are far different. The ebb and flow of human activity are more rapid than ever and continue to accelerate. Consider, for example, the faster pace at which technical innovation is assimilated by society. Television required several decades to come to maturity in the United States. The videocassette recorder required only a few years. Now laser discs, still in their adolescence, are apparently being overtaken by new digital technology.

Social change has been more dramatic although less obvious. In little more than two decades from the onset of the Vietnam conflict, attitudes toward government and institutions have shifted from general trust to pervasive suspicion. The nation's two-party political system has been replaced by a veritable army of special interest groups. Consensus politics have deteriorated into legislative gridlock. The nuclear family has disintegrated, and traditional concepts of ethics and morality have deteriorated at an unprecedented pace.

Economic change has been an equal contributor to social dislocation. Growing interdependency among political subdivisions has primarily been responsible.

Relatively high levels of independence among cities and states has declined precipitously with the onset of the industrial age. The same phenomenon has subsequently occurred continentally, hemispherically, and, most recently, internationally.

The information explosion and the advent of instantaneous worldwide communication has led to an unprecedented level of dynamic complexity that remains to be mastered by governments, institutions, and commercial organizations. Their efforts to cope with fast-changing environments have compounded social and economic stress.

Problems Compounded

The combined impact of these changes has rendered traditional research in the social sciences increasingly difficult. Only recently, for example, has the impact of television on society been fully elaborated in the work of Joshua Myerowitz and others.

History doubtless will one day reflect at least equal social change in the wake of the computer revolution. Public relations practitioners and other social scientists in the interim must deal daily with ill-defined but nevertheless difficult transient circumstances.

Transitions from the industrial to the post-industrial age, from a youth-oriented to a senior-oriented society, and from a manufacturing to a service economy are but a few of the major trends that impact every organization and demand practitioner attention. Accelerating rates of change often render analyses of these trends through traditional research methods little more than exercises in futility.

Contemporary conditions thus demand broadening the scope of "research" to encompass a broader spectrum of activities vital to the successful practice of public relations. These activities include development and maintenance of bodies of knowledge in (1) educational disciplines prerequisite to public relations practice, (2) the practice of public relations, (3) national and international social and economic developments and trends, and (4) organizational environments. Only when these are in place can formal research programs essential to the public relations process be successfully performed.

A BROADER APPROACH

The prerequisites to success in formal public relations research are neither quickly nor easily obtained. They require candidates for the profession to enter into what has been called "lifelong learning." The process replaces episodic acquisition of knowledge and skill with on-going acquisition and synthesis of information from the several environments with which practitioners are necessarily involved. It encompasses many of the traditional steps in the formal education process but requires considerably more. The process may be formal, informal, or a combination of the two techniques.

Beginning Points

Prospective practitioners first must acquire and thereafter maintain state-of-the-art knowledge and skill in the social sciences, logical thinking, and use of the English language. Together with history, these are the primary components of lower division course work in undergraduate college and university curricula.

The term "social sciences" is not amenable to precise definition, and interpretations vary from one college or university to another. Virtually all embrace the three disciplines necessary in public relations: economics, psychology, and sociology. Anthropology, world history, and political science are helpful as well.

Logical thinking is normally engendered through courses in mathematics and philosophy, the latter including studies in logic as well as major philosophical questions. English encompasses literature as well as writing.

Public Relations

English courses engender the fundamental writing skills necessary in learning first journalistic and then public relations writing in the upper division of undergraduate curricula. Public relations courses also include surveys of the profession, strategies or case problems, and research methods.

These should be supplemented by studies in management, marketing, and theories of persuasion before the candidate is prepared for entry level employment. The course work should also launch students into what has come to be called "environmental assessment," an on-going process through which individuals and organizations scan and monitor events and trends in the world around them.

Maintaining Knowledge Levels

Environmental assessment is critical in maintaining knowledge and skill levels that students acquire in their initial studies. The process requires that they identify and track social and economic trends that may influence the organizations with which they are professionally involved.

Identification and tracking are accomplished by monitoring developments in society, public relations, and the commercial, industrial, or institutional sectors in which clients or employers are involved. By acquiring and synthesizing information, practitioners are able to anticipate events, define alternative organizational responses, and provide appropriate counsel to management.

Formal Research

Only when armed with these prerequisites are practitioners adequately equipped to undertake the several formal and informal research tasks intrinsic to public relations practice. These involve monitoring attitude and opinion among organizational constituencies in several contexts.

Knowledge of constituent attitude and opinion is essential in planning public relations programs and in selecting the "right" public relations activities. It also is necessary in determining if public relations programs are achieving their objectives.

The public relations process is essentially cyclical in nature. It begins with research to provide precise information concerning existing conditions. Resultant information is first used in the programming process. Baseline data produced are subsequently used in measuring results achieved.

INFORMAL RESEARCH PROCESSES

The word "informal" is something of a misnomer as applied in public relations research. "Formal" research includes all the processes that employ statistical methods.

Virtually all other forms of research can be labeled "informal." They include activities ranging from systematic media scanning to focus group interviews. Between these extremes are several monitoring or research techniques applied in public relations to insure maintenance of practitioner knowledge levels in diverse subject areas.

Maintaining Knowledge

In today's world nothing is changing as rapidly as man's knowledge and skills. The rate of change in recent years has accelerated to a point where academics have estimated that the half-life of knowledge is as short as five years. "Half-life" is a term taken from nuclear physics to describe the time in which levels of radiation decline by 50 percent.

Applied to post-secondary education, a five-year half-life implies that the bulk of the knowledge and skill gained by students in completion of a baccalaureate degree will be rendered obsolete in less than a decade. The concept is applicable to public relations and every other subject. Practitioner success is highly dependent on individual willingness and ability to maintain knowledge and skill levels through an on-going renewal process.

Educational Renewal

Renewal efforts are concentrated in three primary areas: public relations, the society in which practitioners function, and the commercial/industrial/institutional sectors of which existing and prospective clients and employers are a part. Each is renewed through one or more of several techniques: graduate education, other formal education, and individually designed, self-study courses.

Most successful individual renewal plans or programs are based on understanding systems and communication theory. Systems theory postulates that individuals and organizations are interactive entities—that they influence and are influenced by their environments, and that their behaviors can be best understood in this context. Communication theory deals with individuals as they function within self-constructed sets of perceptions that constitute their realities. These perceptions can be modified by messages originating in individual environments, but the process is beset with uncertainties.

Two Responses

For these reasons educational renewal requires two responses from public relations practitioners. First, they must be conversant with flows of contemporary events that may influence public relations practice or the organizations and individuals with which public relations deals. Second, they must be sufficiently knowledgeable in systems theory to ascertain the potential impact of those events.

These circumstances require practitioners to establish personal environmental assessment programs paralleling those employed in strategic planning. Successful organizations continuously scan the environments with which they are involved to identify events that may signal the onset of trends. Practitioners can readily emulate these efforts.

Individual environmental assessment requires identifying and monitoring sets of information sources—professional and business publications, newspapers, and selected television programs, especially the educational television networks' offerings. Significant events identified through this process are then monitored over time to engender sufficient levels of insight to permit accurate assessment of potential organizational impact.

Monitoring Organizations

Similar informal research techniques also can be used in public relations to monitor conditions within and surrounding organizations. The process is similar to individual educational renewal but deals instead with organizational environments.

As individuals, practitioners monitor events and trends in their professions and in professional environments. As members of organizations, they monitor internal and external organizational environments the same way.

Process Differences

The processes differ only in the sets of information sources involved. They both usually include a set of media, but organizational data, such as sales figures, numbers of service calls, and volume of disputed accounts, also provide information concerning the relative health of relationships with external groups.

Internal environmental scanning similarly requires monitoring diverse sets of variables that may directly or indirectly indicate the onset of organizational problems. Employee morale, for example, is an intangible that defies direct measurement but can be monitored indirectly. Worker attendance records and numbers of employee appeals of managerial decisions, for example, are valid indicators of the relative health of labor relationships. Quality control data in manufacturing and customer complaint trends in service industries also provide insight.

Environmental Differences

External environmental scanning is more complex but involves similar techniques. Complexity arises from the varying nature of organizations and their stakeholder groups. Publicly owned corporations concerned with shareholder relationships, for example, often monitor numbers and sizes of stock transfers. Correspondence from shareholders may be subject to close scrutiny. Volume of securities held by mutual funds and pension trusts and the changing recommendations of analysts also may be tracked.

In governmental or quasi-governmental organizations dependent on public funding, attention is focused on the public utterances of elected and appointed officials, the editorial comments of major news media, and the activities of any pertinent regulatory bodies. Attitude and opinion among these groups are as important to the economic health of the organization as market conditions are to the publicly owned corporation.

Secondary Analysis

All of these activities can be categorized as informal research. The term *secondary analysis* is also applicable. Secondary analysis most commonly refers to reexamining the findings of earlier formal research to identify trends or other insights. Secondary analysis in informal research involves using preexisting data compiled principally for other organizational purposes to illuminate the condition of relationships between organizations and stakeholder groups.

Primary informal research involves another dimension. Where preexisting data are inadequate to engender understanding of stakeholder dynamics, informal research techniques may be applied to produce further findings. They often approach the border between formal and informal but usually fail to meet the critical random sampling test described later.

Informal Research

Techniques used in informal research often are little more than scientific extensions of the monitoring processes discussed earlier. Rather than merely counting numbers of customers' complaints, for example, the researcher may sort them by type or cause. Written complaints might be further subjected to content analysis. The latter is a valid formal research technique when applied, for example, to randomly selected newspapers or magazines. Reports from business and professional publications may be similarly analyzed.

Analyses of existing data can be extended to virtually any area of organizational operation. Some techniques may not be recognized as research although they meet many research criteria. Most organizations, for example, closely monitor sales and profit levels. Manufacturing defect rates, customer complaint rates, absenteeism and tardiness rates, and similar indicators of organizational health are frequently monitored as well. They produce trend data that often can be used to project future performance. The product of such processes more often is referred to as "management information" than as "research data."

More complex approaches to informal research often use advisory boards or panels and focus group interviews. When these techniques are used, practitioners go beyond analysis of preexisting information to develop new data. They are most often sought in industries where sales are a function of appearance rather than utility and where changing customer tastes can quickly influence organizations' economic results.

Advisory boards or panels, consisting of individuals deliberately selected for their experience or knowledge, are convened periodically to provide information to management. Focus groups are also constituted through deliberate selection but usually convene only once to address one or more specific issues of contemporary significance.

Advisory boards and focus groups differ from samples drawn in classical social science research in two ways. First, their members are selected by design based on their presumed knowledge or experience. Second, they are almost always relatively small in size, often constituting a minute fraction of one percent of populations from which they are drawn.

Researchers cross a somewhat hazy line from informal to formal research with more sophisticated analytical processes or by applying random selection techniques to develop larger samples. Consider, for example, sales forecasting based on prior sales records. Where there is no reason to expect significant change in external circumstances, past records probably are the best available indicator of future performance. The process is called *regression analysis*. When such forecasting is done with a least-squares regression procedure (beyond the scope of this text) if falls in the realm of formal research. The process can be more readily accomplished with simple calculations, however, and these often are sufficient to answer the research question involved.

FORMAL RESEARCH

As many public relations questions cannot be answered through informal research, formal strategies become necessary. Knowing when to use the formal rather than the informal is the practitioner's responsibility.

A simple rule usually determines which course to take: *always use informal research if possible*. The logic in the rule will be demonstrated in subsequent chapters, but some key points are worthy of note here.

1. Formal research usually is relatively expensive. Procedures may cost $10,000 to $100,000 and most organizations hesitate before making such financial commitments.

2. Many procedures require considerable time in planning, execution, data analysis, and report preparation. Public relations problems often require faster response time than formal research permits.

3. Formal research involves an element of practitioner risk. Because cost and time factors are extensive, senior managers may expect magical cures for organizational problems. Even when it succeeds, formal research seldom produces such results. Management must be advised accordingly. Failure to do so can result in management disappointment and subsequent damage to practitioner careers.

4. Commercial research firms must often be hired. Few practitioners are adequately experienced in formal research to cope readily with its complexities.

5. Finally, formal research can go awry. The most experienced researchers make mistakes. Studies can be flawed by elementary but undetected oversights. Even carefully planned research schemes can produce data that fly in the face of experience or common sense. Minor quirks of research design or awkward question wording can produce such flawed results. All formal research contains "error" which compounds with design weaknesses. The complexity of formal research continually proves Murphy's Law: If it can go wrong, it will.

Why would practitioners suggest formal research to clients or employers in the face of such risks? Formal research in many instances is the best—or only—way to obtain data necessary to solve public relations problems. Informal research should be used where possible. The formal must be used where the informal process is inadequate.

The rule bears repeating. When needed information can be obtained through informal research, informal procedures are preferable. Otherwise, formal research is appropriate. Well-planned and well-designed formal procedures should not be considered threatening. This text is intended to equip practitioners with adequate knowledge to plan and oversee formal and informal research.

Formal Research Trends

Public relations practitioners annually find hundreds of situations that call for formal research. The number of such circumstances has been increasing steadily. This trend is comparable to the trends that have accompanied the introduction of new technologies.

A decade age virtually every public relations practitioner used a typewriter. It was a necessary and expected tool of the trade. Today almost every practitioner uses a computer for word processing. It is more efficient for individual work and offers multiple advantages including the ability to transmit copy (news releases or reports) over telephone lines to distant points.

Impact of Computers

The computer has changed the way we think, and one of its most dramatic perceptual impacts affects the way we think about research. Today sophisticated programs that run on low-cost home computers can be acquired for less than

$100. The new technology makes it possible for individuals to perform research analyses which only five years ago required mainframe computers priced at $1 million or more and programs costing more than $5,000.

What does this mean in public relations practice? More people today know about formal research analysis, and it has become the accepted way of doing things. Ten years ago it was novel, mysterious, even exotic. Today it is commonplace, relatively well understood, and expected. Business managers, agency executives, and others who turn to public relations practitioners for advice are familiar with formal research. They often find it peculiar, in fact, if formal research tactics are not proposed where appropriate.

Enhanced Sophistication

The adoption of new technology has produced more sophistication in public relations practice as well. Research is half of the public relations acronym R.A.C.E.—*Research, Action, Communication,* and *Evaluation.* It is the beginning and end of the public relations process.

Nevertheless many professionals have not kept pace with the advances that have brought formal research to the forefront. Judges in public relations contests have historically criticized the absence of preliminary and evaluative research. This pattern is quite evident in the annual Silver Anvil Awards competition of the Public Relations Society of America (PRSA) and similar events sponsored by PRSA subunits and other organizations. Entries with outstanding action plans and communication efforts are often devoid of research and evaluation. Even today, some sophisticated public relations programs are ''seat-of-the-pants'' responses to assumed needs. Formal research remains to be adopted at all levels of professional practice.

Those whose practices do not include research are doomed to the fate of dinosaurs because they are operating in an aggressive, rapidly changing environment with yesterday's tools. Their time of effective practice is accordingly limited. Those who hope to succeed must understand and appreciate the principles of research.

Practitioner Responsibilities

Public relations practitioners must know enough about formal research to recognize when it should be used. This text will provide techniques, examples, terminology, and suggestions applicable to public relations problems that can be solved through formal research. Specific examples will necessarily not apply to every public relations need, but the ideas, procedures, terminology, and strategies they illustrate will be useful in almost every public relations situation.

Knowledge Essential

Practitioners must also know enough about formal research to be able to oversee research efforts. Many, if not most, studies are undertaken by consulting research professionals. Such consultants exist in virtually every locale and offer benefits worthy of practitioner attention. They specialize in research and conduct studies on a continuing basis. They have well-tested sampling plans. They have trained interviewers on staff as well as project directors who can suggest proven research strategies. They own or have access to sophisticated computers for analytical purposes, and they are experienced in writing research reports. A great deal of valuable support is thus available to practitioners. Costs are relatively high but a full range of research services is usually available and risk is significantly reduced.

Some research firms, on the other hand, offer little more than advisory services. They do not perform research on a full-time basis and often offer only a few of the above mentioned advantages. They may be less expensive but may not be able to meet all research needs.

Consultant Selection

Selecting the wrong firm can produce additional expense with few benefits. Knowing which commercial research organization to use thus becomes another practitioner responsibility. Practitioners must make it their business to learn the capabilities of local firms and be able to make selections accordingly. The task is not an easy one. The field changes rapidly and today's reliable provider may not be available next year.

The practitioner's most important responsibility, and one of the primary reasons for this text, is to understand enough about formal research methods to recommend and oversee research efforts. Formal research in most cases will not be done entirely in-house. Even experienced public relations researchers often prefer to acquire outside expertise, survey interviewer assistance, or help with data analysis.

The Buck Stops Here

Practitioners are responsible for directing research, however, regardless of the extent of outside contracting. No outside firm can know as much about the organization's current situation and research objectives so practitioners must work hand-in-hand with outside providers. They advise on needs, approve research strategies, maintain communication as projects progress, and assist in analyzing results and reporting them to management. To do less is to abrogate responsibility and court problems that may interfere with successful project completion. Outside providers may be sympathetic when research efforts fail to provide solutions to a public relations problem, but practitioners justifiably carry the bulk of the blame for projects that fail.

As active partners in research efforts, practitioners must have at least a cursory knowledge of formal research terminology and tactics. The language of statistics, sampling methods, error levels, questionnaire design, experimental method, and a host of associated research techniques and jargon are complicated and prone to confusion or abuse. This text will provide guidelines for in-house formal research and for overseeing formal research projects handled under contract through outside firms. Although few practitioners attempt to carry out projects from inception through final report, all must be sufficiently familiar with procedures to evaluate published reports and direct research efforts for clients and organizational managers.

FORMAL RESEARCH STRATEGIES

Most formal research in public relations embraces one of three basic strategies: surveys, experiments, and content analyses. Although essentially different and applicable in solving different problems, the principles involved overlap. Formal research, as subsequent chapters emphasize, requires understanding a few fundamental principles. Many of the remaining procedures are little more than logical extensions of the basic precepts. They can be adjusted when applied to specific public relations problems.

Survey Methodology

The survey is the most prevalent form of formal research used in public relations. This method can provide a rich lode of background and forecasting information. Practitioners who employ survey techniques on a continuing basis can be confident they will always know the interests of stakeholder groups.

Barring unforeseen crises, surveys enable practitioners to keep their fingers on the pulses of constituent groups. Resulting data permit management to keep abreast of the general tenor of feeling among organizational stakeholders.

A Case in Point

A recent example of using research to solve a public relations problem involved the Farm Aid concert in 1985. A record number of farmers went bankrupt between 1982 and 1985, and Farm Aid was an effort to draw national attention to the farmers' problems.

The independent Farm Bureau Federation opposed the message Farm Aid was attempting to get across as it believed Farm Aid sponsors were mistaken about how farmers had gotten into their financial difficulties. The bureau also thought Farm Aid's suggested political solution was incorrect. In all, the bureau sought to counteract Farm Aid's mission every way it could. To assess the impact Farm Aid might have, the bureau invested in a major survey hoping to use survey findings to help it discredit the Farm Aid effort.

One of the survey tactics the bureau used was a public opinion assessment of the Farm Aid concert's main spokesperson: none other than country and western singer Willie Nelson. The bureau hoped to learn if it could convince the American public that Willie Nelson was mistaken about solutions to the farmers' plight. The bureau believed Willie Nelson's association with some very liberal and very outspoken entertainers, several of whom were also to perform at the Farm Aid concert, might be used to discredit his position. Could viewers, especially those in the middle-American farm belt, be persuaded that Nelson's point of view was in error?

Clear Answer

The survey results were in, and the answer was clear: The public considered Willie Nelson the most credible source of information on the plight of farmers. He would be believed and any efforts to counteract his position on the farm problem were doomed to failure. Worse still, if the bureau were linked to an effort to discredit Willie Nelson, it stood to lose considerable good will with its own farm constituency.

The bureau's public relations department had expertly done its job by using survey research. It had determined that battling Willie Nelson on the farm front was equivalent to opposing apple pie and Chevrolet pickups. Some other method had to be used to counteract the views that were likely to be aired during the Farm Aid concert.

The bureau's public relations department recommended a novel solution: The bureau would become a major sponsor of the concert. It worked with the event from the inside and helped organize and promote the concert. The bureau's feelings were, for the most part, consistent with Farm Aid aims as it did favor drawing public attention to the plight of American farmers. At the same time, the bureau made its position clear to the other Farm Aid sponsors: It opposed their political solutions and would be a co-sponsor only if the political message were eliminated from the concert event.

Successful Outcome

The outcome was a public relations success for the bureau. One of the entertainers did give the political message on stage during the live broadcast concert. But this was the only mention the political message received during the entire Farm Aid telethon. Survey research had prevented what might have been a classic public relations disaster for the bureau. The example illustrates only one of the hundreds of diagnostic services survey research performs in public relations every year.

While effective in tracking public and constituent opinion, surveys are only as good as the methodologies researchers apply. They are most successful when the questions produce responses that effectively measure attitude.

The cost and the possible risk of employing formal research can be high, but even higher are the cost and risk of not doing formal research. The farm bureau's experience with Willie Nelson's Farm Aid program is only one example of the possible public relations loss an organization might suffer in ignoring research. Had the bureau tried to publicly discredit this popular entertainer, it might have lost all credibility with its constituency. How effective would the bureau be in the future if midwest farmers remembered it as the group that said Willie Nelson shouldn't be trusted?

Experiments

Social science experiments use different techniques than those applied in the physical sciences because their subjects are human beings. Experiments are used, however, for the same reasons. Practitioners often want to know how stakeholders are reacting to communication strategies.

Advertisers who spend millions of dollars on television commercials rely on experimental research to determine message effectiveness. Will it sell the product or alter opinion in the desired direction? Company policy changes are amenable to testing through similar procedures. The effectiveness of proposed new policies or communication plans can be pretested with selected representatives of target groups rather than being "run up the flag pole to see if anyone salutes." In the same way as commercials are often improved after experiments, public relations practitioners can recommend changes prior to policy enactment or the start of the communication plan. Experiments offer additional fail-safe procedures when they are well planned and flawlessly executed. These are the safety-valve mechanisms that practitioners offer their clients and employers.

Content Analysis

The third formal research tactic often employed is content analysis. It is a systematic method for analyzing change and it is used instead of merely "keeping up with trends" in society generally or in specific fields.

Perhaps the most far-reaching content analysis project in recent years was designed by a Michigan firm in the mid–1970s in response to the Arab oil embargo. The entire news content of several major newspapers was fed into a computer that had been programmed to count stories related to oil prices and availability, auto manufacturing, and public reaction to the gasoline shortage that the embargo produced.

Research Objectives

The researchers had been hired by an auto manufacturers' association in Detroit who wanted to monitor public thinking about car size, mileage rates, and pertinent governmental policies. They hoped the analysis would help them predict when Americans would be ready to return to the larger cars that they traditionally preferred. Because it takes two years to retool auto manufacturing equipment, knowing when to change could mean billions of dollars to the industry.

Although the analysis was launched as a marketing and sales tactic, it was applicable in public relations as well. The domestic auto industry had been a target of public outrage during the gasoline shortage. Manufacturers lost considerable consumer confidence over producing 10-mile-per-gallon gas guzzlers while imported sub-compacts were logging 30 miles per gallon. Many blamed American manufacturers for the gasoline shortage—a peculiarly un-American position for the nation's leading industry.

Cause and Effect

The extent to which loss of confidence contributed to loss of sales is open to question. The manufacturers, anxious to avoid another public relations disaster, invested in sophisticated content analysis procedures to prevent another mistake. The industry could have gained the same insights at less expense by hiring their own experts to read newspapers and discuss trends. That process would have been equally efficient and could have produced the same results. With billions of dollars in good will and car sales at stake, however, the manufacturers elected to invest in formal research. Better results were not guaranteed but the stakes were too high to gamble on educated opinions, even those of their own experts.

The chapter on content analysis will explain how to use formal research procedures to study trends and compare published data systematically and objectively. As with the other formal research strategies, public relations examples will be used to explain the procedures.

Finally, three research strategies called quasi-quantitative approaches will be presented. Focus groups, Delphi studies, and communication audits are among the most frequently used public relations research techniques. An overview of the general purposes of these three information-gathering strategies is offered.

Throughout the formal research section, discussion will focus on research ethics and how to report research results to management. Public relations practitioners are often concerned that clients or chief executive officers will not understand formal research reports. Underestimating management's appreciation of formal research is a serious error. In most cases today, management not only understands research findings but also questions decisions reached without formal research. Modern managers deal with sales projections, new product tests, quality control reports, and a variety of similar forecasts on a daily basis. The public relations professional should be concerned about *how* to present a report effectively, not *whether* one should be made.

SUMMARY

Research in public relations has grown in application and complexity. Changing definitions of social responsibility have forced organizations to deal with increasing numbers of problems originating in their several environments. Increasing costs of public relations programs have concurrently been producing mounting demands for measurable results. Research is necessary to monitor socioeconomic change and to demonstrate public relations accomplishments.

The social environment in the United States has been changing at an accelerating rate. Household incomes, for example, have remained stable as more and more women have entered the work force. As a result, employers have been forced to deal with child care needs, absenteeism, and tardiness problems.

Political and technological changes have been no less pervasive. Armies of special interest groups have created an almost limitless number of issues demanding organizational attention. The information explosion and instantaneous worldwide communication have produced other issues. Collectively these elements have required a broader definition of the term "research" as it applies to public relations.

Research now begins with environmental assessment, an on-going process through which organizations monitor their environments to identify and track trends that may ultimately require response. Practitioners, as a result, require a broader academic base than they needed twenty years ago. They also must expend more time in maintaining that knowledge base in a fast-changing society.

Education and lifelong learning to develop and maintain bodies of knowledge equip practitioners to engage in informal and formal research. The informal include several processes through which organizations and their environments are monitored. Data are gathered from internal and external sources. Worker attendance, production and quality control data, for example, provide insights into organizational health. Advisory boards and panels are among several devices used to track attitude and opinion among stakeholder groups.

When informal research techniques are inadequate to provide precise answers to questions, formal research is used. Formal processes are relatively costly, time consuming, and risky, and may encourage employers or clients to expect magic cures for problems. When cures are not readily forthcoming, practitioner careers may be at risk. Other risks arise out of research process "error" that can produce results of questionable value.

Access to inexpensive computers and increased needs for accurate data nevertheless are encouraging an increasing volume of formal research in two areas. The first measures prevailing conditions in preparation for public relations programming; the second measures program results.

Practitioners in either situation often meet research needs by employing consultant organizations who offer considerable experience as well as access to sophisticated computers, time-tested sampling plans, and the like. Outside consultants require supervision, however, and the ultimate responsibility for research results rests with clients rather than consultants. As a result, practitioners must possess sufficient knowledge to provide necessary supervision.

Most formal research involves surveys, experiments, or content analyses. Surveys, the most common tool of formal research, enable practitioners to keep their fingers on the pulses of constituent groups. Experimental techniques are used primarily in pretesting public relations concepts and campaign components to ascertain constituent group response. Considerable time, effort, and money can be saved through these procedures. Content analyses involve monitoring media content for signs of social change.

ADDITIONAL READING

Baskin, Otis, and Craig Aronoff. *Public Relations: The Profession and the Practice.* 2d ed. Dubuque, IA: Wm. C. Brown, 1988.

Berko, Roy M., Andrew D. Wolvin, and Ray Curtis. *This Business of Communicating.* 3d ed. Dubuque, IA: Wm. C. Brown, 1986.

Brody, E. W. *Public Relations Programming and Production.* New York: Praeger, 1988.

Buchholz, Rogene A., William D. Evans, and Robert A. Wagley. *Management Response to Public Issues: Concepts & Cases in Strategy Formulation.* Englewood Cliffs, NJ: Prentice Hall, 1985.

Canfield, Bertrand R. *Public Relations: Principles, Cases and Problems.* 5th ed. Homewood, IL: Richard D. Irwin, 1968.

Cantor, Bill. *Inside Public Relations: Experts in Action.* New York: Longman, 1984.

Castells, Manuel, ed. *High Technology, Space and Society.* Beverly Hills, CA: Sage, 1985.

Cohen, Paula Marantz. *A Public Relations Primer: Thinking and Writing in Context.* Englewood Cliffs, NJ: Prentice Hall, 1987.

Crable, Richard E., and Steven L. Vibbert. *Public Relations As Communication Management.* Edina, MN: Bellwether Press, 1986.

Cutlip, Scott M., Allen H. Center, and Glen M. Broom. *Effective Public Relations.* 6th ed. Englewood Cliffs, NJ: Prentice Hall, 1985.

Didsbury, Howard F., ed. *Communications and the Future: Prospects, Promises and Problems.* Washington, DC: World Future Society, 1982.

Dilenschneider, Robert L., and Dan J. Forrestal. *The Dartnell Public Relations Handbook.* 3d ed. Chicago: The Dartnell Corporation, 1987.

Dizard, Wilson P., Jr. *The Coming Information Age: An Overview of Technology, Economics and Politics.* 2d ed. New York: Longman, 1985.

Dunn, S. Watson. *Public Relations: A Contemporary Approach.* Homewood, IL: Richard D. Irwin, 1986.

Grunig, James E., and Todd Hunt. *Managing Public Relations.* New York: Holt, Rinehart and Winston, 1984.

Helm, Lewis M., et al., eds. *Informing the People: A Public Affairs Handbook.* New York: Longman, 1981.

Hennessy, Bernard. *Public Opinion.* 5th ed. Monterey, CA: Brooks/Cole, 1985.

Herbert, Walter B., and John R. G. Jenkins, eds. *Public Relations in Canada: Some Perspectives.* Markham, Ontario: Fitzhenry & Whiteside, 1984.

Hiebert, Ray E., ed. *Precision Public Relations.* New York: Longman, 1988.

Hills, J. P. *Trends in Information Transfer.* Westport, CT: Greenwood Press, 1982.

Masuda, Yoneji. *The Information Society as Post-Industrial Society.* Tokyo: Institute for the Information Society, 1980.

Moore, H. Frasier, and Frank B. Kalupa. *Public Relations: Principles, Cases and Problems.* Homewood, IL: Richard D. Irwin, 1985.

Nager, Norman R., and T. Harrell Allen. *Public Relations Management by Objectives.* New York: Longman, 1984.

Nager, Norman R., and Richard H. Truitt. *Strategic Public Relations Counseling: Models from the Counselors Academy.* New York: Longman, 1987.

Newsom, Doug, and Alan Scott. *This is PR: The Realities of Public Relations.* 3d ed. Belmont, CA: Wadsworth, 1985.

Organ, Dennis W., and W. Clay Hamner. *Organizational Behavior.* 2d ed. Plano, TX: Business Publications, Inc., 1985.

Phillips, Charles S. *Secrets of Successful Public Relations.* Englewood Cliffs, NJ: Prentice Hall, 1985.

Reilly, Robert T. *Public Relations in Action*. 2d ed. Englewood Cliffs, NJ: Prentice Hall, 1987.

Robinson, Edward J. *Public Relations and Survey Research*. New York: Appleton-Century-Crofts, 1969.

Rogers, Everett M. *Communication Technology: The New Media in Society*. New York: Free Press, 1986.

Settle, Robert B., and Pamela L. Alreck. *Why They Buy: The American Consumers Inside and Out*. New York: John Wiley, 1986.

Simon, Raymond. *Public Relations: Concepts and Practices*. 3d ed. New York: John Wiley, 1984.

Smith, Judson, and Janice Orr. *Designing and Developing Business Communication Programs That Work*. Glenview, IL: Scott, Foresman, 1985.

Wilcox, Dennis L., Phillip H. Ault, and Warren K. Agee. *Public Relations: Strategies and Tactics*. New York: Harper & Row, 1986.

Williams, Frederick. *Technology and Communication Behavior*. Belmont, CA: Wadsworth, 1987.

Winnett, Richard A. *Information and Behavior: Systems of Influence*. Hillside, NJ: Lawrence Erlbaum Associates, 1986.

Wright, Theon, and Henry S. Evans. *Public Relations and the Line Manager*. New York: American Management Association, 1964.

Part One
Informal Research Methods

2 Foundations of Research

Research is a systematic inquiry or investigation into a subject to discover or revise facts, theories, or applications. The process is designed to create new knowledge. Inevitably, then, it must begin with mastery of existing knowledge.

Fulfilling the latter requirement is no small task. Public relations is an applied social science. It deals with human beings—individually and in groups. The human element precludes use of the traditional methods of scientific inquiry that are used in the physical sciences.

Most physical phenomena can readily be examined in isolation. Environmental influences can be excluded or controlled. With the advent of space travel, physicists, chemists, and biologists can examine their subjects in a vacuum—even beyond the influence of gravity. Laboratory breeding permits them to deal with identical animal subjects as well.

Social scientists enjoy no such luxuries. Studies of human behavior are necessarily undertaken amidst near limitless numbers of subject and environmental variables. They seldom can be controlled but must be known and evaluated to avoid errors in data interpretation. Research in human behavior thus demands command of more diverse bodies of knowledge than research in the physical sciences.

Human behavior essentially is a product of multiple environments, past and present. Individual behavioral predispositions are created through experience. Behavior in any given situation is a product of experience on the one hand and immediate circumstances on the other. Experience and environment are the primary determinants of three factors of primary concern in public relations: human attitude, opinion, and perception.

OBJECTIVES AND OBSTACLES

Most developmental research in public relations practice is designed for one of two purposes. It is primarily undertaken to define attitude and opinion among organizations' stakeholder groups and provide insight into stakeholder perceptions of organizations and issues. Developmental research is also applied in developing programs designed to modify stakeholder attitude, opinion, or behavior. Research studies are also conducted to measure the extent to which objectives have been achieved. These follow-up studies also provide data to adjust on-going public relations programs to enhance future results.

Both types of research are undertaken in dynamic rather than static conditions. Environments are in a constant state of flux. Human experience changes apace. Stakeholder perception, attitude, opinion, and behavior are responsive to these changes as well as to public relations programs. Practitioners thus find it necessary to continuously monitor environmental developments that may influence organizational stakeholders.

Multiple environments are involved in the process that is usually referred to as environmental assessment. Environmental assessment involves two processes. The first is scanning, used by practitioners to identify events that may signal new trends of significance to clients or employers. Isolated shortages of teenage workers during the summer of 1986, for example, signaled the arrival of the "baby-bust generation" into the work force. The second process is monitoring or tracking that enables practitioners to follow developing trends and assess their potential impact on organizations.

Systems Theory

Understanding events and trends requires knowledge of many specialized fields. They can best be understood in terms of systems theory. This concept suggests that organizations are open systems, are composed of subsystems, are part of suprasystems, and are continuously influenced by events taking place in both sectors.

Organizations' suprasystems consist of the natural, technological, human, political, socioeconomic, and market environments in which they function. Change in any of them is apt to require organizational adjustment or adaptation. No organization has escaped, for example, the technological and market changes of recent years. Spurred by computer-based technologies, the United States has been in process of transition from an industrial to a postindustrial society. Many organizational markets have concurrently been changing from national to global in scope.

Subsystems or internal organizational environments exert an equally powerful influence. They include the psychological, social, political, and technological. The technological and psychological have recently been major sources of change. Applied new technologies and organizational "downsizing" have displaced many workers and managers resulting in altered workers' perceptions of organizations. Sense of security and organizational loyalty have deteriorated significantly.

Changes in both the human suprasystem and psychological subsystem suggest significant future problems. Diminishing numbers of workers will necessarily create significant interorganizational competition for their services. Organizational ability to recruit and retain qualified personnel will be undermined, however, by erosion in loyalty and sense of security. Perceptive practitioners already are counseling clients and employers to act now to remedy these problems. The extent to which they succeed will significantly influence future organizational welfare.

Knowledge and Skills

Complex situations such as these are indicative of the extent of knowledge and skill necessary to contemporary public relations practice. These attributes today are developed in postsecondary educational programs. Maintenance of state-of-the-art capabilities, however, requires much more. The era of lifelong learning pragmatically has arrived. The half-life of knowledge has been estimated at five years. Applied to public relations, this concept suggests that 75 percent of the knowledge practitioners obtain in colleges and universities will become obsolete within ten years. Practitioners therefore must continuously hone knowledge and skills acquired in educational institutions through continuing education programs and on-going individual environmental assessment efforts.

COMPONENTS OF SUCCESS

Successful public relations research is dependent on several practitioner attributes. First among them is an adequate educational base dealing with the social sciences as well as public relations. Knowledge and skills thus acquired must be continuously renewed, however, in keeping with the evolution of public relations practice.

Equally important is similarly detailed knowledge of organizations with which practitioners deal. Practitioners must understand the impact of environmental events and trends upon the organizations with which they are involved. Only with this knowledge can they successfully design and implement successful research programs.

Postsecondary Education

Contemporary standards for undergraduate and graduate education in public relations reflect the combined thinking of educators and practitioners. Both participated in the 1987 Commission on Undergraduate Public Relations Education and the 1985 National Commission on Graduate Study in Public Relations. Their curriculum recommendations are contained in reports respectively entitled ''Design for Undergraduate Public Relations Education'' and ''Advancing Public Relations Education: Recommended Curriculum for Graduate Public Relations Education.''

The undergraduate commission report divided its recommended program of study into two parts: general and professional education. The former encompasses 65 semester hours in arts and science courses including English, social sciences and history, psychology and behavioral sciences, natural sciences, mathematics, and foreign languages. The latter includes studies in communication and public relations.

The communication component of the curriculum was defined to include technical/production, historical/institutional, and process/structure components. In the technical/production area, the commission recommended copy preparation and editing, graphic arts and typography, still photography, production for electronic media, and public speaking/oral presentation. Public relations components include principles/practices/theory, writing/message dissemination/media networks, planning/evaluation, strategy/implementation, and supervised public relations experience.

Where curricula create opportunities for a minor area of study, the commission recommended it be undertaken in business with courses in marketing, management, economics, and finances.

Graduate Education

The National Commission on Graduate Study recommended a basic curriculum requiring at least 30 semester hours of study including courses in:

1. Research methodology
2. Communication theory
3. Communication processes
4. Public relations principles, practices, and theory
5. Public relations management
6. Public relations programming and production
7. A public relations specialty option

Suggested specialty options in public relations included courses in government, health care, non-profit organizations, education, and politics.

A minor consisting of six to nine semester hours in courses related to areas of student interest and a thesis or comprehensive examination would complete the master's program.

Continuing Education

Formal continuing education programs in public relations are rare in the United States. One is sponsored in New York City by New York University and the Public Relations Society of America (PRSA). Another is sponsored by PRSA's Counselor Academy. Neither is readily accessible to most practitioners although both PRSA and the International Association of Business Communicators (IABC) offer professional development programs at multiple sites.

Informal programs are more generally available, however, through PRSA, IABC, the American Society for Hospital Marketing and Public Relations (ASHMPR; an American Hospital Association affiliate) and others. Most are professional development sessions conducted in conjunction with annual meetings or conventions.

IABC has traditionally scheduled professional development programs in multiple locales. Local chapters of PRSA and IABC also support their members with seminars and other periodic programs conducted in conjunction with their regular meetings.

In progress during 1987 within PRSA was a series of symposia designed to produce recommendations on how the society might demonstrate member professionalism. The symposia were prompted in part by a Committee on Public Relations Licensure and Certification established by pioneer practitioner Edward Bernays. They addressed a number of alternatives ranging from licensure to enhancement of a previously existing accreditation program. Society action on symposia recommendations was anticipated at the annual meeting of the organization's governing body in late 1988.

Individual Activities

In the absence of, or in addition to formal continuing education programs, public relations practitioners can maintain state-of-the-art knowledge through two techniques: accreditation or certification by professional organizations and extensive self-study.

Accreditation

Both the Public Relations Society of America and the International Association of Business Communicators sponsor accreditation programs consisting of preparatory study, day-long written examinations and, in the case of PRSA, a verbal examination as well.

These programs have strengths and weaknesses. On the one hand, they are relatively rigorous, as demonstrated by low first effort success rates. On the other, they seemingly assume a static body of knowledge as the credentials are granted for life.

Local chapters of both organizations offer preparatory seminars for accreditation candidates and supplement national study guides and extensive bibliographies provided to assist those preparing for examinations. Preparatory processes thus are educational in themselves. Resulting credentials, however, attest only to recipient knowledge and skill levels at the time of the examinations. With one exception, credentials remain effective until death or resignation. (PRSA maintains a disciplinary mechanism through which violators of the society's code of ethics can be expelled from membership, in which case accreditation is lost. IABC has no parallel disciplinary system.)

Certification

A similar program is sponsored by the American Society for Hospital Marketing and Public Relations (ASHMPR). The organization certifies members at two levels of proficiency based primarily on experience, educational attainment, and involvement in professional development activities.

Like the other organizations, the ASHMPR credential requires no periodic renewal. At the senior fellowship level, however, ASHMPR requires candidates to complete a major research project. The project can be practice-based and may focus on professional programs or activities. It must, however, contribute to the body of knowledge used in hospital marketing and public relations.

Self-Study

Unlike physicians, attorneys, accountants, and other professionals, public relations practitioners may or may not engage in activities designed to maintain state-of-the-art knowledge of their fields. PRSA in 1988 appeared to be moving toward a mandatory continuing education requirement. In the absence of an early mandate there will remain relatively low member demand for professional development services. These for the most part are confined to seminars conducted in conjunction with national annual meetings. The majority of those engaged in self-study has no other alternative than to create their own professional development systems.

Most systems involve extensive readings about the business world generally, public relations, and the fields in which their clients or employers are engaged. A few include extensive research and writing as well.

Research and writing are used as professional development techniques primarily by academics and a small nucleus of senior professionals who contribute to the professional development activities of others. Most in public relations education engage in research and writing in compliance with the "publish or perish" dictum of the academic world. Many contribute to the professional development activities of other practitioners as well. They are assisted in the latter effort by senior professionals whose contributions are most often found in educational activities at national conferences and conventions. The preparation of materials may require sufficient study and research to insure preparers' continued proficiency. This result would be all but guaranteed were participant efforts to cover all facets of practice specified in accreditation program study outlines (see Figure 2.1).

Other than for the few, especially academics and those who prepare professional development programs for others, studies suggested by the guide are a one time experience. The guide also contains an extensive set of references periodically updated for new candidates. The references alone are indicative of the transient value of contemporary knowledge in public relations. Most are flagged with asterisks referring to a common footnote: "Current Edition."

The level of change that is occurring in public relations practice is readily demonstrated by examining multiple editions of the same text. The second edition of one of the leading texts in the field, Cutlip and Center's *Effective Public Relations*, published in 1965, contained 438 pages. The sixth edition, published 20 years later, was almost double the size of the second. Change of this magnitude, accompanied by parallel developments in public relations specialties and in society, requires on-going assimilation by practitioners.

PROFESSIONAL READINGS

Most members of the profession maintain necessary levels of knowledge of public relations, of business in general, and of the fields in which they practice through extensive reading. Each area is rich in information sources. Some sources require day-to-day monitoring. Others are issued less frequently. Still others need be consulted only on occasion. They are most readily examined in three specific categories.

Public Relations Publications

Public relations, like most professions, is served by several specialized publications, including magazines, newsletters, and academic journals. The leading magazines in the field are the journals of the three major professional organizations: the Public Relations Society of America, the International Association of Business Communicators, and the International Public Relations Association. The first two publications are monthly and the third appears quarterly.

Two other quarterly publications and three weekly newsletters also serve the profession. One of the publications, *Public Relations Quarterly*, is wholly practitioner-oriented. The other, *Public Relations Review*, is a more academic journal that occasionally publishes material of practitioner interest. The newsletters are *pr review*, *Public Relations News*, and *Jack O'Dwyer's Newsletter*. *pr review*, edited by practitioner Patrick Jackson, arguably is the most valuable of the newsletters to those seeking to stay abreast of practice techniques. *Public Relations News* supplements more traditional newsletter content with case histories while the O'Dwyer publication deals primarily in news of public relations consultancies, their accounts, and their personnel.

Other newsletters are published for members by PRSA's Counselor Academy and several PRSA special interest sections. Similar publications are also issued

Figure 2.1
From the Accreditation Study Guide of the Public Relations Society of America (undated booklet issued for use in the society's 1987 pre-accreditation study program)

ACCREDITATION STUDY GUIDE
Public Relations Society of America

I. BACKGROUND AND BASIC PREMISES OF PUBLIC RELATIONS
  A. Definitions
  B. Objectives or purposes
  C. Benefits
  D. History including events, dates, people, trends, developments
  E. Socioeconomic and political factors influencing practice of public relations.

II. PUBLICS AND PUBLIC OPINION
  A. The Concept of Publics
  B. Public Opinions, Attitudes and Propaganda
  C. Research: Measurement and Interpretation
     sources.
     2. Conditions requiring more formal methods of opinion research; use of research in predicting reaction of publics and in solving problems.
     3. Research methods
     4. Research as a means of program evaluation

III. PUBLIC RELATIONS PRACTICE
  A. The Function of the Public Relations Professional
     1. As employer or officer
     2. As outside counsel
     3. As manager of public relations projects, programs and people
     4. Organizing the public relations staff according to function and according to publics; centralization versus decentralization; methods of control
  B. The Relationship of the Public Relations Professional to Management
     1. As interpreter of the external environmental trends and issues
     2. As evaluator and interpreter of public attitude and opinion
     3. As adviser on the public relations significance of contemplated actions
     4. As communications expert
  C. The Public Relations Program
     1. Defining the basic objectives of the enterprise
     2. Basing a public relations program on an institution's objectives
     3. Defining the publics
     4. Using research in developing the program and in problem solving
     5. Counseling management regarding an institution's performance and policies
     6. Adapting program strategies and tactics; managing the public relations program "by objectives"
     7. Supporting marketing and sales
     8. Determining communications priorities and aims
     9. Staffing
     10. Determining costs and budgeting
     11. Measuring results
     12. Preparing emergency and disaster plans

30

Figure 2.1 Continued

    D.   Areas of Public Relations Practice
        1.   Classified by field of interest of principals
             or clients, for example, business and industry,
             financial, international, nonprofit, government
        2.   Classified by special publics of principals or
             clients, for example stockholders, employees,
             customers

IV.   COMMUNICATIONS
    A.   Communication process; theory and models
    B.   Barriers to effective communications
    C.   Method of communication: visual, auditory, audio-
        visual
    D.   Understanding symbols: verbal, non-verbal
        expression, graphics
    E.   Semantics and readability
    F.   Importance of feedback in effective communication
    G.   Channels of communication that can be controlled by
        the communicator
    H.   Mass media
    I.   Emerging technologies
    J.   Advertising as a public relations tool
    K.   Pre-testing and post-testing of messages

V.   ETHICS, LAW AND REGULATIONS AFFECTING PUBLIC RELATIONS
    A.   Reasons for professional ethics
    B.   The PRSA Code
        1.   "Declaration of Principles"
        2.   "Code of Professional Standards for the
             Practice of Public Relations"
        3.   "Official Interpretations of the PRSA Code"
             (including interpretations for Financial and
             Political Public Relations)
        4.   Enforcement of the Code (PRSA Bylaws, Article
             XII, PRSA Directory)
             a.   Roles of the Board of Directors, the
                 Grievance Board, Judicial Panels
             b.   Nature of the judicial hearing
             c.   Rules of Procedure for Judicial Panels and
                 for Grievance Board
    C.   Laws and Regulations Affecting Public Relations
        Practice

VI.   PROFESSIONAL PUBLIC RELATIONS
    A.   Purpose and value of professional organizations
    B.   The Public Relations Society of America, Inc.
        Qualifications for membership; organizational
        structure; membership services; publications
    C.   A career track for the public relations
        professional; continuing education and professional
        development

VII. PUBLIC RELATIONS FIRMS
    A.   The public relations counsel
    B.   Relationship of counsel to client
    C.   Relations of counsel with internal public relations
        staff
    D.   Procedures in serving clients
    E.   The professional attitude
    F.   Economics of public relations practice such as
        determination of costs, method of compensation,
        billing procedures, need for working capital

by specialized public relations groups such as the American Society for Hospital Marketing and Public Relations.

In addition, there is an almost limitless number of publications that occasionally publish articles on public relations. Most are listed for practitioner convenience in one or both of two annual public relations bibliographies. One is issued in mimeographed form by PRSA. The other, considerably more extensive, is compiled by Professor Albert Walker at Northern Illinois University and is published as part of an annual bibliography issue of *Public Relations Review*. The latter publication covers articles in more than 100 business and professional journals, including most of the leading social sciences publications.

Professional Publications

Although the bibliographies list articles in business publications dealing with public relations, they fall short of meeting narrower practitioner needs. Those practicing in specific industries find it essential to maintain an overview of industry-related events and trends. These can best be monitored through general and specialized publications that serve those industries.

In the health care sector, for example, practitioners read an extensive list of publications dealing with hospitals and the several health care professions. The primary hospital publications are the journals of the American Hospital Association, the Federation of American Hospitals, and the American Academy of Healthcare Administrators. They are supplemented by several commercial publications such as *Modern Healthcare* and *Healthcare Management Review*.

Virtually all of the allied health professions, including nursing, respiratory therapy, physical therapy, pharmacology, and a host of others, also publish numerous journals and newsletters. Most deal with subject matter of interest to public relations professionals from time to time. Those for whom they are published are members of the stakeholder groups with which public relations deals. Their publications deal with professional issues and problems which necessarily concern their employers.

Business Publications

Issues of concern in health care or among associated professional groups often are external to the health care industry. They arise as often within organizations' suprasystems as in their subsystems. This requires public relations practitioners also to monitor a set of general business publications.

Preeminent among these is the *Wall Street Journal*. Other publications often read by public relations practitioners include *Business Week*, *Industry Week*, the *Harvard Business Review*, *Fortune*, and *Forbes*. They provide insight into trends with which large organizations are dealing as well as reports of seemingly isolated incidents that may require practitioner attention.

Chemical spills, environmental problems, energy shortages, product tampering, and similar incidents may signal the onset of potentially troublesome trends. They require continuous monitoring and, perhaps, preventive measures to minimize potential impact on practitioners' clients or employers.

General Publications

At least three newspapers often are part of the "required reading" of public relations. One is the *New York Times*, which specializes in in-depth reporting and often is among the first to identify emerging social, business, and political trends. Another, for practitioners whose clients or employers deal frequently with the Federal government, is the *Washington Post*.

The *Christian Science Monitor* performs a similar function for multinational organizations. The *Monitor* is known for its unparalleled coverage of international events and trends.

Other Resources

A number of specialized publications and services are also worthy of practitioner attention. Some focus on specific bodies of knowledge. Others provide an overview of contemporary events that can add significantly to practitioner knowledge.

Foremost among the specialized publications is *American Demographics*, which exclusively interprets demographic trends in the United States. Major trends are identified and analyzed on both national and sectional bases.

Public Opinion, in contrast, deals with the latest survey results. They are analyzed in historical context for lay audiences. Survey techniques as well as results are the primary subject matter for *Public Opinion Quarterly*, a more academically oriented publication which nevertheless is a consistent provider of information of interest in public relations practice.

Finally, there are numerous newsletters issued by major polling or survey research organizations that also can be of help. They include the Roper Organization's *Roper Reports*, Louis Harris and Associates' *Harris Perspective*, and Opinion Research Corporation's *Public Opinion Index*.

Specialized Services

A number of specialized services, created to keep clients abreast of contemporary trends in our fast-changing society, also are available through research organizations. Among the better known are several published by the Naisbitt Group, an organization that deals primarily in media content analysis.

The Naisbitt organization monitors some 200 newspapers as well as other publications and issues a national *Trend Report* as well as several regional quarterly or semi-annual reports. PR Data Systems of Wilton, Connecticut and the News Analysis Institute of Pittsburgh provide similar services.

A somewhat similar annual service is provided to members by the Public Relations Society of America. Working with Opinion Research Corporation, the society surveys leading practitioners, organizational executives, and governmental leaders about their perceptions of emerging problems. Resultant reports are available to members through PRSA's New York office.

Some consider the environmental assessment techniques described above to be components of what has come to be called *issues management*, a process that advocates hold apart from public relations practice. More realistically the techniques are components of on-going informal research processes that practitioners have long used to achieve dual objectives: maintain practitioner knowledge levels in a fast-changing world and anticipate environmentally generated problems of concern to clients and employers.

ISSUES MANAGEMENT

Issues management involves environmental assessment. Most who consider themselves issues managers, however, cling to two distinctions between their practices and public relations. First, they consider "issues" to be matters which ultimately can be or will be amenable to governmental intervention. Second, they argue that "issues" and "problems" differ and therefore require separate handling. Neither argument, on close examination, appears wholly convincing.

Governmental Involvement

Issues managers apparently assume that social problems must inevitably lead to public policy. They are only in part correct. Abortion, equal rights, and similar questions logically fall in the public policy arena. Problems arising out of change in demographic trends or definitions of social responsibility are another matter.

Legislation and/or regulation may be logically applied to resolve questions over the legal standing of a fetus, equal employment opportunity, and the like. Neither device is applicable, however, where organizations attempt to deal with labor shortages arising out of the "baby bust" or conflicting claims on organizational resources.

Issues versus Problems

Attempts to differentiate between problems and issues are no more successful. Advocates of differentiation submit that problems are amenable to solutions satisfactory to all parties involved while issues defy mutually acceptable resolution.

History suggests the matter is far more complex. Many issues are man-made, especially within the context of our nation's quadrennial electoral cycle. Others are "non-issues," little more than smoke screens thrown up to shield those acting out of self interest.

The "missile gap," which preoccupied John F. Kennedy during his election campaign and thus became a subject of national debate, literally disappeared subsequent to his election. "Human rights" was a similar "issue" during the Carter administration and problems in Central America came to the fore during the Reagan years. The "issues" involved changed little, if at all, during the periods in question. Their development and subsequent return to obscurity were more a matter of political agenda setting than reality.

The health care issue of the late 1980s in large part evolved in similar fashion. The aging of the national population may have been a factor but the principal social and economic questions were far from new. Should health care be a matter of privilege or right and, if the latter, who will pay? Rather than address the former question, the issue was drawn over the latter. Government, corporations, and health care providers each sought to shift the burden to the others.

The ritual dances of politicians over the health care issue are especially demonstrative of self interest at work. All proclaim themselves advocates of the poor and disadvantaged yet none is willing to support a functional comprehensive health care program. Instead they attempt to force others to assume the burden. They pressure hospitals into providing more care to indigents, enact legislation that forces employers to extend health insurance to former employees and their dependents as well, and leave millions still without adequate care.

Issues or problems such as these impact all organizations regardless of attempts to differentiate between them. To best serve clients and employers, public relations practitioners must be conversant with organizational environments and the events and trends that influence them. Individually or organizationally, they must monitor events in the world around them and successfully anticipate the nature and extent of their prospective impacts.

Semantics aside, the latter objectives can best be achieved through informal and formal research. The two basic types and their techniques are discussed in the ensuing chapters.

SUMMARY

Research in the social sciences differs significantly from research in the physical sciences. As environmental influences can be eliminated in research in the physical sciences, researchers can examine their subjects under pristine laboratory conditions in a physical vacuum, and even in the absence of gravity. In the social sciences, which include public relations, this is not possible.

Individuals and groups with whom public relations deal are constantly exposed to external influences beyond the control of the researcher. They are engendered by multiple environments to which individuals and organizations both respond and adapt.

Success in both public relations research and public relations practice requires functional knowledge of environmental variables that may influence results. The variables include factors internal and external to the organization that may govern individual and organizational activities.

Where individuals are involved, internal factors are primarily psychological while the external originate in the environments in which humans function. One of them is the organization, which also is influenced by internal and external environments or systems.

Organizations are open systems. They are parts of a set of suprasystems and consist of subsystems. External environments or suprasystems include the natural, technological, human, political, socioeconomic, and market. The internal are psychological, social, political, and technological.

Students acquire knowledge of systems, subsystems, and suprasystems through comprehensive academic curricula at undergraduate and graduate levels. These studies equip students with knowledge of the arts and sciences, especially the social sciences. Emphasizing the knowledge and skills required of public relations professionals, these courses initially equip students as practitioners.

Knowledge and skills acquired in academic settings are transient and require continuous renewal. The half-life of knowledge has been estimated at five years. Seventy-five percent of the product of higher education therefore becomes obsolete within ten years of graduation. On-going renewal is essential, to meet practice as well as individual needs.

Successful practitioners monitor changing environments on behalf of client and employer organizations and to fulfill their own needs. Only in this manner they can anticipate professional opportunities and practice problems. Most professionals engage in one or more of several renewal processes, including formal and informal education and environmental assessment programs.

Formal continuing education programs in public relations are geographically limited. The informal, somewhat more extensive, are sponsored by national and local professional organizations through their meetings and conferences.

The Public Relations Society of America and the International Association of Business Communicators offer accreditation programs for members. Rigorous study is required to successfully complete the comprehensive examinations. Credentials involved, however, essentially are granted for life and require no subsequent educational pursuits.

Successful practitioners must develop their own information-gathering systems to maintain and enhance their ability to best serve clients and employers. At least three bodies of knowledge are involved: knowledge of public relations, the organizational world in general, and the segments of that world in which practitioners are engaged.

Several sets of publications can provide necessary information, and additional data can be obtained through research services. The process might be termed on-going ''environmental assessment'' but some consider it a component of what has been called ''issues management.''

Issues management involves environmental assessment. Distinctions between issues management and the research component of public relations practice, however, are hazy at best. Efforts have been made to differentiate between problems and issues in order to establish issues management as a separate function. Many consider, however, that issues management is little more than the component of public relations that most resembles governmental relations.

ADDITIONAL READING

Baskin, Otis, and Craig Aronoff. *Public Relations: The Profession and the Practice.* 2d ed. Dubuque, IA: Wm. C. Brown, 1988.

Berko, Roy M., Andrew D. Wolvin, and Ray Curtis. *This Business of Communicating.* 3d ed. Dubuque, IA: Wm. C. Brown, 1986.

Brody, E. W. *Public Relations Programming and Production.* New York: Praeger, 1988.

Buchholz, Rogene A., William D. Evans, and Robert A. Wagley. *Management Response to Public Issues: Concepts & Cases in Strategy Formulation.* Englewood Cliffs, NJ: Prentice Hall, 1985.

Canfield, Bertrand R. *Public Relations: Principles, Cases and Problems.* 5th ed. Homewood, IL: Richard D. Irwin, 1968.

Cantor, Bill. *Inside Public Relations: Experts in Action.* New York: Longman, 1984.

Castells, Manuel, ed. *High Technology, Space and Society.* Beverly Hills, CA: Sage, 1985.

Coates, Joseph F. *Issues Management: How You Can Plan, Organize, & Manage for the Future.* Mt. Airy, MD: Lomond Publications, 1986.

Cohen, Paula Marantz. *A Public Relations Primer: Thinking and Writing in Context.* Englewood Cliffs, NJ: Prentice Hall, 1987.

Cutlip, Scott M., Allen H. Center, and Glen M. Broom. *Effective Public Relations.* 6th ed. Englewood Cliffs, NJ: Prentice Hall, 1985.

Didsbury, Howard F., ed. *Communications and the Future: Prospects, Promises and Problems.* Washington, DC: World Future Society, 1982.

Dilenschneider, Robert L., and Dan J. Forrestal. *The Dartnell Public Relations Handbook.* 3d ed. Chicago: The Dartnell Corporation, 1987.

Dizard, Wilson P., Jr. *The Coming Information Age: An Overview of Technology, Economics and Politics.* 2d ed. New York: Longman, 1985.

Grunig, James E., and Todd Hunt. *Managing Public Relations.* New York: Holt, Rinehart and Winston, 1984.

Heath, Robert L., and Richard A. Nelson. *Issues Management: Corporate Public Policymaking in an Information Society.* Beverly Hills, CA: Sage, 1986.

Hennessy, Bernard. *Public Opinion.* 5th ed. Monterey, CA: Brooks/Cole, 1985.

Herbert, Walter B., and John R. G. Jenkins, eds. *Public Relations in Canada: Some Perspectives.* Markham, Ontario: Fitzhenry & Whiteside, 1984.

Hiebert, Ray E., ed. *Precision Public Relations.* New York: Longman, 1988.

Lerbinger, Otto. *Managing Corporate Crises: Strategies for Executives.* Boston: Barrington Press, 1986.

Mitroff, Ian I. *Business NOT as Usual: Rethinking Our Individual, Corporate and Industrial Strategies for Global Competition.* San Francisco: Jossey-Bass, 1987.

Moore, H. Frasier, and Kalupa, Frank B. *Public Relations: Principles, Cases and Problems.* 9th ed. Homewood, IL: Richard D. Irwin, 1985.

Nager, Norman R., and T. Harrell Allen. *Public Relations Management by Objectives.* New York: Longman, 1984.

Nager, Norman R., and Richard H. Truitt. *Strategic Public Relations Counseling: Models from the Counselors Academy.* New York: Longman, 1987.

Newsom, Doug, and Alan Scott. *This is PR: The Realities of Public Relations.* 3d ed. Belmont, CA: Wadsworth, 1985.

Organ, Dennis W., and W. Clay Hamner. *Organizational Behavior.* 2d ed. Plano, TX: Business Publications, Inc., 1985.

Phillips, Charles S. *Secrets of Successful Public Relations.* Englewood Cliffs, NJ: Prentice Hall, 1985.

Reilly, Robert T. *Public Relations in Action.* 2d ed. Englewood Cliffs, NJ: Prentice Hall, 1987.

Robinson, Edward J. *Public Relations and Survey Research.* New York: Appleton-Century-Crofts, 1969.

Rogers, Everett M. *Communication Technology: The New Media in Society.* New York: Free Press, 1986.

Rothman, Jack. *Using Research in Organizations: A Guide to Successful Application.* Beverly Hills, CA: Sage, 1980.

Settle, Robert B., and Pamela L. Alreck. *Why They Buy: The American Consumers Inside and Out.* New York: John Wiley, 1986.

Simon, Raymond. *Public Relations: Concepts and Practices.* 3d ed. New York: John Wiley, 1984.

Smith, Judson, and Janice Orr. *Designing and Developing Business Communication Programs that Work.* Glenview, IL: Scott, Foresman, 1985.

Ward, Jean, and Kathleen A. Hansen. *Search Strategies in Mass Communication.* New York: Longman, 1987.

Wheelen, Thomas L., and J. David Hunger. *Strategic Management and Business Policy.* Reading, MA: Addison-Wesley, 1983.

Wilcox, Dennis L., Phillip H. Ault, and Warren K. Agee. *Public Relations: Strategies and Tactics.* New York: Harper & Row, 1986.

Williams, Frederick. *Technology and Communication Behavior.* Belmont, CA: Wadsworth, 1987.

Wright, Theon, and Henry S. Evans. *Public Relations and the Line Manager.* New York: American Management Association, 1964.

3 Environmental Monitoring

Successful public relations practice requires mastery of multiple bodies of knowledge. Practitioners must be conversant with contemporary developments in three areas: public relations, fields in which employers or clients operate, and the several environments in which individuals and organizations function. The process through which these bodies of knowledge are maintained is called environmental monitoring or environmental assessment. The former term is used here because the latter is more commonly associated with issues management.

Advocates of issues management apply the term environmental assessment to what they contend is a new discipline—developing and maintaining early warning systems to enable organizations to deal systematically with emerging problems rather than merely reacting to them as they intrude upon organizational affairs. Issues management process models differ significantly from those of public relations because they assume issues will become subject to legislation and litigation. Legislation and/or litigation are assumed in issues management. Public relations practitioners make no such assumptions. The two disciplines apply essentially identical methodologies in environmental assessment and monitoring and are equally concerned with social and demographic trends that often defy legislative or judicial intervention.

Environmental monitoring is a process applied in public relations at practitioner, organizational, and societal levels. At the practitioner level, it enables individuals to maintain state-of-the-art knowledge and skills. At the organizational level, it is the first step in a strategic management process that serves to identify emerging problems and define alternative responses. At the societal level, it identifies broader trends that may impact organizations and permits them to be systematically monitored on a continuing basis. In each case, the process involves three components:

1. Identifying, tracking, and analyzing trends that may ultimately impact individuals or organizations.
2. Interpreting and defining the implications of identified trends and alternative responses.
3. Developing strategies and plans through which individual and/or organizational response can best be managed.

The environmental monitoring process proceeds under a set of general assumptions which may or may not hold true in any given situation. Their validity in any specific case is a function of the abilities of individuals involved.

OPERATIONAL ASSUMPTIONS

Considerable time and effort are necessary to develop and maintain efficient environmental monitoring systems. The costs involved are justified on the basis of three primary assumptions.

Trends that impact organizations can be identified earlier, more completely, and more reliably than in the past.

Early identification broadens the range of practical organizational responses.

Awareness enables organizations to assume an active rather than a reactive role in dealing with emerging trends.

The principles are generally applicable, but their application provides no blanket immunity to potentially damaging problems. The monitoring process nevertheless can be beneficial to individuals and organizations by enabling them to avoid some of the hazards created by contemporary society. The impact of demographic trends, for example, can be forecast with a high degree of accuracy. Organizational responses can therefore be planned and implemented with relative confidence. Potential energy shortages, in contrast, are much less predictable. Geopolitical and economic variables defy precise analysis. "Worst case" disasters are beyond rational anticipation. No amount of environmental monitoring could rationally have signaled Johnson & Johnson to prepare for the first Tylenol product tampering incident. Neither could Union Carbide have anticipated the Bhopal disaster. Environmental monitoring and disaster planning must go hand in hand in contemporary public relations practice.

Trend Identification

There is no question that trends can be identified earlier than in the past. Today computer technology makes more information available more rapidly to organizations than ever before. Data compiled by the U.S. Commerce Department's Bureau of the Census, for example, are now compiled by computer and available within months rather than years of the decennial count. Sophisticated computer systems have also provided researchers with analytical tools beyond the wildest dreams of their predecessors.

These and other technologies, however, are also producing accelerating rates of organizational and societal change. Early trend identification is essential if organizations are to do no more than hold their own. Environmental monitoring thus is necessary but not sufficient to survival in competitive environments. Organizations and individuals must successfully apply resulting knowledge.

Creating More Options

Environmental monitoring functions can create more action alternatives in only one way: by lengthening elapsed time between problem identification and organizational impact. Existence of environmental monitoring is no assurance that individuals or organizations will deal better with the demands of a changing world. The process creates opportunities for enhanced response, however, and over time tends to encourage such behavior.

Missed opportunities can be constructive experiences. They encourage those who have suffered the penalties of procrastination to become more responsive. What has been called the ''squeaking wheel approach to management'' becomes progressively less attractive when practitioners and their employers are consistently beset by crises that might have been resolved through preemptive action.

The monitoring process is designed to provide insight into what the future may hold—foresight, if you prefer—for organizations and individuals. It is productive only to the extent that they act on the information that the process produces.

Action Versus Reaction

Organizations, like individuals, have traditionally been reactive rather than active in dealing with problems and opportunities. Environmental monitoring is predicated on an assumption that both can be identified earlier and handled better.

Early identification of trends that may impact organizations at minimum permits a greater level of preparedness. At best, it permits conversion of prospective difficulties into competitive advantages.

Enhanced preparedness would occur, for example, when organizations anticipate another petroleum crisis and minimize vulnerability by developing systems through which they can use alternative fuels. Conversion of an impending problem into a competitive advantage is exemplified by organizations that installed employee-oriented management systems in response to impending labor shortages. Those that recognized the prospective impact of the ''baby bust'' on the work force in the mid–1980s are significantly more successful today in recruiting and retaining personnel than their competitors.

Generating Information

Benefits develop for organizations and individuals only where environmental monitoring is managed in a manner that generates useful information. Successful information-gathering processes share several characteristics. They are systematic and comprehensive, embrace a broad range of data of varying quality, and generate comprehensive sets of developmental alternatives rather than specific predictions of future events.

Data generated through information-gathering permit precise answers to multiple critical questions.

What problems are developing that may impact the organization or its stakeholder groups?

What unforeseen problems may arise if the organization maintains existing policies?

What policy alternatives might be more appropriate under the circumstances?

What policy inconsistencies arise as a result of change?

What prospective difficulties do other organizations' problems imply?

What research may be necessary or appropriate in the decision-making process?

The foresight generated by environmental monitoring in essence creates a point of departure for individual or organizational response. Data gathered in the process may occasionally permit users to make relatively accurate forecasts or predictions. More often, the information requires extensive analysis in the context of historical and/or other current data.

Labor problems arising out of the arrival of the baby-bust generation in the work force, for example, will ultimately impact virtually every organization. The extent to which this problem receives priority managerial attention, however, is another matter. The health care, accommodations, and other labor-concentrated industries should logically be greatly concerned. Manufacturing organizations, in which humans can be successfully supplanted by computers and robots, may find potential impact of negligible significance.

Environmental monitoring, according to Joseph F. Coates, can be directed toward at least ten objectives:

1. Identifying environmental events significant to organizations
2. Identifying their nature and significance
3. Defining prospective threats and opportunities as well as changes to which it may be necessary to respond
4. Informing organizational personnel
5. Inducing more detailed assessment and analysis
6. Promoting a future orientation
7. Providing guidance for planning and action
8. Directing attention to subjects that might otherwise be neglected

9. Informing the organization of the need for anticipatory rather than reactive performance
10. Alerting the organization to change in direction or intensity among multiple trends.

SCANNING AND TRACKING

Environmental monitoring consists of two basic processes and an extensive set of specialized techniques. The processes are scanning and tracking. Scanning involves on-going examination of organizational horizons in search of events that may signal the beginning of significant trends. Tracking is a constant watch on development in identified areas of interest that may generate threats or opportunities.

Events and trends can originate or occur in any number of settings. Coates suggests that they can be conveniently categorized as social, political, scientific, ecological, economic, technological, biological, international, and others. Wheelen and Hunger propose that they originate in three environments: societal, task, and internal. Their societal environment includes sociocultural, economic, political-legal, and technological forces. Their task environment includes what public relations practitioners would define as an organization's stakeholder groups: stockholders, suppliers, governments, employees, customers, competitors, trade associations, creditors, and communities. Their internal environment consists of the organization's structure, culture, and resources.

A Systems Approach

A generic alternative approach comes from systems theory. Systems theory suggests that organizations are open systems—they are parts of six suprasystems and composed of four subsystems. Events and trends can originate or occur in any of them.

The suprasystems are natural, human, political, social, market, and technological. The natural suprasystem includes raw materials, humans who work in the organization, the air they breathe, and the water they drink. The human suprasystem includes individuals with whom organizations deal and their abilities, skills, educational levels, attitudes, and opinions. The political suprasystem includes an almost unlimited number of special interest groups in addition to traditional political and governmental components. The social or socioeconomic suprasystem involves the obligations and responsibilities of individuals and organizations to society and each other. The market suprasystem encompasses consumer behavior, changing consumer values, and similar elements. The technological includes the collective aspects of machines as well as their ancillary and support systems.

The subsystems are psychological, social, political, and technological. The psychological includes individual motivations, needs, values, attitudes, perceptions, beliefs, emotions, and personality structures. The social involves the collective aspects of human behavior in groups of all sizes. The political generates the power and influence wielded by natural rather than formal leaderships. The technological consists of the attributes of machines as well as the humans and systems which support them.

The systems approach is most appropriate as significant events can occur in any environment. Any effort to limit scanning or monitoring in any of them creates undue risk.

The Scanning Process

Scanning, or the systematic examination of published material, can be performed by (a) individuals, (b) an organized team, (c) a group of individuals functioning under direction of a chief scanner, and (d) an organized group coupled with an organizational review panel. With the exception of the last option, these alternatives differ in essence only in their mechanical complexity.

The least sophisticated of the alternatives involves assigning an individual scanner to read selected publications. Material deemed potentially significant to the organization is abstracted and summarized for managerial or administrative review.

The same process is usually used by groups of scanners. They may or may not meet to discuss their findings but a summary of abstracts is usually produced.

Using the third option, a scanner supervisor organizes volunteers generally representative of the organization. They collectively identify a set of publications—usually 30 to 100—to be monitored, and agree on reading assignments. Each reports using a brief descriptive scanning form to which original materials may be attached. The reports are consolidated in a summary document compiled by the supervisor.

More complex procedures are often adopted where organizational review panels are added to the process. Panels may request further information, formal research, reports to upper organizational echelons, and linkages with strategic planning processes. Complex filing systems, often employing computer-assisted information retrieval, are usually used in such programs.

The Tracking Process

Tracking and on-going assessment of developing trends can be more complex than scanning. Tracking keeps organizations abreast of evolving conditions and their potential consequences. Some two dozen identified techniques can be productively applied in the tracking process. They vary, however, in application and effectiveness.

Many research techniques used in tracking also fall logically within informal or formal research categories (see Figure 3.1). Others involve information-gathering and associated analytical processes that can logically be classified as extensions of the scanning process. Still others involve applying technology to

Figure 3.1
Issue Analysis Worksheet Used by Dow Chemical Company, Midland, MI (reproduced with permission of Dow Chemical Company)

This worksheet is intended as a guide in developing constructive company programs for dealing with emerging and/or current issues. It is not meant to be distributed widely throughout the company. Ideally, it should tell us what we know – and don't know – about the dynamics of a particular issue. Completion of the worksheet might logically lead to the following steps:

1) An Issue Overview Statement or executive summary which describes the scope, intensity and direction of an issue; no more than two typewritten pages.

2) A Public Affairs Strategy Proposal which spells out a particular course of action for management review and support.

3) A Company Position Paper which defines, in a paragraph or two, the company's response and/or policy on the issue; this should be particularly useful in handling media queries.

CONCERNING: _____

Figure 3.1 Continued

ISSUE ANALYSIS

Issue: _____

Management responsibility for the issue:

Who is in *overall* charge? _____

Public Affairs: _____   Research: _____

Commercial: _____   Government Affairs: _____

Manufacturing/Division: _____   U.S. Area Management: _____

Legal: _____   Corporate Management: _____

Who is responsible for handling media calls on this issue?

1. Primary _____   3. Back-up _____

2. Back-up _____   4. Back-up _____

Why is this issue of concern to Dow?

_____
_____
_____
_____

Describe the level and intensity of media interest to date. Who are the key reporters and their organizations? Are any "themes" emerging from the news coverage?

_____

_____

_____

_____

What is the potential impact of this issue on the company's operations and/or its reputation?

Short-term: _____

_____

_____

_____

Long-term: _____

_____

_____

_____

Figure 3.1 Continued

Describe any state or federal *legislative* implications:

_____

_____

_____

_____

What, if any, are the state or federal *regulatory* implications?

_____

_____

_____

_____

Who are our key *adversaries* in this matter, and what are their agendas or strategies?

_____

_____

_____

_____

What do we know about public opinion on this issue? Does the evidence suggest that public opinion is (or can be) susceptible to change?

_____

_____

_____

What are the geographic considerations of this issue?

_____ Washington focus

_____ State capital (Name: _____)

_____ Single state (Name: _____)

_____ Single region of the U.S. (Name: _____)

_____ Single town/city (Name: _____)

_____ National issue

_____ International concern

_____ Global

What are the key *legal* implications, e.g., litigation filed or trial dates pending?

_____

_____

_____

_____

Figure 3.1 Continued

How is our position perceived by:

Customers: _____   Key regulators: _____

Employees: _____   General public: _____

Plant communities: _____   Scientific community: _____

Financial community: _____   News media: _____

Key legislators: _____

What have Dow employees been told about the issue?

_____

_____

_____

On a scale of 1-10 (10 being the worst), what is our vulnerability to:

_____ Bad publicity   _____ Regulatory action

_____ Significant lawsuits   _____ Drop in stock price

_____ Customer backlash   _____ Network television coverage

_____ Employee morale problems   _____ Community unrest/fear

_____ New legislation   _____ Security concerns

_____ Congressional testimony   _____ Product recall/ban

_____ Plant shut-down   _____ Terrorist activity

50

STRATEGIC CONSIDERATIONS

What are the toughest questions we will be asked by key parties in this controversy? What are our answers?

_____

_____

_____

_____

What are Dow's basic strengths in this controversy?

_____

_____

_____

_____

_____

Figure 3.1 Continued

What non-Dow resources will be asked for advice and counsel on this issue?

_____

_____

_____

What might Dow say and/or do to defuse or minimize this issue? How might it be turned into a plus?

_____

_____

_____

In what key respects are these strategies likely to conflict with other parts of Dow's organization?

_____

_____

_____

Are there opportunities for a *coalition* approach to the issue? Who are our likely allies, and how can they help us?

_____

_____

Are there opportunities for compromise or joint study of the problem? If this issue has not yet flared, what steps might be taken to begin or accelerate dialogue with our adversaries?

_____

_____

What innovative, *unexpected* approaches might Dow consider?

_____

_____

What related issues should *Dow initiate* for the public agenda?

_____

_____

53

Figure 3.1 Continued

Who are Dow's most persuasive speakers on this issue?

Name	Department	Media-Trained?

What help can you obtain from colleagues who are involved in the Visible Scientist and/or Media Account programs, or from the various regional Public Affairs managers, etc.?

Do your proposed Public Affairs strategies and responses meet important "New Dow" criteria?

_____ Compassionate, caring   _____ Open-minded, receptive to appropriate compromise

_____ Restrained   _____ Give adversaries' motives the benefit of the doubt

_____ Solution-driven   _____ Poised

_____ Concerned about public perceptions

Are there top management *speech* possibilities related to this issue?

_____

_____

_____

_____

What specific actions must be taken (and by whom) to improve our understanding of this issue?

_____

_____

_____

_____

_____

Prepared by: _____

Date: _____

information-gathering and information management processes. A great deal of contemporary research thus involves multiple techniques. The informal precedes the formal in most circumstances for several reasons. Primary among them are relative speed and lower costs. These benefits are obtained, however, only at the expense of programmatic complexity.

The organization of this text makes it inappropriate to consider in detail at this point all the techniques that can be applied in the tracking process. Those that can be categorized as formal or informal research techniques will be considered in greater detail in later chapters. It is appropriate here, however, to categorize and characterize those techniques when they are applied in information-gathering rather than informal or formal research.

Gathering Information

The several techniques that are most readily characterized as information-gathering begin with the scanning and tracking processes described above. Others include networking, precursor analysis, executive opinion juries, expert panels, Delphi techniques, and several small group processes.

Analytical Techniques

The value of data accumulated through information-gathering often can be enhanced through application of any of several nontechnical analytical techniques. "Nontechnical" here refers to human analyses rather than those applied through use of computers or other technological devices.

Analytical techniques include cross-impact analyses, scenario building, trend extrapolation, decision analysis, sensitivity analysis, and key player analysis.

Technological Processes

A number of computer-assisted techniques also can be applied in tracking. Most involve modeling or simulations in which data from multiple sources are manipulated by computer to produce "if–then" forecasts.

Informal Research

A number of informal research techniques or strategies are also used in the environmental monitoring process. Perhaps the most common are tracking methodologies applied in the legislative and media areas.

Formal Research

Systematic information-gathering and analyses are the primary characteristics of formal research. The several techniques involved earn the formal research label only as traditional scientific methods are applied. The nature of environmental monitoring necessarily excludes experimental research but most other formal techniques are applicable.

They include content analysis, polls and surveys, factor analysis, correlation, regression, and others. Computers usually are used in analyzing data generated by formal research but only to facilitate analyses involved.

INFORMATION-GATHERING

The information-gathering process can be viewed as an extension of the scanning component of environmental monitoring. Several simpler information-gathering techniques are basically the same as scanning. Others are considerably more complex.

The simpler or basic processes include networking, trigger event identification, and precursor analysis. Expert panels, executive opinion juries, and Delphi techniques are somewhat more complex.

Basic Information-Gathering

Basic information-gathering processes come into play as scanning produces results. As observed events suggest potential trend development, independent confirmation and further information are necessary. Both are most readily obtained through basic information-gathering procedures.

Networking

Networking refers to the internal and external relationships public relations practitioners maintain in their profession, their own organizations, and their clients' and employers' organizations. These relationships yield information concerning emerging issues. They also enable practitioners to compare the results of their scanning with those that colleagues have obtained. Alternative response strategies and other helpful information may also be obtained in the process.

Professional and internal networks are usually most helpful. The professional enable practitioners to confirm their observations and judgments before engaging organizational response mechanisms. Internal networks assist by providing informal feedback from individuals who, by the nature of their positions and responsibilities, are highly knowledgeable in specific subject areas.

A strike by chromium miners, for example, is a potentially significant event for any manufacturing organization. Level of significance, however, necessarily relates to multiple intervening variables that would include, for example, volume of chromium used, extent of current inventory, availability of alternative materials, and costs of alternatives. Information on these and related topics would be necessary to enable any scanner to discern potential organizational impact of the strike.

The same sort of informational need can develop in a professional context. When the "baby-bust" generation started coming into the work force in the mid–1980s, for example, employers found obtaining skilled manpower more competitive. Worker recruitment and retention became more critical and many organizations instituted major changes in human resource systems as a result.

Much of the attendant "how-to-do-it" information was shared through professional networks.

Trigger Events

The relatively ambiguous term *trigger events* is common in issues management practice. Scanners necessarily are alert to any event or activity that might focus public concern or produce potentially troublesome responses. No standardized process exists, however, by which such events are identified. Identification is a matter of instinct and judgment.

Significant events nevertheless are often easy to identify. The first federal court decision supporting the "comparable worth" concept was one of these. The concept, espoused by a union, suggested that the relative worth of jobs could be precisely calculated and that workers should be paid accordingly. It has slowly been spreading in governmental employment in the United States but has made few inroads in for-profit organizations.

The Soviet Union's Chernobyl nuclear reactor accident also was easy to classify as a significant event. It produced a greater awareness among other reactor operators of potential for mishap. They presumably reassessed their circumstances in light of the logical premise that they were at similar risk. In much the same manner, the Three Mile Island nuclear incident in the United States alerted public relations practitioners to potential communication problems attendant to such events.

Precursor Analysis

What has come to be called *precursor analysis* is similar to the trigger event concept. Precursor analysis is based on "trickle-down theory" and suggests that identifiable leaders establish trends, and that these patterns will ultimately be replicated.

Significant evidence exists to support the concept but precursor analysis nevertheless must be handled with considerable care. Among nations, for example, those in Scandinavia and Europe as well as Japan, Canada, and the United States lead in different areas. Changing consumer and environmental policies, for example, have tended to originate in Scandinavia and Europe before moving to North America. Within the United States, California, Connecticut, Florida, Oregon, Washington, and Colorado are considered by some to be bellwether states. There is little uniformity, however, across the several states. Health and privacy issues often arise first in Florida while Oregon often leads in environmental matters.

The value of precursor analysis thus is a function of precursor identification. Considerable time and effort are required to develop appropriate bodies of knowledge and skill in organizations but external assistance is available in many instances. The Naisbitt Group, for example, publishes The *Bellwether Report*, a newsletter based on analysis of social developments in California, Florida,

Washington, Colorado, and Connecticut. The National Center for Legislative Research provides similar information in *State Policy*.

Complex Techniques

The complexity of precursor analysis can vary with the techniques employed. The process can range from purchase of reports such as those mentioned above to extensive organizational efforts. This is not the case where more complex techniques such as executive opinion juries, expert panels, and Delphi techniques are applied. All of them require considerable organizational time and effort.

Executive Opinion Juries

Many organizations use panels of senior executives and/or managers in tracking processes that can contribute to overall organizational processes in several ways. Executives and managers by the nature of their work frequently may identify emerging problems early. They often are called upon in any event to establish priorities in handling identified trends.

In larger organizations, panels or juries may serve as intermediary bodies. In this role, they review and evaluate reports from subordinates and prepare recommendations for boards of directors or chief executive officers. Occasionally, they also may direct and coordinate the work of subordinate managers.

Executive panels benefit from two attributes of their members. First, members inevitably are most knowledgeable concerning their organizations and thus are highly credible. Second, the individuals involved often become responsible for implementing organizational responses. They then benefit from earlier involvement in the tracking process.

Expert Panels

Use of expert as opposed to executive panels can prove troublesome. Expert panels can be configured in several ways. They may be composed wholly of organization members, entirely of outsiders, or some of each. In any case, those empaneling experts always are faced with critical determinations as to which individuals indeed are expert on the subject at hand.

Few issues are so narrowly defined that they fall entirely within the realm of a single body of knowledge as personified in one or several experts. Almost without exception, multiple disciplines are required. A toxic waste problem, for example, might require the knowledge of chemists, toxicologists, geologists, and hydrologists as well as experts in consumer and public affairs, government, and communication.

Experts nevertheless can be helpful because they bring new perspectives on existing or potential organizational problems. Their expertise need not be limited, however, by application only on panels. Delphi techniques often are appropriate. They are especially applicable where distances compound costs or where exceptionally large panels are indicated. The latter circumstances readily can arise in the case of complex problems.

Delphi Techniques

Cost and distance are only two of the factors that led to development of the Delphi technique. Physically bringing together panels of experts is expensive and difficult. The Delphi approach is comparable to a group discussion handled by mail. The first step in the multistep process involves circulating a questionnaire whose results are tabulated and arranged on a continuum. Respondents at either extreme are asked to explain their positions. The explanations and the first set of responses then are communicated to all respondents with a request that they answer a second time. Consensus usually begins to develop by the end of the third round. By eliminating the need to bring panel members together, the Delphi technique also minimizes potential for dominance on the part of one or more members (see Chapter 16).

While mechanically attractive, the traditional Delphi presents several problems. Low validity, difficulty in framing questions, and limitations on response are among them. These obstacles can be overcome through a variation on the technique called a conversational Delphi.

The conversational Delphi involves sets of structured interviews conducted in person or by telephone. While more time-consuming than the conventional technique, the conversational Delphi destroys any limitation on responses, permitting amplification and clarification of complex points.

ANALYTICAL TECHNIQUES

As the evolution of issues and their potential for impact on organizations requires more than the mere accumulation and assimilation of information, a number of analytical techniques often are applied. They vary in applicability and extent of use but often are critical in anticipating the prospective impact of events and trends. Most frequently used analytical techniques include trend extrapolation, cross-impact analysis, economic analysis, key player analysis, scenario building, and decision analysis.

Trend Extrapolation

Market research and technological forecasting long have applied formal trend extrapolation in efforts to gain insight into the future. The process involves making projections of the future on the basis of historical data.

Trend extrapolation has become progressively more sophisticated in recent years, especially as applied in trend analysis. Critical to this progression has been the introduction of interactive computer software packages that permit analysts and organizational managers to define trends in any context they wish and then proceed to an almost limitless number of "what if" analyses. Perhaps the most frequently employed technique is cross-impact analysis that can be used with or without computers.

Cross-Impact Analysis

The term "cross-impact analysis" is somewhat misleading. It accurately implies that one event or trend may be interrelated with another. It misleads, however, because more than two trends or events may interact together. No event occurs in a vacuum. As Newton's third Law of Motion tells us, for every action there is an equal or opposite reaction.

Cross-impact analysis is applied in efforts to predict accurately the results of two or more interacting trends or factors. At the extreme, the process is manifested in formal research in an analytical technique called "cross tabs" which will be discussed in the chapter on formal research. At this juncture, cross-impact analysis is considered in a more general sense. It is advanced as a technique through which public relations researchers can extend their understanding of potential trend impacts.

Complex Issues

The process requires addressing a single but potentially complex question: What are the prospective impacts of an event or trend beyond the organization with which the practitioner is primarily involved? Consider, for example, the case of the chromium mine strike mentioned earlier in somewhat simplistic fashion. The results can impact a manufacturing organization in one or several ways.

The earlier discussion referred to volume of usage, extent of supplies on hand, and prospective alternatives. These would logically be among managers' immediate concerns. Many other concerns might develop, however, were the strike to continue over an extended period of time. Chromium is used in the machine tool industry, which produces the equipment used in manufacturing, as well as in manufacturing generally. A lengthy strike could limit a manufacturer's ability to acquire spare parts and equipment. Tolerance of a shortage of raw chromium might thus be quite limited. Plants might ultimately be shut down through the secondary results of the strike.

Results of a mine strike halfway around the globe can become even more pervasive over time. Extended plant shutdowns lead to economic losses among workers. These, in turn, are reflected in retail sales in plant communities. Unemployment benefit costs increase and tax revenues decline, ultimately creating governmental economic problems.

Linearity of Process

Although superficially complex, the example above is essentially simplistic. The shortage of chromium, for example, might be accompanied by developments that would render the cost of substitute materials less expensive. These circumstances would produce the reverse of conditions described above, but in different communities.

The process described is far from linear. There is no practical limit to the number of trends that influence an organization at any given moment. The trends frequently interact, in the process diminishing or compounding the consequences of any one of them. These complexities often obscure structural changes that can influence the economic welfare of organizations. Economic analysis therefore often accompanies cross-impact analysis.

Economic Analysis

Although often used in strategic planning and resource allocation, economic analysis is equally appropriate in tracking. Anticipated economic impact of trends, prospective cost of organizational responses, and interests of stakeholder groups often are subjected to economic analysis.

Prospective Impacts

The economic consequences of emerging trends are major variables in organizations. The nature of individual trends and organizations governs the extent of the prospective impacts. The Clean Air Act, for example, created major difficulties for the nation's steel industry but few problems for hospitals. A developing shortage of professional personnel, on the other hand, may create problems for hospitals without influencing steelmakers or other manufacturers. Variations such as these are determinants of organizational response.

Organizational Responses

Organizations, like individuals, establish priorities. They deal first with matters perceived as most pressing or having the greatest potential to create damage. Organizations also examine alternative responses and inevitably assess relative costs.

Steelmaker responses to clean air legislation, for example, varied widely. Emission control equipment was installed in some plants while others were closed. Some steelmakers, partly as a result of environmental regulation, moved with deliberate haste to shift resources to other endeavors. Other organizations, through similar economic reasoning, built new "minimills" to establish competitive positions in steelmaking.

These actions should have been predictable through economic analysis. The extent to which this was the case will probably never be known but the range of potential responses is illuminating. Most significant is the fact that economic analysis permits relatively accurate predictions of individual and organizational action.

Stakeholder Groups

It is axiomatic in physics, as in systems theory, that no event occurs in a vacuum. The principle applies to events and trends as well as to organizations and their responses. Around each trend, as around each organization, a set of stakeholder groups assembles. Each has its own interests. Many, if not most of them, are economic or economically related.

In the steelmaker example above, shareholders, employees, vendors, customers, and communities all had economic stakes in the impact of the Clean Air Act. The stakeholder concept, generally accepted in public relations, is especially noteworthy here. No event or trend can be fully appreciated by any organization without considering stakeholder perspectives and economic interests.

Key Player Analysis

The same rationale applies in what has somewhat ambiguously been called *key player analysis*. This term refers to identifying parties, organizations, or stakeholder groups that may play a role in resolving issues that can arise out of emerging trends. It refers especially to those in a position to influence outcomes.

Key player analysis is in large part economic. Other factors, however, must be included as well. Individuals and organizations can be identified by their interests, responsibilities, concerns, and other elements that may induce them to behave in predictable fashion.

Key player analysis should follow established public relations procedure in identifying and characterizing stakeholder groups. Characterization enables practitioners to anticipate stakeholder responses. Organizational ability to track key player responses as trends develop is enhanced as well.

Scenario Building

Information developed through cross-impact, economic, and key player analyses often is further refined through scenario building. The term *scenario* was defined by Kahn and Wiener as "a hypothetical sequence of events" developed to analyze causes and decision points. Scenarios assume the future is only partially formed and can be partly controlled. They bring sets of trend projections together in holistic form to suggest alternative future realities.

Alternative developments in organizations' internal and external environments can be examined in almost endless variety as scenario building proceeds. Taken to an extreme, however, this level of flexibility also can create complexity and confusion. Analysts must focus their efforts on developing most likely and/or most desirable outcomes if scenario building is to assist in guiding organizational response.

Other Analytical Approaches

At least one other analytical technique—decision analysis—can be applied in tracking. The process and its reciprocal, policy capturing, can also provide insights into the prospective development of trends. Decision or judgment theory can occasionally be helpful as well.

Use of the word "analysis" in some terms is misleading. The phrases "sensitivity analysis" and "factor analysis" suggest these techniques might also be included among what we have termed "analytical techniques." The terms refer, however, to procedures that are better characterized as formal research. They will be addressed later in that context.

TECHNOLOGICAL FACTORS

Computer and other technological devices are useful in several of the research techniques described in the preceding sections. The computer, for example, is often used in cross-impact analyses. Several computer programs have been developed that permit concurrent analyses of 20 or more factors. Other programs permit analysts to manipulate models incorporating as many as 100 events and 50 trends.

Other technology-based devices are becoming equally prevalent. They range from the Consensor, used to facilitate information-gathering techniques, to audience monitoring devices used by television rating services.

Computer-Assisted Techniques

Computers are used to enhance many information-gathering and analytical processes. They are especially useful in what have come to be known as decision support systems. These are interactive computer-based systems that help decision makers use data and models in solving unstructured problems. Decision support systems are especially useful in linking databases with spread sheets. This marriage enables analysts to quickly explore alternative trend impacts and the relative effectiveness of response options. It also permits rapid exploration of areas in which additional data may be necessary.

These capabilities are derived from the computer's ability to develop and store multiple analytical models that are readily applied to collected data. The systems essentially are similar to those used in database management.

Computer-based interactive analytical programs also enhance the value of data obtained through Delphi studies and from other sources. Once confined to simple extrapolations, computers equipped with these programs can now quickly assimilate alternative assumptions and generate sets of extrapolations.

Consensors

A markedly different technology is applied in information-gathering through the Consensor system, essentially an electronic facilitator of small group processes. The Consensor functions in the same manner as scoring equipment used in Olympic competition. Group members are equipped with hand-held devices linked to a display screen at the head of the table. Moderators ask members at appropriate times to indicate responses in terms of a point scale. When all have responded, a histogram of individual responses is displayed on the screen.

The system permits anonymous response and encourages candor on the part of group members. It also enables moderators to move rapidly through extended series of questions, exploring subject matter from multiple perspectives.

SUMMARY

Environmental monitoring is a process through which public relations practitioners identify and interpret events and trends that may create change in personal, professional, and organizational circumstances. Conducted formally or informally, the process enables practitioners to respond more efficiently and effectively to the demands of fast-changing environments.

In organizational settings, the process is usually formalized and designed to achieve several specific objectives. Organizations, as a result, can assume active rather than reactive roles in dealing with emerging trends. Early identification creates a broader range of response options. It enables organizations to identify:

Developing problems and potential impacts

Penalties that may attach to inaction

Prospective policy inconsistencies

Parallel problems in other organizations

Need for research prerequisite to decision making

Environmental monitoring consists of two basic processes and involves an extensive set of specialized techniques. The processes are scanning and tracking. The techniques are applied during the tracking process to define and characterize trends that organizations elect to monitor.

Scanning can be undertaken through examination of and extrapolation from published information in one of several ways. Individuals, scanning teams, and relatively complex organizational subunits all can be successfully used in the process.

Tracking or on-going assessment is more complex. The process keeps organizations abreast of evolving conditions and their potential consequences and enables them to evaluate alternative responses and select the most productive ones. Some two dozen identified tracking techniques can be applied in different circumstances. Most fall into one of five categories: information-gathering, analytical, technological processes, informal research, and formal research.

Information-gathering is an extension of the scanning process. Networking, trigger event identification, precursor analysis, expert and executive panels, and Delphi techniques often are used as information-gathering tools.

Analytical processes applied to accumulated data include trend extrapolation, cross-impact analysis, economic analysis, key player analysis, scenario building, and several other techniques.

Technology is interjected into the environmental monitoring process through the application of computers and other technical devices. Computers are used to enhance information-gathering and analytical processes. Interactive analytical programs enable trackers to link databases and spread sheets. That linkage, in turn, permits extensive modeling to explore an almost unlimited number of alternative developments.

Mechanical devices similar to scoring systems used in Olympic competition also are applied in environmental monitoring. Called Consensors, they are used in small group settings to provide anonymity for individual participants and permit rapid group response to multiple questions.

ADDITIONAL READING

Baskin, Otis, and Craig Aronoff. *Public Relations: The Profession and the Practice.* 2d ed. Dubuque, IA: Wm. C. Brown, 1988.

Berko, Roy M., Andrew D. Wolvin, and Ray Curtis. *This Business of Communicating.* 3d ed. Dubuque, IA: Wm. C. Brown, 1986.

Brody, E. W. *The Business of Public Relations.* New York: Praeger, 1987.

Buchholz, Rogene A., William D. Evans, and Robert A. Wagley. *Management Response to Public Issues: Concepts & Cases in Strategy Formulation.* Englewood Cliffs, NJ: Prentice Hall, 1985.

Canfield, Bertrand R. *Public Relations: Principles, Cases and Problems.* 5th ed. Homewood, IL: Richard D. Irwin, 1968.

Cantor, Bill. *Inside Public Relations: Experts in Action.* New York: Longman, 1984.

Castells, Manuel, ed. *High Technology, Space and Society.* Beverly Hills, CA: Sage, 1985.

Chase, W. Howard. *Issues Management: Origins of the Future.* Stamford, CT: Issue Action Publications, 1984.

Coates, Joseph F., et al. *Issues Management: How You Can Plan, Organize & Manage for the Future.* Mt. Airy, MD: Lomond, 1986.

Cohen, Paula Marantz. *A Public Relations Primer: Thinking and Writing in Context.* Englewood Cliffs, NJ: Prentice Hall, 1987.

Crable, Richard E., and Steven L. Vibbert. *Public Relations as Communication Management.* Edina, MN: Bellwether Press, 1986.

Cutlip, Scott M., Allen H. Center, and Glen M. Broom. *Effective Public Relations.* 6th ed. Englewood Cliffs, NJ: Prentice Hall, 1985.

Destanick, Robert L. *Managing to Keep the Customer: How to Achieve and Maintain*

Superior Customer Service Throughout the Organization. San Francisco: Jossey-Bass, 1987.

Didsbury, Howard F., ed. *Communications and the Future: Prospects, Promises and Problems*. Washington, DC: World Future Society, 1982.

Dilenschneider, Robert L., and Dan J. Forrestal. *The Dartnell Public Relations Handbook*. 3d ed. Chicago: The Dartnell Corporation, 1987.

Dizard, Wilson P., Jr. *The Coming Information Age: An Overview of Technology, Economics and Politics*. 2d ed. New York: Longman, 1985.

Hamilton, Seymour. *A Communication Audit Handbook: Helping Organizations Communicate*. New York: Longman, 1987.

Harrison, Michael I. *Diagnosing Organizations: Methods, Models and Processes*. Newbury Park, CA: Sage, 1987.

Heath, Robert L., and Richard A. Nelson. *Issues Management: Corporate Public Policymaking in an Information Society*. Beverly Hills, CA: Sage, 1986.

Hennessy, Bernard. *Public Opinion*. 5th ed. Monterey, CA: Brooks/Cole, 1985.

Herbert, Walter B., and John R. G. Jenkins, eds. *Public Relations in Canada: Some Perspectives*. Markham, Ontario: Fitzhenry & Whiteside, 1984.

Hiebert, Ray E., ed. *Precision Public Relations*. New York: Longman, 1988.

Kahn, Herman, and Anthony Wiener. *The Year 2000: A Framework for Speculation on the Next Thirty-Three Years*. New York: Macmillan, 1967.

Kilmann, Ralph H. *Beyond the Quick Fix: Managing Five Tracks to Organizational Success*. San Francisco: Jossey-Bass, 1985.

Martel, Leon. *Mastering Change: The Key to Business Success*. New York: Simon & Schuster, 1986.

Merriam, John E., and Joel Makower. *Trend Watching: How the Media Create Trends and How to Be the First to Uncover Them*. New York: AMACOM, 1987.

Moore, H. Frasier, and Kalupa, Frank B. *Public Relations: Principles, Cases and Problems*. 9th ed. Homewood, IL: Richard D. Irwin, 1985.

Nagelschmidt, Joseph S., ed. *The Public Affairs Handbook*. New York: AMACOM, 1982.

Nager, Norman R., and T. Harrell Allen. *Public Relations Management by Objectives*. New York: Longman, 1984.

Nager, Norman R., and Richard H. Truitt. *Strategic Public Relations Counseling: Models from the Counselors Academy*. New York: Longman, 1987.

Newsom, Doug, and Alan Scott. *This is PR: The Realities of Public Relations*. 3d ed. Belmont, CA: Wadsworth, 1985.

Organ, Dennis W., and W. Clay Hamner. *Organizational Behavior*. 2d ed. Plano, TX: Business Publications, Inc., 1985.

Phillips, Charles S. *Secrets of Successful Public Relations*. Englewood Cliffs, NJ: Prentice Hall, 1985.

Reilly, Robert T. *Public Relations in Action*. 2d ed. Englewood Cliffs, NJ: Prentice Hall, 1987.

Rogers, Everett M. *Communication Technology: The New Media in Society*. New York: Free Press, 1986.

Rydz, John S. *Managing Innovation: From the Executive Suite to the Shop Floor*. Cambridge, MA: Ballinger, 1986.

Settle, Robert B., and Pamela L. Alreck. *Why They Buy: The American Consumers Inside and Out*. New York: John Wiley, 1986.

Simon, Raymond. *Public Relations: Concepts and Practices*. 3d ed. New York: John Wiley, 1984.

Smith, Judson, and Janice Orr. *Designing and Developing Business Communication Programs That Work*. Glenview, IL: Scott, Foresman, 1985.

Ward, Jean, and Kathleen A. Hansen. *Search Strategies in Mass Communication*. New York: Longman, 1987.

Wheelen, Thomas L., and J. David Hunger. *Strategic Management and Business Policy*. Reading, MA: Addison-Wesley, 1983.

Wilcox, Dennis L., Phillip H. Ault, and Warren K. Agee. *Public Relations: Strategies and Tactics*. New York: Harper & Row, 1986.

Williams, Frederick. *Technology and Communication Behavior*. Belmont, CA: Wadsworth, 1987.

Wright, Theon, and Henry S. Evans. *Public Relations and the Line Manager*. New York: American Management Association, 1964.

4   Informal Research

Information acquisition employs one or more of three research strategies: primary, secondary, informal and research. Primary or formal research creates new information. (Formal research processes are described in Part Two of this text.) Secondary research involves gathering and analyzing previously published data or information. Informal research encompasses all other organized information-gathering efforts.

Informal research may be on-going or episodic. On-going informal research, commonly called environmental monitoring, was described in Chapter 3. The monitoring process described generates a knowledge base that meets most practitioners' needs for information concerning the environments in which and with which they work. Episodic research, in contrast, deals with gathering detailed information on specific subjects, usually to fill temporary needs. The most common episodic research involves in-depth information required in preparation for writing reports or proposals.

Public relations practitioners use several resources to obtain information. Their needs in most cases relate to an industrial, commercial, or institutional sector, to an organization, or to a stakeholder group. Their interests in any case may be local, regional, national, or global in scope. Needs may be immediate or less pressing, and economic resources may vary as well. Each of these elements suggests use of specific information sources ranging from personal libraries to computer databases. The nature of the need usually suggests appropriate information sources.

PROBLEM DIAGNOSIS

Applying diagnostic procedures in public relations yields clues about the information sources that should first be investigated. These procedures pinpoint one or more organizations and/or stakeholder groups. Acquiring information about specified organization(s) and group(s) thus is the first step in the process.

The second step deals with related organizations and groups, which may be parents or affiliates of the primary actors. They also may be legislative, regulatory, or other agencies with which primary or secondary groups deal.

A third step is occasionally necessary as well—delving into the industries, businesses, or activity sectors in which organizations or stakeholders are involved.

Organizations and Stakeholders

Although organizations are diverse by nature, their stakeholder groups are relatively uniform. Virtually all organizations have workers, managers and supervisors, vendors, and consumers of their products or services. All operate in one or more communities and deal directly or indirectly with several governmental and/or regulatory agencies.

Larger organizations may deliver products or services through intermediaries. Manufacturers often work with distributors as well as dealers. Many insurance companies sell their products through agencies. Publicly owned corporations also deal with shareholders and the financial community. Members are a major concern for business, professional, social, and philanthropic groups.

Public relations is a process through which organizations achieve accommodation with stakeholder groups. The process deals with specific issues of interest to the organization and one or more stakeholder groups. Information-gathering processes logically begin with the organization and groups involved in any specific issue.

Organizational Perspectives

Organizations gather and maintain considerable information about their stakeholders. Human resources departments, for example, have abundant data concerning the demographic characteristics of workers, organizational expenditures on wages and benefits, and other factors that may bear on employee or labor relations problems.

Sales and marketing departments maintain extensive records about consumers and prospective consumers of products or services. Purchasing departments are major sources of information about vendors. Legal departments are usually knowledgeable about organizational relationships with legislative and regulatory bodies.

When public relations problems arise, practitioners begin by gathering all pertinent information from these sources. The process often is extended to encompass any consultants retained by the organization, such as accounting firms, management consultants, and any others to whom the organization turns for specialized guidance.

Stakeholder Perspectives

With all internally available information in hand, practitioners next turn to external sources. Many can be of assistance when information is needed concerning individual stakeholder groups. Although the information varies considerably in specificity with different groups, it can be valuable in many situations.

External sources include the media, trade and professional associations, competitors, and governmental agencies. Each provides different kinds of information.

The mass media are helpful where stakeholder group activities have been newsworthy. Labor organizations, environmentalist groups, and consumer organizations often make news. Much of it may deal with tactics they have used in dealing with other organizations. Business, professional, or trade associations to which practitioners' clients or employers belong often have similar information available. Competitors who have dealt with similar problems may also be helpful. Competitors' assistance is usually readily forthcoming if they perceive their interests to be involved.

Governmental and regulatory bodies can also provide massive amounts of information. Financial data concerning every publicly owned firm are available from the Securities and Exchange Commission. Extensive information about unions can be obtained from the Department of Labor and the National Labor Relations Board. The Federal Communications Commission, Occupational Safety and Health Administration, Environmental Protection Agency, Federal Aviation Agency, and others can also be helpful. Most of their records are open to the public under the Freedom of Information Act.

Stakeholder-Related Groups

Many of the sources listed above can be used only indirectly. This occurs with some frequency in the financial relations and labor relations sectors. Many corporations, for example, are subsidiaries of holding companies. Holding companies may or may not file separate financial reports for their subsidiaries. Local union records similarly may be inaccessible but those of their national parents are readily available.

Information concerning special interest groups may be more difficult to find but can usually be obtained. Most advocacy groups are corporations. Corporate charters are issued by the secretary of state of the several states and copies are available from their offices. In some cases, corporate by-laws are also on file and open to inspection.

Many if not most special interest groups maintain extensive governmental relations or lobbying programs. The federal government and many states require that lobbyists be registered and that their clients be publicly identified. Pertinent records can be obtained in Washington and state capitals.

Industrial Intelligence

Still further information can often be obtained through industrial intelligence techniques. Few special interest groups confine their activities to one industry, business sector, or locality. Most operate nationally or internationally and across industrial or commercial boundaries. Public relations practitioners are only rarely unfortunate enough to represent their "first target" in a given industry. When this is the case, the information-gathering process becomes more rigorous still.

Clues as to "where they come from" are most readily obtained from the mass media but can often be found elsewhere. Local media libraries, or "morgues," and the regularly issued index to the *New York Times* often provide beginning points for the information-gathering process. The U.S. Chamber of Commerce, the Conference Board, and other national business organizations can also be helpful.

Once an organization's prior activities are known, additional information is more easily acquired. Logical sources include business, trade, or industry associations in sectors in which it has previously been involved. Associations' informational resources may be less than adequate. Their executives nevertheless may be able to provide names of members who have dealt with the group in question.

Experiences of others in similar circumstances are often helpful in public relations practice. This is especially so where practitioners take advantage of information available directly and indirectly from colleagues. The bulk of this information is contained in libraries of several types.

PERSONAL LIBRARIES

Over time most public relations practitioners build "minilibraries" that quickly become major information sources. They usually contain periodicals as well as books. Both are valuable as information sources and as "beginning points" for extended information-gathering efforts.

All these resources have become increasingly important with growth in the body of knowledge that supports public relations practice. As in law, medicine, accounting, and other professions, practitioners can no longer carry in their heads all of the information their practices require. Like other professionals, however, they must be sufficiently knowledgeable to quickly find information that a specific problem may require. Current editions of public relations books, supplemented by periodicals and newsletters, often provide that information.

Books

Students' textbooks often form a beginning point for a library as most obtain writing, research, and case problems books as well as introductory texts during their academic careers. A number of graduate-level texts are also worthy of inclusion in these libraries. So are some basic public relations reference tools.

Basic Texts

Cutlip, Center, and Broom's *Effective Public Relations*, Wilcox, Ault, and Agee's *Public Relations: Strategies and Tactics*, and Grunig and Hunt's *Managing Public Relations* arguably are the preeminent basic texts in public relations. Newsom and Scott's *This is PR: The Realities of Public Relations*, Crable and Vibert's *Public Relations as Communication Management*, and Aronoff and Baskin's *Public Relations: The Profession and the Practice* are also worthy of inclusion in practitioner libraries.

All of these books are in general use in colleges and universities. They are supplemented in many courses by several other texts that are also of value to practitioners. These include Nager and Allen's *Public Relations Management by Objectives*, Cantor's *Inside Public Relations: Experts in Action*, and Nager and Truitt's *Strategic Public Relations Counseling: Models from the Counselors Academy*. These texts are more specialized in nature and more oriented to senior practitioners.

Other Texts

Some writing texts, notably Newsom and Carrell's *Public Relations Writing: Form and Style*, and Brody and Lattimore's *Writing for Public Relations*, are worthy of inclusion in personal libraries. They qualify, however, on the basis of chapters describing the principles of persuasion and public relations theory. While writing techniques presumably become ingrained in practitioners, accessibility to pertinent theory is valuable.

Other public relations texts that should be included in practitioner libraries include several used in undergraduate research, case problems, and campaigns classes. These include Simon's *Public Relations Management: A Casebook* and Pavlik's *Public Relations: What Research Tells Us*.

Several books written primarily for use in graduate public relations courses as well as a number that deal with organizational communication should also be included. Two books by Brody, *The Business of Public Relations* and *Public Relations Programming and Production*, fall in the former category. The latter include books by Goldhaber and Kreps bearing the same name—*Organizational Communication*.

Also of value are recent editions of public relations handbooks and more specialized texts that have been published over the years. Most recently revised among the handbooks is *The Dartnell Public Relations Handbook*. The third edition, written by practitioners Robert L. Dilenschneider and Dan J. Forrestal, was published in 1987. Simon's *Public Relations Law*, although several years old, also should be part of practitioner libraries.

Periodicals

Although books are helpful for their bibliographic listings and their content, they are limited by their periodicity. A year or more can elapse between completion of a manuscript and publication of a book. Considerable change can occur in the interim.

Public relations professionals stay abreast of contemporary events through periodicals. These fall into two general categories: magazines or journals and newsletters. A host of periodicals highly valuable in public relations research are described in detail on p. 33.

OTHER LIBRARIES

When personal resources are exhausted, practitioners usually turn to other libraries. Practitioners make best use of them when armed with one or more of several current public relations bibliographies that are readily available.

With bibliographic data in hand, researchers find contemporary libraries more "user friendly" than they once were. Today many have their collections listed on computers and their number is growing.

Types of Libraries

Several types of libraries are directly or indirectly available to researchers. Their usefulness is governed by several factors in addition to the extent of researchers' lists of bibliographic citations. Physical proximity is a major variable. Information not available in local libraries can often be obtained from others but only over a period of days or weeks.

Libraries most readily accessible to practitioners are usually components of public library systems. In larger communities, their resources are supplemented by college and university libraries. Many business and professional organizations also maintain libraries for members and occasionally make collections accessible to others.

Public Libraries

The quality of public libraries is a major variable. The size and value of their collections usually vary with community size and budgetary constraints. Their personnel, however, tend to be exceptionally helpful.

Public libraries usually house limited numbers of technical and professional books and periodicals. Available books, more frequently than in college and university libraries, are often not the most recent editions. Many public libraries, however, maintain working relationships with libraries in larger cities and can obtain needed materials on loan.

Academic Libraries

The quality of academic libraries is no less a variable than in public libraries. Most academic library holdings are of relatively current vintage. Breadth and depth of material tends to be inconsistent, however, in specific subject areas.

Two factors produce the inconsistencies. One is the specialty of the college or university involved. The other is the scope of curricular offerings. Library holdings expand as graduate degree programs come into being. Libraries at colleges and universities offering master's degrees are usually superior to those offering only undergraduate curricula. They are better still where doctoral programs are offered. Improvement occurs, however, only in those disciplines in which the graduate degrees are offered.

Library collections in public relations, both books and periodicals, are usually superior at schools that offer degrees in journalism or public relations. Existence of master's or doctoral programs in these subjects suggests the presence of even better resources. Neither undergraduate nor graduate curricula in other disciplines are apt to produce improvement in library holdings in public relations.

The same principles apply in other disciplines. Researchers seeking data on management or marketing, for example, will probably find what they are seeking at universities offering business degrees. Their needs are unlikely to be met at typical liberal arts colleges.

Specialized Libraries

When specialized information is necessary, still other libraries on college and university campuses and elsewhere may prove valuable. Most universities and some colleges maintain professional schools and centers for specialized study in one or more academic disciplines. They often maintain branch libraries separate and apart from the main library.

Schools of medicine, dentistry, law, veterinary medicine, accounting, architecture, and engineering usually maintain their own libraries on university campuses. Within these schools, public relations practitioners occasionally find academics whose research interests prompt them to maintain specialized personal libraries.

Other specialized libraries are often maintained in the offices of business, trade, and professional associations, including the Public Relations Society of America (PRSA). These can be most readily identified through the yellow pages of local telephone directories.

The PRSA library, maintained at the society's headquarters at 33 Irving Place in New York City, is accessible at nominal cost through a telephone and mail request service. The library publishes a list of holdings by subject area. Materials range from samples of brochures and newsletters to complete entries in the society's annual awards competition. Requests for specific information are filled by mail. PRSA is also planning to incorporate its library content into a computer database that will provide more rapid access to content.

Using Libraries

A number of specialized services and facilities available in many libraries can be helpful to researchers. Library cooperatives or interlibrary loan services and computer systems are the most valuable.

Library Access

Except for libraries maintained by associations, researchers usually experience little difficulty in gaining access to libraries. Community libraries are open to all. College and university libraries usually make their resources available to area residents by special permission which seldom is withheld.

Such permission can be valuable to researchers even if library collections are inadequate for their needs. Many public libraries and almost all college and university libraries are part of a library cooperative. Usually referred to as interlibrary loan systems, the cooperatives enable librarians to obtain books or copies of periodical articles that may not be in their own collections. Many libraries also subscribe to computer databases containing research papers and other unpublished material of interest to researchers. Fees for database searches are usually low although copies of requested materials may take several days to arrive (see Chapter 5).

Library Computers

Libraries equipped with "in-house" computers are easily used and typically list all of the library's books by subject, author, and title with a brief description and the publication date. Equipped with multiple terminals, such systems are replacing traditional card catalogs in larger libraries. In a few of the largest, systems are accessible externally through microcomputers equipped with modems (modulator/demodulators) and hooked to telephone lines.

Computer systems are especially helpful when researchers have compiled "starting point" bibliographies before going to libraries or "dialing up" library computers. A complete search of a million-volume collection can be completed in minutes when lists of subjects, authors, and titles are compiled in advance.

OTHER RESOURCES

An almost limitless array of information sources comes into play as researchers move beyond the scope of community resources. Sources generally can be classified as governmental, business/professional, and not-for-profit. In some cases, as in not-for-profit research and development subsidiaries of trade or professional associations, they may defy easy classification.

Some resources are not readily identified and located. A huge volume of information generated by and available from the federal government is a classic example. Most can be had for the asking, but finding who to ask is another matter. Federal departments and their subsidiaries are so large, so many, and so geographically diverse that identifying the office that has the desired information can be a research task in itself.

Information from business/professional and not-for-profit organizations is more readily found, but researchers nevertheless must know where to look. Unfortunately, no existing search strategy will generate uniformly successful results. There are several, however, that can be used as starting points to launch usually successful efforts.

Search Strategies

Successful information search strategies are developed by applying logic or common sense to limited knowledge. Two assumptions, the first general and the second tentative, are usually applicable: (1) The information is available—somewhere; (2) the information is most likely to be found in the geographic locale where the activity is most common.

Each assumption suggests a search strategy. Available information is in the hands of some organization. The researcher need only find the appropriate organization. If the activity involved is centered in one or more geographic areas, companies active in the field under study usually exist in that area. Alternative strategies thus involve looking for organizations by type and/or in geographic context.

Identifying Organizations

Virtually every field of human endeavor produces organizations, such as individual businesses, trade associations, and governmental or quasi-governmental groups with which the others inevitably deal. Information of potential value to researchers is available from organizations that researchers should be able to identify in each of these groups.

The most detailed information available about organizations is found in directories. Directories are published, usually at annual intervals, by a host of for-profit firms. There is even a directory of directories for those who experience difficulty in identifying types of organizations in which they are interested.

Many directories of a general nature are found in libraries. Others can be obtained through business or professional organizations. Some may be available only through an organization's members. Most U.S. manufacturers, for example, are listed in national buyers guides such as the *Thomas Register*. Virtually all of the nation's mass media are listed in the several directories published by Standard Rate and Data Service. Names of daily newspapers' editorial executives can be found in *Editor & Publisher's* yearbook.

National directories often have their counterparts at state and, occasionally, local levels. The chambers of commerce and industrial development boards of all the states publish directories, as do many city and county chambers of commerce. Although seldom all-inclusive because they charge for the space involved, telephone yellow pages also can be used in identifying business, trade, professional, and philanthropic groups.

Geographic Strategies

Organizations of specific types are often readily identified geographically. Governmental offices are usually situated in principal cities within their jurisdictions. Most national business, trade, and professional groups are headquartered in Washington although some are in New York, Chicago, and, to a lesser extent, other cities.

Organizations that serve agricultural interests are usually close to their members. Trade organizations dealing with the citrus industry, for example, are generally in Florida, California, and Texas. Most of those serving the cotton industry are in Memphis, Tennessee. Tobacco interests are concentrated in the Carolinas and Virginia; most automotive organizations are in Michigan. Basic knowledge of this sort would lead logically to contacts with industrial or agricultural agencies in the states involved.

Alternative Approaches

Geographically oriented searches in many cases also lead to governmental agencies. Virtually every industry in the United States is regulated in some manner and some must cope with multiple legislative and regulatory bodies. Many of the agencies conduct research in the industries they serve. Virtually all agencies maintain extensive records concerning firms with which they deal.

When researchers want information concerning agricultural chemicals, for example, the U.S. Department of Agriculture might be a logical starting point. Depending on the nature of information being sought, other agencies might be better sources. At minimum, inquiries might be productively directed to:

1. Federal and state departments of transportation that regulate safety in the transportation of agricultural chemicals, many of them toxic.

2. The Occupational Safety and Health Administration that regulates the handling of these materials in manufacturing plants, at distribution points, and in their ultimate application.

3. The Environmental Protection Agency that is involved from a different perspective in manufacturing, distribution, and application.

Depending on the nature of information being sought, further inquiries might be addressed to other governmental units. When researchers are concerned with air or water pollution, for example, multiple jurisdictions are often involved. The nation's major rivers border multiple states and air movement knows no boundaries.

Some libraries are logical starting points in seeking information from federal agencies. Many libraries, especially on college and university campuses, house large collections of government documents.

IDENTIFYING PROSPECTIVE MEDIA

The information-gathering process arms public relations practitioners for communication tasks ahead. Data obtained in identifying and characterizing stakeholder groups serve in part to establish criteria for message content and media selection.

Group characteristics are indicative of media usage habits. Demographic and socioeconomic factors, for example, suggest the extent to which print and electronic mass media can be successfully used. The nature of stakeholder groups usually suggests using specific controlled communication channels as well.

Media Characteristics

Because of audience fragmentation in recent years the mass media infrequently are efficient message delivery vehicles. The mass media focus primarily on issues of interest to every consumer or voter. Such issues are relatively rare among the many concerns that organizations must address in the context of specific stakeholder groups. More selective channels of communication therefore must be found if organizational messages are to be efficiently conveyed.

Employees and, to a lesser extent, shareholders are readily identified. Employee names and addresses are known. The bulk of shareholders can be similarly identified. Members of both groups can be readily reached by mail. Employees are even more accessible through organizational communication channels.

Other stakeholders are more difficult to reach, especially when they are dispersed over large geographic areas. Specialized media, such as trade and professional journals, then become preferred communication channels. Information-gathering processes in these circumstances should include analyses of available communication channels and their applicability in terms of public relations problems at hand.

Alternative Channels

Most business and professional groups are served by multiple media, as indicated by the previous listing of those serving public relations. Analyses of stakeholder groups should involve a study of their media habits, including an examination of the characteristics of media they are prone to use.

Media habits are most readily identified through publications such as those of the Standard Rate and Data Service of Skokie, Illinois. SRDS, as it is commonly called, publishes multiple advertising media directories designed to supply rate information and mechanical specifications to advertising agencies.

Directory content often includes two features of interest in public relations practice. The SRDS business publication directory, for example, often provides geographic distributions of magazine readers and categorizes them by job title within their organizations.

Since organizational decision-making patterns vary, differences in magazine readership can be critical to public relations success. Information concerning a new manufacturing technique, for example, usually is better placed in the hands of engineers or plant managers than chief executives or chief operating officers. SRDS readership analyses for competing publications may readily indicate which will prove most effective in given circumstances.

APPLYING DATA

Data produced through informal research or information-gathering processes are of real but limited value. They enable practitioners to define contemporary conditions, and provide historical insights into the behaviors of stakeholder groups in given circumstances. They are lacking, however, in one significant respect: They cannot be used with any degree of accuracy in predicting future events.

Knowledge of current conditions enables practitioners to prepare comprehensive reports to senior managers. Anecdotal information concerning past behavior of stakeholders permits historical analyses that can be helpful, to some extent, in suggesting alternative organizational responses. Precise statistical information is necessary, however, to analyze trends that can more accurately suggest how specific problems may evolve.

Appropriate statistics can be obtained in only two ways. The first, secondary analysis of previously published data, is discussed in Chapter 5. The second, primary research to produce new data, is the subject of later chapters.

SUMMARY

Informal research is one of three methods practitioners use to obtain information necessary in solving public relations problems. The others are secondary and primary research.

Informal research begins with problem diagnosis, a process through which a problem or problems are analyzed and the involved stakeholder groups are identified. Once the stakeholders are known, practitioners turn to other components of their organizations and external sources to obtain basic information about each group.

Considerable information concerning employees, shareholders, vendors, consumers, and other groups is available within organizations. Additional data are readily available through the news media, trade and professional associations, competitors, and governmental agencies that deal with these groups.

Regulatory bodies can be especially valuable sources. Labor organizations, publicly owned corporations, and others that fall within the jurisdiction of federal or state regulatory bodies are usually required to file reports concerning their activities. Most reports are accessible under the Freedom of Information Act.

Business and trade organizations also are valuable information sources. The U.S. Chamber of Commerce, the Conference Board, and a host of other organizations that serve specific segments of the business and industrial communities maintain extensive records and research programs. Records include information such as labor contracts, the history of environmental movements and groups, and the like.

With basic information in hand, practitioners usually turn to libraries for further information. Personal, public, and college or university libraries are most helpful. Informational resources of the Public Relations Society of America and similar professional groups also can be of assistance.

Personal libraries, often built upon academic texts used in undergraduate and graduate public relations curricula, should be maintained and enlarged by adding current text editions and specialized books in public relations and organizational communication. Periodicals published for practitioners and academics in public relations—both magazines and newspapers—are valuable resources. Collectively, the content of a personal public relations library should yield a wealth of bibliographic citations that can be used in obtaining information from other sources.

Most public and almost all college and university libraries offer multiple sources of information. College and university libraries maintain extensive collections in academic areas in which their students are engaged. Many libraries participate in interlibrary loan programs through which they can obtain books they do not own.

Specialized libraries often are maintained by business and professional schools and by centers for specialized study within colleges and universities. These are usually housed apart from central libraries.

Access to multiple computer databases is available through many libraries. Skilled librarians in most cases will perform searches for clients at nominal cost. These yield lists of books, periodicals, and other materials that can then be obtained by researchers.

Beyond libraries, there exists an almost limitless volume of information stored primarily in the archives of governmental and not-for-profit organizations. The information is so voluminous, in fact, that retrieval is a major difficulty.

One of several search strategies can make the retrieval process more manageable. The first involves identifying organizations with which stakeholder groups are apt to be involved. Business, trade, and professional groups often are most helpful. The second strategy deals with governmental or regulatory bodies with which stakeholders may be involved. Extensive information is available, for example, concerning labor unions and virtually any group that engages in lobbying activities at federal or state levels.

Information obtained from these sources enables public relations practitioners to prepare relatively detailed analyses of stakeholder groups, their objectives, their strategies, and their likely courses of action in any given set of circumstances. This information, however, is relatively weak in its predictive value as it will be largely historical and anecdotal. It seldom will be indicative of any significant long-term developmental trends.

Information of the latter sort can be obtained in one of two ways: secondary analysis, which involves reexamining previously published statistical data, and formal research, which creates new information concerning stakeholders and contemporary circumstances. These subjects are addressed in subsequent chapters.

ADDITIONAL READING

Aronoff, Craig E., and Otis W. Baskin. *Public Relations: The Profession and the Practice.* 2d ed. Dubuque, IA: Wm. C. Brown, 1988.

Berko, Roy M., Andrew D. Wolvin, and Ray Curtis. *This Business of Communicating.* 3d ed. Dubuque, IA: Wm. C. Brown, 1986.

Brody, E. W. *The Business of Public Relations.* New York: Praeger, 1987.

———. *Public Relations Programming and Production.* New York: Praeger, 1988.

———. *Communicating for Survival: Coping with Diminishing Human Resources.* New York: Praeger, 1988.

Brody, E. W., and Dan L. Lattimore. *Writing for Public Relations.* New York: Praeger, 1989.

Buchholz, Rogene A., William D. Evans, and Robert A. Wagley. *Management Response to Public Issues: Concepts & Cases in Strategy Formulation.* Englewood Cliffs, NJ: Prentice Hall, 1985.

Canfield, Bertrand R. *Public Relations: Principles, Cases and Problems.* 5th ed. Homewood, IL: Richard D. Irwin, 1968.

Cantor, Bill. *Inside Public Relations: Experts in Action.* New York: Longman, 1984.

Center, Allen H., and Frank E. Walsh. *Public Relations Practices: Managerial Case Studies and Problems*, 3d ed. Englewood Cliffs, NJ: Prentice Hall, 1985.

Cohen, Paula Marantz. *A Public Relations Primer: Thinking and Writing in Context.* Englewood Cliffs, NJ: Prentice Hall, 1987.

Crable, Richard E., and Steven L. Vibert. *Public Relations as Communication Management.* Edina, MN: Bellwether Press, 1986.

Cutlip, Scott M., Allen H. Center, and Glen M. Broom. *Effective Public Relations.* 6th ed. Englewood Cliffs, NJ: Prentice Hall, 1985.

Degan, Clara, ed., *Communicators' Guide to Marketing.* New York: Longman, 1987.

Didsbury, Howard F., ed. *Communications and the Future: Prospects, Promises and Problems.* Washington, DC: World Future Society, 1982.

Dilenschneider, Robert L., and Dan J. Forrestal. *The Dartnell Public Relations Handbook.* 3d ed. Chicago: The Dartnell Corporation, 1987.

Dizard, Wilson P., Jr. *The Coming Information Age: An Overview of Technology, Economics and Politics.* 2d ed. New York: Longman, 1985.

Goldhaber, Gerald M. *Organizational Communication.* 4th ed. Dubuque, IA: Wm. C. Brown, 1986.

Grunig, James E., and Todd Hunt. *Managing Public Relations.* New York: Holt, Rinehart and Winston, 1984.

Hamilton, Seymour. *A Communication Audit Handbook: Helping Organizations Communicate*. New York: Longman, 1987.

Hennessy, Bernard. *Public Opinion*. 5th ed. Monterey, CA: Brooks/Cole, 1985.

Hiebert, Ray E., ed. *Precision Public Relations*. New York: Longman, 1988.

Glossbrenner, Alfred. *How to Look It Up Online*. New York: St. Martin's Press, 1987.

Kelly, John M. *How to Check Out Your Competition: A Complete Plan for Investigating Your Market*. New York: John Wiley, 1987.

Kreps, Gary L. *Organizational Communication*. New York: Longman, 1986.

Moore, H. Frasier, and Kalupa, Frank B. *Public Relations: Principles, Cases and Problems*. 9th ed. Homewood, IL: Richard D. Irwin, 1985.

Nager, Norman R., and T. Harrell Allen. *Public Relations Management by Objectives*. New York: Longman, 1984.

Nager, Norman R., and Richard H. Truitt. *Strategic Public Relations Counseling: Models from the Counselors Academy*. New York: Longman, 1987.

Newsom, Doug, and Alan Scott. *This is PR: The Realities of Public Relations*. 3d ed. Belmont, CA: Wadsworth, 1985.

Newsom, Doug, and Bob Carrell. *Public Relations Writing: Form and Style*. 2d ed. Belmont, CA: Wadsworth, 1986.

Patton, Michael Q. *Creative Evaluation*. 2d ed. Beverly Hills, CA: Sage, 1987.

Pavlik, John V. *Public Relations: What Research Tells Us*. Beverly Hills, CA: Sage, 1987.

Phillips, Charles S. *Secrets of Successful Public Relations*. Englewood Cliffs, NJ: Prentice Hall, 1985.

Reilly, Robert T. *Public Relations in Action*. 2d ed. Englewood Cliffs, NJ: Prentice Hall, 1987.

Rogers, Everett M. *Communication Technology: The New Media in Society*. New York: Free Press, 1986.

Settle, Robert B., and Pamela L. Alreck. *Why They Buy: The American Consumers Inside and Out*. New York: John Wiley, 1986.

Simon, Morton J. *Public Relations Law*. New York: Appleton-Century-Crofts, 1969.

Simon, Raymond. *Public Relations Management: A Casebook*. Columbus, OH: Publishing Horizons, 1986.

Smith, Judson, and Janice Orr. *Designing and Developing Business Communication Programs That Work*. Glenview, IL: Scott, Foresman, 1985.

Ward, Jean, and Kathleen A. Hansen. *Search Strategies in Mass Communication*. New York: Longman, 1987.

Wilcox, Dennis L., Phillip H. Ault, and Warren K. Agee. *Public Relations: Strategies and Tactics*. New York: Harper & Row, 1986.

Williams, Frederick. *Technology and Communication Behavior*. Belmont, CA: Wadsworth, 1987.

5   Secondary Research

Secondary research is the analysis of existing statistical data to produce insights into public relations problems. Considerable data applicable to any given problem often is encountered during the informal research process. Additional data can be obtained through deliberate searches oriented toward specific organizations, types of organizations, and stakeholder groups as well as problems with which researchers are dealing.

Search strategies are dictated by the nature of problems and stakeholder groups involved. Most focus on researchers' organizations, organizations with which researchers' employers or clients are concerned, or with one or more stakeholder groups. Different strategies are indicated in each case.

VALIDITY OF DATA

Search strategies are governed by the nature and validity of available data. Informal research efforts usually generate significant amounts of statistical material that varies in value. Speeches by corporate officers, for example, often are sprinkled with statistics that defy interpretation. Corporate annual reports, on the other hand, are more reliable and are most helpful when researchers obtain copies for several consecutive years.

The quality of information is governed by the context. Corporate officers' speeches are invariably designed to impress their audiences. Annual reports may be similarly oriented, but they contain audited financial statements that are necessarily more candid in nature. Comparison of annual financial statements and other statistical data over a period of years produces still more enlightening insights. Data contained in these documents vary, however, both qualitatively and quantitatively.

Qualitative Variables

The word "qualitative" refers to two factors: source credibility and statistical accuracy. Speeches by corporate officers are not necessarily misleading. They nevertheless can create distorted impressions unless examined with special care.

Several factors contribute to potential researcher problems. First, speeches are designed for specific audiences and seldom provide balanced overviews of the speaker's organization. Second, the data presented often are ambiguous. Data in corporate reports are more precise but require more care in interpretation.

Speeches

Two major interpretive problems are usually encountered in analyzing speech content. First, speakers almost invariably deal in percentages rather than specific quantities. Percentages are used in speeches because their meanings are more readily grasped by audiences. As base data often are lacking, however, the percentages are meaningless.

Published reports of oil company profits during the Arab oil embargoes were typical of misleading statistics. Headlines dealt with profit increases of 100 to 300 percent and produced considerable resentment among motorists waiting in lines to buy gasoline. Few paused to consider a logical question: "One-hundred to three-hundred percent of what?"

Petroleum industry profits are notoriously volatile. A 300 percent increase in net profit is not unusual from a bad year to a good year. A 600 percent increase, in fact, could hardly be called unconscionable if prior year's profits were only one percent of sales. Current year's profits would then be six percent, which few executives would find satisfactory.

Annual Reports

Oil company annual reports for the years in question provided more balanced pictures of their true profitability. The pictures varied, however, with the data provided and the abilities of report readers.

Descriptive portions of annual reports can be deceptive. Most take a "best foot forward" approach. Messages of chairmen and chief executive officers are cast in positive terms. The primary objective of annual reports, from their perspective, is to enhance the image of the organization in the eyes of shareholders and members of the financial community. As a result, they tend to gloss over any bad news while exaggerating any positive results.

Financial statements, audited and certified by accounting firms, are more accurate but require careful examination. Poor operating performance, for example, can be offset by "one time" profits on sale of assets. Careful analyses focused on differences in comparable year-to-year data quickly reveal such statistical anomalies.

Quantitative Variables

Ability to compare year-to-year or period-to-period performance compounds the value of data in every situation. Comparability, however, is in itself a variable that requires researcher attention. Some data obviously are beyond valid comparison. Other data may be comparable only in part. The differences usually are quantitative and arise out of different data collection procedures that render results incomparable.

This can occur even where serial statistics are involved. Although data produced by agencies of federal and state government, for example, appear universally comparable, this is not always the case. Debate during the late 1980s over the consumer price index points up this issue. On one side were those who believed the "market basket" on which the Consumer Price Index was based had become obsolete. On the other was a group resisting change on grounds that it would destroy comparability.

Researchers must carefully examine all data they propose to analyze through secondary research. Results of different studies require exceptionally close scrutiny but potential problems in serial data must be considered as well.

Separate Studies

Differences in separate studies dealing with the same basic subject matter arise in two primary areas. One encompasses original researchers' population parameters and sampling techniques. The other is geographic differences. Both elements require special attention in academic research.

A great deal of academic research is geographically limited. It may deal with a single community, state, or region. Differences between populations in these areas and the area in which the secondary researcher is concerned can be considerable. Studies of public transportation systems, for example, almost inevitably will produce different results because population density varies among areas served.

Serial Studies

In some circumstances differences in data produced in serial studies are more difficult to discern. Most data published by federal agencies are extensively footnoted to indicate any inconsistencies that may render individual figures less than wholly comparable. Information compiled by business, professional, and trade associations often is published without note of such variations.

Changes in reporting and record-keeping procedures also can produce inconsistencies. These are often found, for example, in health agencies' reporting of communicable disease cases. Data collected in the nineteenth century are notoriously less reliable than those of the twentieth. Haphazard physician reporting rather than agency record keeping usually is at fault, but the data are nevertheless unreliable. Researchers working in medical and other technological areas should also be wary of change in data quality produced over time by ever-improving diagnostic and measurement techniques. Apparent increases in death and disease rates in the past have been attributed to such improvements.

ORGANIZATIONAL RESEARCH

Data gathered by organizations for internal use are usually relatively reliable. Most are available in serial form. Data often are limited, however, by the number of years for which they are available.

Most organizations are averse to unnecessary record keeping, but their records for recent years usually are more voluminous than those of earlier decades, often as a result of changes in governmental requirements. The advent of the Occupational Safety and Health Administration and the Environmental Protection Agency, for example, brought a myriad of new record-keeping requirements. Although requirements are considered burdensome by managers, resulting data often are valuable to public relations practitioners.

Secondary research within organizations is almost invariably oriented toward one of several specific stakeholder groups. Specific research projects often deal with employees and prospective employees, managers and supervisors, shareholders, distributors and dealers, customers and prospective customers, and vendors. Considerable information concerning each of these groups is available from multiple organizational sources. Much of it, however, may not be obviously applicable to practitioner needs. Sorting out the pertinent from the inapplicable thus becomes the researcher's first task.

Types of Data

Public relations practitioners' concerns usually focus on attitude and opinion within stakeholder groups. These elements are amenable to indirect as well as direct measurement. Direct measurement can be expensive and does not necessarily produce superior results.

Applicability of measurement techniques varies across stakeholder groups and in keeping with researcher needs. Variation among groups is a function of the extent of existing bodies of knowledge. Organizations necessarily know more about employees than customers. Researcher need is a more volatile factor. It varies with conditions among stakeholder groups. Some of them are predictable while others are not.

Direct Measurement

Communication audits, surveys, and other direct measurement techniques vary in application. Many organizations use them consistently to track prevalent conditions among stakeholder groups. Others apply them regularly to limited numbers of stakeholder groups. Still others use direct measurement only occasionally in response to specific needs.

Needs often are a function of emerging problems. Some can be anticipated while others defy prediction. When problems, such as the labor shortage in the late 1980s, can be anticipated, appropriate attitude and opinion monitoring devices can be put in place on a timely basis. A wildcat strike, on the other hand, defies advance preparation.

Audit results are more enlightening when conducted regularly rather than erratically. Periodic audit data accurately reflect attitude/opinion change. Individual audits conducted in response to isolated problems often are less productive than already available indirect indicators.

Communication audits covering multiple stakeholder groups are favored among larger, more affluent organizations that function in volatile environments. Smaller organizations often use audit techniques in monitoring attitude and opinion among individual stakeholder groups. Where resources are limited, organizations often turn to indirect measurement.

Indirect Measurement

An almost limitless number of indicators are available within most organizations that accurately reflect attitude and opinion among stakeholder groups. The word ''reflect'' is appropriately applied as the indicators involved do not measure attitude or opinion. They consist instead of data concerning elements that logically can be assumed to relate directly to attitude and opinion.

Absenteeism and tardiness rates, for example, are generally accepted as accurate indicators of employee attitude and opinion. Change in these indicators, for better or worse, can safely be taken as indicative of improvement or deterioration in attitude and opinion. A host of other indicators are equally useful in assessing organizational relationships with employees and other groups.

Workers

Employee turnover rates often are high on researchers' lists of worker attitude and opinion indicators. Quality control data can be equally valuable. Productivity levels and defects in manufactured products tend to increase as morale deteriorates. Volume of customer complaints is similarly considered an accurate indicator of employee morale.

Managers and Supervisors

Indicators of worker satisfaction or dissatisfaction are also considered accurate predictors of supervisory and managerial proficiency. Each of the factors noted above becomes an even better indicator when data involved are examined across operational units. Many consider worker performance to be the most accurate measure of managerial and supervisory proficiency.

Shareholders

Satisfaction among shareholders was formerly considered to vary directly with organizations' fiscal performance and therefore require little monitoring. This is no longer the case. Shareholders increasingly are holding organizations accountable for performance in areas such as environmental protection and involvement with unpopular governments. Shareholder turnover rates thus have become a major indicator of attitude and opinion.

Customers

Like shareholders, customers are increasingly influenced by multiple factors. While customer votes are counted in sales dollars, organizations have found it necessary to monitor attitude and opinion in other areas as well. Domestic automotive manufacturers, for example, constantly monitor buyer satisfaction with product quality.

Dealers/Distributors

Auto manufacturers' buyer monitoring programs are also a component of their dealer-distributor assessment systems. Manufacturers are dependent on dealers to sell their products and develop customer loyalty. Manufacturer concerns in this area have produced extensive monitoring of customer complaints through indirect as well as direct research. The indirect involves tracking such factors as numbers of buyers who use dealer service departments and numbers who change brands when trading automobiles.

The number of indirect attitude and opinion indicators available within organizations is virtually limitless. Researchers' primary task in applying such indicators is twofold: First, they must be found; second, their validity must be accepted by senior managers.

INDUSTRY RESEARCH

Public relations practice frequently requires information about organizations' competitive positions or relative stature in the commercial, industrial, or institutional sectors in which they operate. Practitioner concerns usually relate to two factors. First, much of their work deals with differentiating their clients and employers from similar organizations in the minds of customers or consumers. Second, while attempting to ensure that organizations they represent are perceived in as salutary a manner as possible, they must adhere religiously to truth and accuracy.

The latter requirement is especially important. Stakeholder respect and confidence are perishable commodities. Both are especially susceptible to deterioration through release of misleading information. Questionable organizational claims for products or services can create unacceptable risk. Risk can be eliminated only through factual data.

Needed information can be gathered from a host of sources, but most fall within three categories: trade sources, government sources, and third party sources. Collectively, these sources can provide an almost limitless volume of information.

Trade Sources

The term "trade sources" is somewhat misleading as it implies organizations such as trade and professional associations as well as business publications. Considerably more is involved.

Information about organizations can also be obtained by direct inquiry, observation, site visits, and examination of published materials.

Trade Groups

Business, trade, and professional associations are a major source of information. Such groups exist in almost every area of human endeavor. They are often known only to their members. They exist, however, in virtually every field of interest.

Efforts to obtain data from these groups is a two-step process. First, organizations must be identified. Second, members with client or employer organizations must be found.

Directories of trade and professional associations are published by Columbia Books, Inc. (777 14th Street NW, Washington, D.C. 20005); the Gale Research Co. (Book Tower, Detroit, Michigan 48226); and R. R. Bowker Co. (1180 Avenue of the Americas, New York, New York 10026). Many libraries have copies of these directories.

Publications

Virtually every business, trade, and professional group publishes at least one membership magazine or newsletter. Those that accept advertising are listed by Standard Rate and Data Service. Others are listed in public relations directories. Subscriptions are usually included in members' dues and are available at commercial rates to others.

Many organizations also publish membership directories, industry surveys, and technical reports that can be of value in public relations practice. Like publication subscriptions, they are usually available without cost to members and at a nominal charge to others.

Copies of industry publications, including those of membership groups, are or should be available in most organizations. Many are accessible through college or university libraries as well (see Chapter 4).

Meetings and Shows

Business, professional, and industrial trade shows and meetings can be equally enlightening. They are especially valuable as sources of information concerning competitors' products, services, and capabilities.

Literature and technical specifications for products usually are distributed to all attendees of trade and industrial shows. Literature usually includes information on competitor promotional efforts and technical data indicative of relative product strength and weaknesses.

Other Sources

A surprising amount of valuable information can be obtained from many organizations for the asking. Annual and quarterly reports can be as helpful as product literature. While essentially self-serving, reports often provide insights into organizations' strategic plans.

Still more information can be obtained by taking plant tours, attending open houses and, sometimes surprisingly, by merely asking. Many organizations have weak or nonexistent policies concerning release of information. A letter or telephone call to an appropriate party often produces information that the company in question would have been better advised to protect.

Governmental Sources

Governments are the largest single source of information used by public relations practitioners. Virtually every government in the world collects business information. Most is used for governmental purposes but a great deal is compiled to assist organizations.

In the United States, more than two dozen national regulatory agencies and the several cabinet departments gather and distribute information. Some can be obtained for the asking. Other data may require special efforts.

Available Data

Summaries of published and readily available information can be obtained on request from the Superintendent of Documents, U.S. Government Printing Office, Washington, D.C. 20406. Categories in which researchers are interested should be specified.

The Department of Commerce is the largest compiler of business information. The department's Census of Manufacturers, published at five-year intervals, and supplemental special studies can be especially helpful.

The Securities and Exchange Commission and Department of Labor are often consulted by public relations practitioners. The SEC can provide copies of periodic financial filings required of all publicly held corporations. The Department of Labor requires annual reports from labor unions that can be helpful in labor relations problems.

Other sources are the National Reference Center at the Library of Congress, the U.S. Coast and Geodetic Survey, the Internal Revenue Service, the Interstate Commerce Commission, the Bureau of Labor Statistics, and the Patent and Trademark Office. A university librarian experienced in government documents can be of invaluable assistance in guiding researchers to specific information.

Other Information

While most information compiled by the federal government is available for the asking, some can be obtained only through pressure. When requests are refused, researchers may file formal petitions under the Freedom of Information Act, an act that requires the government to make non-classified documents available to all citizens.

During the past ten years, Freedom of Information Act users have obtained considerable information from governmental agencies that otherwise would have been beyond their reach. FOI petitions, for example, produced information for Hancock Laboratories about rival Pfizer Pharmaceuticals' production processes. Competitors obtained one of Monsanto's herbicide formulas from the Environmental Protection Agency in the same manner. And information about Control Data Corporation's capabilities and costs was obtained by other computer manufacturers after the firm received a multimillion dollar computer services contract.

Third Party Sources

Although more often employed in areas other than public relations, several additional sources of business information are noteworthy. They often are used in developing data for strategic planning and marketing. These are areas in which public relations practitioners are increasingly becoming involved.

The process by which these information sources are used is more often called *industrial intelligence* than research. It involves systematically soliciting information from groups that, by their nature, are apt to have valuable data. They include customers, suppliers, intermediaries, and competitors.

Customers

Competitors' customers have been a major source of information for many organizations. IBM, for example, long has employed field personnel as well as sales representatives as information-gatherers. Information IBM gained concerning consumer perceptions of competitive products has enabled the company to define and profitably fill a number of product niches.

Other information-gathering techniques applied to obtain data from customers are regular calls by organizational executives. They are designed primarily to solicit responses to two questions: "How can we serve you better?" and "How are our competitors failing to meet your needs?" Competitor weaknesses create opportunities. Seminars and conferences for customers and prospective customers on contemporary topics of mutual interest also serve to elicit such information.

Suppliers

A great deal of information concerning competitors' plans can be extrapolated from data about their purchases of products and services. Vendors obtain considerable information that customers erroneously assume to be confidential. Much of it ultimately finds its way to competitors.

More valuable are the organization's own contacts in several service industries, especially banking and insurance. Absolute confidentiality among bankers is more perceived than real. A request from a valued customer often produces substantial information about a competitor or competitors. The same technique can be productive with insurance agents, especially when questions deal with common industry risks and coverages.

Intermediaries

Wholesalers, distributors, manufacturers' agents, and others in similar intermediary positions often know a great deal about markets and individual firms. They frequently know what products are selling or not selling, and why.

"Why" can be especially significant. Products and services usually fail to sell because they lack a specific feature or fall short of promised performance in a given area. Either symptom can suggest an effective communication strategy.

Competitors

Competitors are not apt to provide information that might be used to their disadvantage. A significant exception to this rule, however, can be productively applied.

Where company A competes with company B and company B competes with company C, A may be more than willing to assist C in competing with B. Competition, like politics, can create strange bedfellows.

STAKEHOLDER RESEARCH

Information concerning specific stakeholder groups external to the organization is available from diverse sources. Competitors often perceive their interests to be coincident in some situations. Labor relations problems and/or difficulties arising from the activities of special interest groups, for example, often are viewed as common problems.

These conditions produce what might be described as "permanent limited alliances" that arise out of shared interests or concerns. They are unlike the "temporary total alliances" that often are created by transient emergencies.

Permanent limited alliances bring members of a commercial, industrial, or institutional group together to fight a common foe. Temporary total alliances result when groups that otherwise may be adversaries find themselves momentarily allied out of necessity or convenience. Such alliances do not preclude competition in other areas.

External stakeholders with whom most organizations are concerned include prospective employees and shareholders, multiple governmental agencies, and an assortment of special interest groups. Each is important to the organization for different reasons. Information about all of them is vital to effective planning as well as communication efforts.

Prospective Employees

Information of vital importance concerning prospective employees is available to organizations. The importance of the data arises from demographic trends indicating significant labor shortages through the early years of the twenty-first century. These conditions suggest that organizations will be forced to identify and establish early communication with prospective employees, especially in professional and technical categories.

Labor Categories

Organizational human resources departments are logical starting points for pertinent research. Many of them deal extensively in manpower-need projections by vocational area. These projections are then examined in context with existing and prospective resources.

Labor supplies will vary across occupational categories. By the mid–1980s, the nation was experiencing a major shortage of nurses. Nursing school enrollments were down as well, indicating that the shortage would become still more critical. Similar shortages were also being predicted for teachers. Surpluses were being forecast, however, for physicians, for attorneys, and in other professions.

Information Sources

Labor supply data are available from multiple governmental and quasi-governmental agencies at national, state, and local levels. Federal and state departments of labor maintain extensive records by occupational category. Data for smaller areas are available through industrial development agencies, chambers of commerce, and similar organizations.

While these sources deal primarily with existing labor supplies, data from colleges and universities can provide insight into short-term changes and long-term trends. Existing enrollment levels in specific academic programs are accurate indicators of numbers of students who will graduate in the ensuing four to five years. These data can be supplemented with information from many academic organizations that monitor enrollment trends. The Association for Education in Journalism and Mass Communication, for example, monitors enrollments in advertising and public relations as well as print and electronic journalism.

Prospective Shareholders

Organizational interest in prospective shareholders is equally significant. Securities prices are a function of supply and demand. Organizational ability to raise funds is governed by demand for securities. Organizational growth through acquisitions or expansion therefore may be significantly limited by securities prices.

The bulk of the nation's demand for investment securities originates in two areas. The greater portion of the total is generated by mutual funds and pension or retirement funds that are managed by a relatively small number of investment managers or advisers.

The remaining demand is from individuals who buy and sell through brokerage houses. Some of them hold securities in their own names. Others have their brokers hold them in house or "street names."

Information concerning these groups is limited. Profiles of potential individual investors might be developed by analyzing lists of existing shareholders. Prospective shareholder characteristics presumably would be similar to those of existing holders. Data obtained in this manner can be rendered more useful by information published periodically by the major stock exchanges' research departments. This information includes data about the demographic characteristics of shareholders generally as well as trends in securities ownership.

Governmental Agencies

Information about governmental agencies is only marginally more precise. Administrators and managers who direct their operations can be identified by name. Agency responsibilities and their past activity patterns can be determined from pertinent statutes and reports the agencies must submit to legislative bodies.

Agencies' existing and prospective behavioral patterns are more difficult to ascertain and predict as they are governed by political parameters established by the party in power, economic limitations imposed by legislative bodies, and the predispositions of their administrators.

Data contained in their activities' summaries and other reports nevertheless are most helpful to public relations practitioners. Analyses of the content of these documents on a continuing basis and under changing administrations best indicates the thrust of their programs.

Special Interest Groups

Every organization today is susceptible to unsolicited attention from a broad range of special interest groups. They include a host of "rights" organizations as well as environmentalists, conservationists, consumerists, and others. Each has its own agenda and may prove rational or irrational in its demands and activities.

Potential problems arising out of special interest group activity are determined by the nature of individual organizations and their activities. A substantial part of the problem potential can be minimized through compliance with contemporary laws and regulations. Little can be done to avoid the attentions of more militant organizations. Preparedness, however, can minimize the impact of their activities. Two steps are essential. First, those groups that may become interested in the organization must be identified. Second, their tactics must be cataloged in order to take appropriate preventive measures.

Identification

The nature of organizations' activities governs the extent to which they may be besieged by special interest groups. Organizations in the wood and wood products industries, for example, inevitably come under the scrutiny of the Sierra Club. Those in the petrochemical industry necessarily attract the attention of environmentalists. Biological research organizations should expect confrontations with animal rights groups.

Monitoring

The activities of each of these groups are well known. Three sources of information are of special significance to vulnerable organizations. Business, trade, and professional organizations are foremost among them. These membership groups invariably monitor the activist organizations that create problems for members. Regular and detailed reports of activist behavior often are circulated to members.

Similarly, individuals within organizations that have become entangled with activists can be rich sources of information. Their identities or, at minimum, the identities of their organizations, can be readily obtained through the news media. The *New York Times*, the *Wall Street Journal*, and the *Christian Science Monitor* all publish extensive news stories on the many areas of social responsibility.

Information obtained through these sources should be analyzed by organizations in the context of their own situations to determine how specific activist groups might behave at their plants or business sites. Appropriate emergency plans then can be implemented to handle pickets, sit-ins, and other demonstrations.

DATA ANALYSIS

Secondary research requires sifting masses of information. A small percentage proves invaluable to the researcher; a somewhat larger portion is enlightening but of marginal statistical value. The bulk of the information is anecdotal rather than statistical and defies further analysis. Very little, however, should be arbitrarily discarded.

All information should be retained until a set of complex analyses have been completed. Most of those classified as informal research were described in Chapter 3. Others, categorized as formal research, are covered in subsequent chapters.

Statistical Analyses

Valid, comparable data can be analyzed using traditional statistical tests. The words ''valid'' and ''comparable'' are important. Validity in this case refers not only to the data but to the manner in which they were gathered. Both conditions must be fulfilled before further analysis can be justified.

Comparability is equally important. Accusations concerning "apples and oranges" can readily be leveled against those who subject incomparable data to statistical testing and claim valid results.

Where both conditions are met, and in one other set of circumstances, formal statistical examination is justified. The other set of circumstances deals with correlational tests (see Chapter 13). Correlational tests are undertaken when analysts seek to establish relationships (but not causality) between two separate but perhaps interdependent variables.

A correlational analysis might be attempted, for example, to establish a relationship between supervisory or managerial behavior and employee turnover rates. Other factors would be involved, of course, but some correlation probably exists.

Nonstatistical Analyses

Other data collected in preparation for secondary research can be subjected to alternative studies. Several large corporations, for example, demonstrate the effectiveness of public relations programs by gathering and analyzing media content.

All published and broadcast material is categorized as affirmative, negative, or neutral. Numbers of items in each category are tabulated periodically and compared across periods to determine whether programmatic results have improved, deteriorated, or remained the same.

Results of such nonstatistical analyses necessarily are less precise but no less valuable in public relations practice than their statistical counterparts. Factors such as attitude and opinion are inherently difficult to measure without costly formal research. Improvement—or deterioration—can often be readily discerned in the absence of formal tests. Where rates of change can be established through continuing use of such indicators, results can be as satisfactory as where traditional statistical measures are used.

SUMMARY

Secondary research is the gathering and analysis of existing statistical data to generate information applicable to specific public relations problems. The process and search strategies focus on three components of public relations practice: the problem, organization(s), and stakeholder group(s) involved.

Analyses of these factors dictate the strategies of data-gathering. The data require close scrutiny, however, to insure their validity and applicability. A great deal of information contained in the speeches of corporate officers and organizational promotional material may contain data of questionable value. These data can mislead the unsuspecting researcher.

Information contained in the statistical components of corporate annual reports and certified by accountants, in contrast, can be assumed to be relatively accurate.

Organizational reports to regulatory agencies and other data compiled and available from governmental agencies also are generally accurate and credible.

Valid data can vary in comparability. Difficulties are frequently caused by differences in data collection procedures. They arise even where serial statistics compiled by federal agencies are involved. Over time, governmental agencies change their procedures for collecting and analyzing information. When changes occur, one series of comparable figures ends and another begins. Federal agencies diligently footnote their data to warn of the changes but other groups are not so meticulous.

Problems are compounded when proposed secondary research involves multiple sets of data generated by different researchers under varying circumstances. Those who anticipate reusing data from multiple studies should be especially careful to insure that sampling as well as analytical techniques were adequate to insure validity.

A great deal of data amenable to secondary analysis originates in organizations rather than in prior research or governmental statistics. These data usually relate to specific stakeholder groups and, more specifically, to attitude and opinion within those groups.

Attitude and opinion can be measured directly or indirectly. Communication audits, surveys, and other direct measurement techniques usually are used sparingly in organizations because they are relatively expensive and ample indirect indicators of stakeholder attitude and opinion often exist in organizations.

Indirect indicators exist in multiple forms. Absenteeism, tardiness, and turnover rates relate directly to employee morale. These indicators of worker satisfaction also reflect the efficacy of their managers and supervisors. So do productivity and quality control data in operational units they control.

Shareholder satisfaction is readily measured through volume of stock changing hands. Customer reactions can be calculated through their continued patronage. The number of available indicators in context with any stakeholder group is more than adequate for analytical purposes in most organizations.

Further information amenable to secondary analysis is available to researchers from the commercial, industrial, or institutional sectors in which organizations operate. Trade sources include the many business and commercial associations that exist in most sectors. Their publications, ranging from membership journals to industry survey reports, often provide valuable data.

Information about products and services is readily gathered at conventions, trade shows, and related meetings. Provider organizations' annual reports and other public documents are similarly valuable. Many organizations sponsor meetings of their own to further information.

Extensive governmental resources can be tapped to produce data for secondary research. Prime sources include the U.S. Government Printing Office, the Department of Commerce, the Securities and Exchange Commission, and the Department of Labor. Their information usually is available for the asking. Documents that may not be readily given often can be obtained under the Freedom of Information Act. The act requires that all nonclassified information in governmental files be made available to citizens on request.

Third party sources also contribute to the information available to secondary researchers. Information from customers can be invaluable to organizations. Suppliers, other vendors, and a host of other firms also can provide information.

Data relative to specific stakeholder groups can be gathered from another set of sources. Information concerning prospective employers is available from multiple governmental and quasi-governmental agencies. Data regarding prospective shareholders is published by securities exchanges and may be extrapolated from organizational data on existing shareholders.

Information about special interest groups can be obtained from business and industry associations, from mass and industry media, and from other organizations in the researcher's industry.

When all available data have been gathered, sorting and analytical processes can begin. Only a small percentage of the data gathered is usually useful in secondary analysis. A somewhat larger proportion is enlightening but of marginal statistical value. The remainder consists largely of anecdotal information that may be of interest but defies statistical analysis.

ADDITIONAL READING

Baskin, Otis, and Craig Aronoff. *Public Relations: The Profession and the Practice.* 2d ed. Dubuque, IA: Wm. C. Brown, 1988.

Brody, E. W. *Public Relations Programming and Production*, New York: Praeger, 1988.

Buchholz, Rogene A., William D. Evans, and Robert A. Wagley. *Management Response to Public Issues: Concepts & Cases in Strategy Formulation.* Englewood Cliffs, NJ: Prentice Hall, 1985.

Canfield, Bertrand R. *Public Relations: Principles, Cases and Problems.* 5th ed. Homewood, IL: Richard D. Irwin, 1968.

Cantor, Bill. *Inside Public Relations: Experts in Action.* New York: Longman, 1984.

Cohen, Paula Marantz. *A Public Relations Primer: Thinking and Writing in Context.* Englewood Cliffs, NJ: Prentice Hall, 1987.

Crable, Richard E., and Steven L. Vibbert. *Public Relations as Communication Management.* Edina, MN: Bellwether Press, 1986.

Cutlip, Scott M., Allen H. Center, and Glen M. Broom. *Effective Public Relations.* 6th ed. Englewood Cliffs, NJ: Prentice Hall, 1985.

Dilenschneider, Robert L., and Dan J. Forrestal. *The Dartnell Public Relations Handbook.* 3d ed. Chicago: The Dartnell Corporation, 1987.

Dunn, S. Watson. *Public Relations: A Contemporary Approach.* Homewood, IL: Richard D. Irwin, 1986.

Glossbrenner, Alfred. *How to Look It Up Online.* New York: St. Martin's Press, 1987.

Grunig, James E., and Todd Hunt. *Managing Public Relations.* New York: Holt, Rinehart and Winston, 1984.

Hamilton, Seymour. *A Communication Audit Handbook: Helping Organizations Communicate.* New York: Longman, 1987.

Hennessy, Bernard. *Public Opinion.* 5th ed. Monterey, CA: Brooks/Cole, 1985.

Herbert, Walter B., and John R. G. Jenkins, eds. *Public Relations in Canada: Some Perspectives.* Markham, Ontario: Fitzhenry & Whiteside, 1984.

Kelly, John M. *How to Check Out Your Competition: A Complete Plan for Investigating Your Market.* New York: John Wiley, 1987.

Moore, H. Frasier, and Kalupa, Frank B. *Public Relations: Principles, Cases and Problems.* 9th ed. Homewood, IL: Richard D. Irwin, 1985.

Nager, Norman R., and T. Harrell Allen. *Public Relations Management by Objectives.* New York: Longman, 1984.

Nager, Norman R., and Richard H. Truitt. *Strategic Public Relations Counseling: Models from the Counselors Academy.* New York: Longman, 1987.

Newsom, Doug, and Alan Scott. *This is PR: The Realities of Public Relations.* 3d ed. Belmont, CA: Wadsworth, 1985.

Patton, Michael Q. *Creative Evaluation.* 2d ed. Beverly Hills, CA: Sage, 1987.

Phillips, Charles S. *Secrets of Successful Public Relations.* Englewood Cliffs, NJ: Prentice Hall, 1985.

Reilly, Robert T. *Public Relations in Action.* 2d ed. Englewood Cliffs, NJ: Prentice Hall, 1987.

Rogers, Everett M. *Communication Technology: The New Media in Society.* New York: Free Press, 1986.

Settle, Robert B., and Pamela L. Alreck. *Why They Buy: The American Consumers Inside and Out.* New York: John Wiley, 1986.

Simon, Raymond. *Public Relations: Concepts and Practices.* 3d ed. New York: John Wiley, 1984.

Ward, Jean, and Kathleen A. Hansen. *Search Strategies in Mass Communication.* New York: Longman, 1987.

Wilcox, Dennis L., Phillip H. Ault, and Warren K. Agee. *Public Relations: Strategies and Tactics.* New York: Harper & Row, 1986.

Williams, Frederick. *Technology and Communication Behavior.* Belmont, CA: Wadsworth, 1987.

Wright, Theon, and Henry S. Evans. *Public Relations and the Line Manager.* New York: American Management Association, 1964.

6 Computers In Research

Computers have become indispensable tools in public relations research. Long used in analyses of survey data, they are applied today in environmental assessment, information-gathering, and informal research.

Today's applications are usually performed with microcomputers rather than their larger cousins. "Microcomputer" is a somewhat misleading term as it applies to a growing family of physically small devices with ever-increasing mechanical capabilities.

As microcomputers' capabilities have increased, software designed primarily for mainframes has been modified for use on the smaller machines. The Statistical Package for the Social Sciences (SPSS) is a good example. SPSS was created as a mainframe program and used for decades on sophisticated college and university systems. The program was adapted for microcomputers in the mid–1980s and is as popular among public relations practitioners as it is in the academic world (see Chapter 13).

By far the greatest part of computer-based public relations research activities, however, involves no statistical analyses. Most deal with online databases. These are masses of information accessible to any individual. Access requires five components: a microcomputer, a modem, a communication software package, a telephone line, and the price of one or more subscriptions.

HARDWARE REQUIREMENTS

Three of the five elements specified above—microcomputer, modem, and telephone line—can be considered generic hardware requirements for computer-based research. Each involves several variables.

Computers come in a host of types and sizes. Modems are available in several types and a broad range of capabilities. The term "telephone lines" also involves several variables.

Computers

Virtually any computer can be used in online research. In practical terms, a computer becomes little more than a dumb terminal in this application. Only the screen and keyboard are essential although other components can be helpful as well.

With only screen and keyboard in use, the computer serves as a remote extension of the mainframe that houses the database being accessed. Keyboards are used to activate a communication software package that instructs the modem to "dial up" the mainframe. Access codes then can be inserted automatically or manually and specified information is displayed on the screen. The computer need be no larger than the TRS 100, a miniature Radio Shack unit with a single-line display.

Miniature and laptop computers seldom are used in computer research, however, because few of them are equipped with *hard drives*. These are relatively bulky containers for computer data that can be used to capture any document or other information that the user may want to retain in electronic form for future use.

Modems

Computers use telephone lines to communicate with one another. Linking a computer to a telephone line requires a connecting device called a modulator/demodulator or *modem*. Modems come in two basic types and in a broad range of capabilities.

The basic types are internal and external. Internal modems are installed in the central processing unit or box that houses the major components of the computer. External units plug into the box.

Modems vary operationally in the speeds, called *baud rates*, at which they transmit or receive information. Baud rates are expressed in bits per second (bps) and range from 300 to 9600 in most modems designed for microcomputer applications.

Higher speed modems are seldom used extensively in public relations practice. They are designed to transmit large volumes of data rapidly. A 300 bps modem, for example, will display information on a computer screen at a rate that can be comfortably read as received. At 1200 baud, information flashes across the screen so rapidly that it can not be traced and assimilated by the human eye and brain.

Higher speeds are convenient where long files are being downloaded from databases. Convenience seldom creates major economies, however, because higher transmission rates usually involve higher database charges.

Telephone Lines

With a modem-equipped computer, public relations researchers need only a telephone line to access any of thousands of databases. The term "telephone line" is somewhat deceiving, however, because more than one may be involved.

A computer researcher's first requirement is a private line that is free or can be made free of "call waiting" services. The tones these services use to indicate calls are waiting will interrupt and may cut off computer communication.

Home or office telephone lines may connect directly or indirectly to database computers. In large cities major databases are accessible through local telephone numbers that represent direct access lines leased by database operators for user convenience.

Direct access lines involve no long distance charges to the user. Database operators' telephone costs are built into user charges. In smaller communities, where direct access lines are not available, database users gain access by long distance or through one of several telephone services that specialize in data transmission. Telephone numbers are provided to subscribers by database operators.

SOFTWARE REQUIREMENTS

Software requirements for online database access are less complex in operation than they appear on paper. Two programs are involved: one by which users access the database and another by which they navigate within the database.

In practical terms, the communication program that the computer uses to take you to the database "hands you off" to the program used within the database. Users seldom notice the transition but it is nevertheless there.

Computer Programs

Many computer communication programs are available. Most are relatively inexpensive, especially when purchased through software discounters who advertise regularly in computer magazines. Some public domain or free software packages also are available but many lack the features of those offered commercially. CrossTalk and SmartComm are the leading commercial packages. QModem and NewKey are generally comparable "freeware" packages.

Database users universally want two features contained in all of these packages. The first is a capture system through which, at the stroke of a key, every word appearing on the computer screen is transcribed onto the computer's hard drive. Capture systems are helpful in scanning database content and eliminate the possibility that users may have to download information already seen on their screens.

The second feature is a download protocol, a program within a program through which mainframe files can be quickly copied onto searchers' hard drives. Downloading documents usually can be completed more rapidly than on-screen viewing.

Database Programs

Several database producers and vendors have created specialized proprietary software. Usually called *front end* packages, the programs are intended to make database use easier.

Producers of DIALOG, NEXIS, Wilsonline, and other databases have developed such programs. They are most valuable to those who regularly use individual databases and want to handle searches as rapidly as possible. Speed in database use reduces costs because almost all charges are based on usage time as well as information retrieved.

RESEARCH APPLICATIONS

Online databases of different kinds can be used productively in every aspect of public relations research. They are applicable in environmental assessment and in informal, secondary, and primary research. They also are used extensively by practitioners in monitoring contemporary news flows relative to events in which clients or employers may be involved.

Each online database application requires a different search strategy. Strategies, in turn, may imply use of different databases.

Online Databases

Using online databases too early in research can be a frustrating process. Frustration occurs due to the sheer volume of information accessible. In late 1979, for example, more than 400 databases were available. By 1987, the number had increased to more than 3,000 and more have been added almost daily.

Virtually everything a public relations practitioner needs to know at any moment can be obtained from one or more of the online databases. That knowledge often is of little consolation, however, to those preparing to embark on a database search. Knowing the information is there and knowing where to look for it are two very different things.

The task is not a simple one even when the correct database has been selected. A single database can cover hundreds of information sources. One magazine file within one database can contain hundreds of articles published over a period of years.

Fortunately, learning to become a proficient researcher is not very difficult because of the nature of the database industry. The most commonly used information in online research is concentrated in a few databases. These include DIALOG, BRS/SEARCH, NEXIS, ORBIT and Dow Jones News/Retrieval Service.

Gateway Services

Many of the leading databases are accessible through *gateways*. A gateway is a system that gives users access to other systems. In some cases, gateway systems are accessible through still other systems often referred to as computer utilities.

The major computer utilities include CompuServe Information Service, The Source, and Delphi, a product of General Videotex Corporation. Each serves, to a greater or lesser extent, as a gateway. In addition, each provides a host of other services to users.

CompuServe Information Service (CIS), for example, enables users to buy and sell listed securities, make airline reservations, and purchase a broad range of merchandise. CIS is also "home" to a number of special interest groups or forums of interest to public relations practitioners.

PRSIG, the Public Relations and Marketing Forum, and AEJMC, a special interest group consisting of members of the Association for Education in Journalism and Mass Communication, are both accessible through CIS. In addition, CIS is home to IQuest, a gateway database created by Telebase Systems, Inc., of Narberth, Pennsylvania.

IQuest, otherwise known as EasyNet, provides access to BRS, DIALOG, and other services. Used in conjunction with PRSIG, AEJMC and other forums or SIGs, as they are often called, these services enable public relations practitioners to conduct a large part of their research through CompuServe. Environmental assessment, information-gathering, and informal research are readily conducted through many of the basic CIS services. IQuest provides access to a great deal of statistical data applicable in formal research and the CompuServe Executive Service enables practitioners to monitor developing events as well.

ENVIRONMENTAL ASSESSMENT

Environmental assessment, as discussed in Chapter 3, is an on-going, two-part process accomplished by monitoring and tracking. Monitoring involves scanning organizational horizons for events that may signal the start of trends significant to the organization. Tracking involves following those trends to ascertain the speed with which and extent to which they are developing.

Environmental assessment in public relations is carried out in two contexts. One involves the profession. Successful practitioners must maintain state-of-the-art knowledge concerning their profession. The other is organizational, dealing with the organizations with which practitioners are involved as counselors or employees.

Professional Assessment

The professional aspects of environmental assessment will be the focus of this discussion although the same methodology is applicable in organizational settings. Professionals usually maintain knowledge by attending professional development meetings and seminars and by reading publications in public relations and associated fields.

PRSIG, however, can make a significant contribution to the process. Several techniques are involved, as evidenced by the material from CompuServe and PRSIG shown in Figure 6.1. Readers should note that commands entered after exclamation points are entered by the user, in this example one of the authors. Users are first shown CompuServe's introductory menu. In this case, rather than a selection from the introductory menu, the computer was told "GO PRSIG." Had there been messages waiting for the user within the forum, an appropriate message would have appeared "on arrival."

Use of the carriage return <CR> after the second exclamation point leads to the forum menu. The libraries' submenu(3) was then selected, and the Desktop Publishing submenu was selected from the set of libraries (again, no. 3). The computer was instructed to (1) browse through all the files (neither keywords nor dates were provided). Since one of the authors was planning to buy a laser printer at the time, a *string* or series of messages concerning laser printers was displayed.

Message strings taken from bulletin boards are shifted to libraries by system operators when their content will be of continuing interest. Otherwise, the libraries contain a host of documents on all of the topics indicated. Included are many summary transcriptions of on-line conferences retained for reference by those who were unable to be present. Conference content is essentially original material "written" and "published" by PRSIG and CompuServe and appearing nowhere else.

CompuServe also acts as a gateway for IQuest, an "information utility" that contains some 70 databases arranged by topic. Several informational documents taken from IQuest's entry menu are shown in Figure 6.2. These documents include the IQuest introduction as well as search tips, and the directory of databases. At the end of Figure 6.2 readers will find the word "off" entered after an exclamation point. That word tells the computer that the user is finished and that the line can be disconnected.

It is impossible to include here a summary of all the information available through PRSIG or CompuServe. Several databases, however, are worthy of special note by those concerned with public relations research. The CompuServe Executive Service includes a mechanism whereby users can establish electronic file folders to capture information moving through the networks maintained by news services. Users of this service type in key words and the CompuServe system then puts an electronic copy of every news item containing the selected words into the user's file. File content can be checked periodically, examined, and either retained or discarded on an item-by-item basis. The service is especially valuable to practitioners dealing with breaking news stories concerning their clients or employers.

CompuServe is also home to hundreds of SIGs (special interest groups) akin

Figure 6.1

Exchange of Information Concerning Laser Printers for Desktop Publishing Systems from the Desktop Publishing Library on CompuServe's Public Relations and Marketing Forum (PRSIG) (copyright 1988, CompuServe Information Systems, reprinted by permission)

```
          A Visit To CompuServe Information Service's
          Public Relations and Marketing Forum (PRSIG)

     The following information is reproduced exactly as it
appeared on a microcomputer screen at the time and on the
date specified below.  It is reproduced here with the
permission of CompuServe Information Service.


CompuServe Information Service
15:15 CDT Thursday 07-Jul-88 P

Last access: 13:32 07-Jul-88

     Copyright (C) 1988
   CompuServe Incorporated
     All Rights Reserved

CompuServe                      TOP

 1 Subscriber Assistance
 2 Find a Topic
 3 Communications/Bulletin Bds.
 4 News/Weather/Sports
 5 Travel
 6 The Electronic MALL/Shopping
 7 Money Matters/Markets
 8 Entertainment/Games
 9 Home/Health/Family
10 Reference/Education
11 Computers/Technology
12 Business/Other Interests

Enter choice number !GO PRSIG

  CompuServe                    PRSIG



One moment please...
Welcome to PR & MKTG FORUM, V. 4D(36)

Hello, E.W. Brody
Last visit:  07-Jul-88  13:01:48

Forum messages:  30330 to  31843
Last message you've read:  24855

Section(s) Selected: [ 0 1 2 3 5 6 7 8 9 10 11 12 13 14 15 17 ]

Press <CR> !
PR & MKTG FORUM Forum Menu

 1 INSTRUCTIONS
 2 MESSAGES
 3 LIBRARIES (Files)
 4 CONFERENCING (0 participating)
 5 ANNOUNCEMENTS from sysop
 6 MEMBER directory
 7 OPTIONS for this forum
```

Figure 6.1 Continued

```
Enter choice !3
PR & MKTG FORUM Libraries Menu

Libraries Available:
 0 GENERAL/SYSOP
 1 ON YOUR OWN
 2 RESOURCE CO-OP/EBT
 3 DESKTOP PUBLISHING
 4 SAVTIM
 5 POTPOURRI/PRODUCTS
 6 TEACHING PR
 7 MARKETING
 8 PR BOOK
 9 HIGH TECH ALERT
10 INTELNET
11 PRL:INFO/NEWS
12 PRL:JOBS ONLINE
13 PRL:SEMINARS/CONF'S
14 WORK IN PROGRESS
15 PRL: BUSINESS
17 MEDIA RELATIONS


Enter Choice !3

PR & MKTG FORUM Library 3

DESKTOP PUBLISHING

 1 BROWSE thru files
 2 DIRECTORY of files
 3 UPLOAD a new file
 4 DOWNLOAD a File
 5 LIBRARIES

Enter choice !1
Enter keywords (e.g. modem)
or <CR> for all:

Oldest files in days
or <CR> for all:


[76703,575]
LASER.STR                03-Jul-88 5236              Accesses: 1

    Keywords: PRINTERS LASER ENVELOPES DESKTOP OPTIONS MESSAGE
STRING BULLETIN BOARD

    For those interested in purchasing a printer for their desktop
operation, they'll want to read this message string from the
bulletin board concerning their options.  Also includes some
exchanges on how to best print envelopes using the DTP printers.

Press <CR> for next or type CHOICES !choices

PR & MKTG FORUM Library Disposition

 1 READ this file
 2 DOWNLOAD this file
 3 RETURN to library menu

Enter choice or <CR> for next !1
```

Figure 6.1 Continued

CompuServe PR & MKTG FORUM

Laser printers
S 3 / DESKTOP PUBLISHING

Date Range: 12-May-88 to 24-Jun-88

#30695
Fm: Katharine Pierce 72460,214
To: All
Dt: 12-May-88

Hi gang -- Am taking the plunge into DTP and would appreciate
feedback on printers. Hardware consultant is putting together
system to upgrade IBM equipment and is offering a NEC LC 890. (I
read good things all around about it.) Software consultant is
arguing for an Apple Laserwriter "because it's been around so
long." Same price range for both, no Mac on the horizon in my
office, limited networking with a few other PCs possible within the
year. Any experience with either printer with an IBM system would
be appreciated. Most output will be words-heavy documents or
numbers graphs/charts. Thanks ...

        -- Katharine

#30782 reply to #30695
Fm: Daniel Janal Asst. Sysop 76004,1046
To: Katharine Pierce 72460,214
Dt: 17-May-88

I use an HP Laserjet II and am quite happy with it. Postscript
print would be nice, but it costs about $2,000 more. The Apple has
it, but it does not have HP compatibility, which is important if
you decide to use a program that doesn't support Postscript. I've
heard good things about the NEC, also.

#30788 reply to #30782
Fm: Katharine Pierce 72460,214
To: Daniel Janal Asst. Sysop 76004,1046
Dt: 17-May-88

Dan -- Thanks for the input. I looked at the HP series but really
need to be able to handle a wide variety of type and graphics
styles. We seem to be leaning toward the NEC (tech support is
good, I hear). I'll find out soon enough. -- Katharine

#31116 reply to #30788
Fm: Nelson Ramos 75076,615
To: Katharine Pierce 72460,214
Dt: 04-Jun-88

109

Figure 6.1 Continued

Am in same situation, but I'm working with MAC equipment. I looked
at NEC but disqualified it because it is not capable of doing
envelopes. Right now, I'm "holding" on my purchase. At MacWorld
conference in San Francisco in February, General Computer demoed a
clone of the Apple Laserwriter which is supposed to be released
this month at a retail price of $4,200. Graphics and text shown
were excellent. Company claims this will be lowest priced
Postscript printer with Appletalk, serial and parallel interfaces.
Can call them at General Computer, Waltham, Mass. for info.

#31168 reply to #31116
Fm: Bill Weylock 76012,3026
To: Nelson Ramos 75076,615
Dt: 06-Jun-88

Nelson - YOu can do envelopes on the NEC, but only one at a time.
What laser printers do better at this stage? I'm told none have an
envelope feed that is reliable. - BW

#31192 reply to #31168
Fm: Mike Gentry 73310,1170
To: Bill Weylock 76012,3026
Dt: 07-Jun-88

We just purchased a DataProducts LZR 1230 at our company because of
its envelope capability. Did a small mailing last week (800
letters) and didn't have any problems with the envelope feed. The
printer wasn't cheap but I have been impressed by it. Mike Gentry
PS: It is HP compatible, but doesn't do PostScript for DTP

#31208 reply to #31192
Fm: Bill Weylock 76012,3026
To: Mike Gentry 73310,1170
Dt: 08-Jun-88

Mike - How much was the LZR 1230? I really envy your being able to
do envelopes. What a nightmare they are on other systems.
   - BW

#31210 reply to #31208
Fm: Nelson Ramos 75076,615
To: Bill Weylock 76012,3026
Dt: 08-Jun-88

ANOTHER SOLUTION TO ENVELOPES, THOUGH NOT CHEAP IS TO PURCHASE AN
AUXILIARY PAPER FEEDER. IF YOU DON'T NEED POSTSCRIPT AND CAN
JUSTIFY IT THEN YOU CAN GET A 2 PAPER BIN/1 ENVELOPE BIN FEEDER
THAT ATTACHES TO AN HP LASERJET FOR ABOUT $1,600. DOES ANYONE OUT
THERE HAVE ANY EXPERIENCE WITH THESE, PARTICULARLY ON A NETWORK?

#31215 reply to #31208
Fm: Mike Gentry 73310,1170
To: Bill Weylock 76012,3026
Dt: 08-Jun-88

Figure 6.1 Continued

We paid $5,500 for our LZR 1230. This included installation and a
half day training session for all our secretaries. In addition, to
the envelope feed, it also has three other paper trays. We use one
for letter-head, one for second sheet, and one for plain white
bond. I thin it will pay for itself just in eliminating the "paper
shuffle" our secretaries were doing.

Regards,

Mike Gentry

#31217 reply to #31215
Fm: Bill Weylock 76012,3026
To: Mike Gentry 73310,1170
Dt: 08-Jun-88

Thanks for the info, Mike. Sounds like a good system.

   - BW

#31434 reply to #31116
Fm: Katharine Pierce 72460,214
To: Nelson Ramos 75076,615
Dt: 20-Jun-88

Hi -- Been out of town and away from my computer. As an update, I
went ahead with the NEC and have not run into any major problems
... yet. I did pick up a routine (either here or one of the tech
forums) for running envelopes through. Haven't yet tried it,
because the typewriter is so safe. I'll let you know, though. Let
me know what you end up with. -- Katharine

#31437 reply to #31434
Fm: Bill Weylock 76012,3026
To: Katharine Pierce 72460,214
Dt: 20-Jun-88

K - If you run into trouble with the NEC, give a holler. I have an
890. Happy to help if I can. Do you get three dots in the upper
right hand margin of each first page in a given run? You'll like
the printer, I think. Especially for the low maintenance.

   - BW

Figure 6.2
Introductory Information to CompuServe Information System's IQuest Data Base, Downloaded on 7 July 1988 (copyright 1988, CompuServe Information Service, reproduced with permission)

```
                    An Introduction to IQuest
                    The On-Line Data Base of
                  CompuServe Information Service

        [The following information concerning IQuest was
           downloaded from CompuServe on 7 July 1988 and
           is reproduced here with the permission of CompuServe
           Information Service]


CompuServe                      IQUEST

IQuest

   1 Introduction to IQuest
   2 Search Tips
   3 IQuest Pricing
   4 IQuest Database Directory (W)
   5 More Information About IQuest
   6 Access IQuest ($)
   7 IQuest Scan Feature

Enter choice !1
CompuServe                      IQU-4
```

Welcome to IQuest (pronounced "I Quest"), one of the most
comprehensive information and reference services available
anywhere. IQuest gives you access to over 800 publications,
databases and indices spanning the worlds of business, government,
research, news - even popular entertainment and sports. Extremely
easy to use, IQuest is a menu-based service which prompts you for
your information needs and then goes to work for you. Accessing
databases through online services such as Dialog, BRS, NewsNet, and
Vu/Text, among others, IQuest executes the search and displays the
results to you.

IQuest offers two simple methods for finding information of
interest, IQuest-I and IQuest-II. IQuest-I guides you through a
series of menus which define your topic of interest. Then IQuest
determines which database is right for your search and prompts you
for words to search for in that database. If you already
know the database you want, IQuest-II allows you to specify the
name of the database and bypass the menus.

IQuest features two types of databases: bibliographic and full
text. Bibliographic databases provide complete reference
information for an article including title, author, publication and
date. Often this is enough for research purposes, but many
bibliographic databases also provide a summary of an article,
called an abstract, that may eliminate the need to see the entire
contents of an article. Full text databases, on the other hand,
provide access to the entire text of an article but are often
narrower in scope than bibliographic databases. Many full text
databases cover specialized newsletters.

Figure 6.2 Continued

The cost to perform a search on IQuest is $7 (although a few databases carry a surcharge of $4 to $25 which is clearly indicated before a search is requested). If the database is bibliographic, you are shown up to 10 titles of articles that contain your search terms. Each of the titles come with bibliographic information for further research. If your search has generated more than 10 hits, you are shown the most recent 10 and may request the next group of 10 titles for an additional $7 (plus surcharge if applicable). You may display an abstract for any title for a $2 charge.

If you've searched a full text database you are shown up to 15 titles. In addition you are entitled to see the full text of one of the titles as part of your search fee (the full text for additional titles in a group of 15 is available for $7 per article, plus surcharge if applicable). If your search has turned up more than 15 hits, you may view the next most recent 15 titles for a $7 charge (plus surcharge if applicable).

A small number of IQuest databases are unavailable at certain times on weekends. Typically the number unavailable at any time is less than 10 of the 800 total databases. When possible, IQuest tells you when a database will be back online. You are not charged for requesting a database that is unavailable.

Most of the IQuest databases are textual in nature and will be displayed at either 40 characters or 80 characters per line, depending on your terminal setting. However, a few databases contain tabular information (most notably in the financial area) and are set to display at 80 characters per line. These reports will be difficult to read on monitors with less than 80 column display.

IQuest displays current session charges on every menu. Remember that CompuServe base connect rates are in effect at all times, but only IQuest transaction charges are shown on the menus. You are encouraged to use the help facility which is available at almost every prompt in IQuest and you should print or capture items of interest. If you need help in structuring a search request, just type SOS and a trained researcher will come online and provide suggestions.

Because of the advanced nature of this product and the extensive help facilities, credits will not be given for user errors (however, errors caused by verifiable system problems will be credited).

IQuest is brought to you as a joint effort of CompuServe and Telebase Systems, Inc. of Bryn Mawr, Pennsylvania and Western Union Corp.

Last page !
CompuServe   IQUEST

IQuest

    1 Introduction to IQuest
    2 Search Tips
    3 IQuest Pricing
    4 IQuest Database Directory (W)
    5 More Information About IQuest
    6 Access IQuest ($)
    7 IQuest Scan Feature

Figure 6.2 Continued


```
Enter choice !2
CompuServe              IQU-11
```

There are some simple guidelines to follow in entering search terms
for IQuest:

Simplify your entry by omitting common words such as OF, THE, FOR,
AT, BY, TO, etc. Example: STATE UNION instead of STATE OF THE
UNION.

Retrieve only the most relevant articles by using words and phrases
that are unique and specific. Example: CONVERTIBLE rather than
AUTOMOBILE.

Don't worry about using upper or lower case letters. Example:
Brazil, brazil, and BRAzil will all be treated the same way.

Retrieve all words that begin with the same letters by using a
slash (/) as a "wild card" at the end of a word. Example: COMPUT/
will retrieve COMPUTE, COMPUTERS, and COMPUTING.

Narrow your search by using AND. Example: ASTRONAUT AND GEMINI
will retrieve only items which include both of these keywords.

Broaden your search by using OR. Example: ASTRONAUT OR COSMONAUT
will retrieve items which include either phrase. This is
especially helpful when using synonyms e.g. DATSUN OR NISSAN.

Exclude a concept from your search with NOT. Example: WIMBLEDON
NOT SINGLES will retrieve all items with the word "Wimbledon"
except those that contain "singles". Note that NOT is exclusive.
This search would ignore an article like: "Wimbledon Singles Crown
Awarded - Doubles Play Moves to Center Court".

Indicate which concepts are to be considered together by using
parentheses () around groups of words that you have combined with
AND, OR, or NOT. Example: ASPEN AND (DOWNHILL OR CROSS COUNTRY) is
different than (ASPEN AND DOWNHILL) OR CROSS COUNTRY. The former
will retrieve every article that includes "downhill" or "cross-
country" along with "Aspen". The latter will retrieve information
about cross-country skiing anywhere, along with every story about
downhill skiing in Aspen.

You are encouraged to review the sample search terms available at
the search prompt in IQuest. In addition, you may type SOS and
consult with a trained researcher if you have difficulty in finding
items of interest. Remember that no credits will be given for
errors in entering search terms. IQuest is very forgiving in most
cases - the first search you request which gets no hits is free and
subsequent no hit searches cost only $1.


```
Last page !
CompuServe              IQUEST
```

IQuest

Figure 6.2 Continued

```
1 Introduction to IQuest
2 Search Tips
3 IQuest Pricing
4 IQuest Database Directory (W)
5 More Information About IQuest
6 Access IQuest ($)
7 IQuest Scan Feature

Enter choice !4
CompuServe                 IQU-492

IQuest Directory
```

The following five menu pages list subject categories which include
all IQuest databases. Each database is listed under the
appropriate category with a brief description. Source of
information, frequency of updates, and content are given
for most of the IQuest databases.

```
DATABASE DESCRIPTIONS
 1 Accounting     12 China
 2 Aerospace      13 Civil Engineering
 3 Agriculture    14 Computers
 4 Anthopology    15 Corporate Data
 5 Art/Arts/Humanities
 6 Banking/Finance
 7 Biography
 8 Biology
 9 Business Management
10 Canada
11 Chemistry

DATABASE DESCRIPTIONS (continued)
16 Earth Sciences
17 Economics/Statistics
18 Education
19 Electrical/Electronics
20 Employment
21 Energy          27 Germany
22 Environment     28 History
23 Film
24 Foundations/Grants
25 France
26 General Reference

DATABASE DESCRIPTIONS (continued)
29 Industry        40 Mech. Engineering
30 Insurance       41 Medicine
31 Int'l Affairs   42 Metals
32 Int'l Business  43 Music
33 Investments/Securities
34 Japan
35 Law
36 Library/Information Science
37 Literature
38 Marketing
39 Mathematics
```

Figure 6.2 Continued

```
DATABASE DESCRIPTIONS (continued)
44 Newspapers - Regional/National
45 Newspapers - International
46 Paper        55 Religion
47 Patents      56 Rubber
48 Pharmacy     57 Science
49 Philosophy   58 Social Science
50 Physics      59 Sociology
51 Plastics     60 Soviet Union
52 Psychology   61 Sports
53 Public Affairs/Government
54 Real Estate

DATABASE DESCRIPTION (continued)
62 Taxation
63 Telecommunications
64 Television/Radio
65 Textiles
66 Theater
67 Trademarks
68 Transportation
69 United Kingdom

Last menu page, enter choice !
CompuServe                 IQUEST

IQuest
 1 Introduction to IQuest
 2 Search Tips
 3 IQuest Pricing
 4 IQuest Database Directory (W)
 5 More Information About IQuest
 6 Access IQuest ($)
 7 IQuest Scan Feature

Enter choice ! off
-----------------------------------------------------------------
```

to PRSIG but dedicated to other subjects. They are devoted to a broad range of interests, including computer hardware and software of all kinds. Most significantly, most of their memberships are open to any CompuServe subscriber and their system operators (SYSOPs) literally are walking libraries concerning members' areas of interest. Responses to questions are quickly answered.

SUMMARY

Microcomputers and databases have become major resources for every public relations practitioner. They are especially valuable in research. Necessary equipment includes a microcomputer, a modem, and a telephone line that will not be interrupted by call waiting services. Researchers also need one of the available broad-range communication software packages.

Both online databases and information utilities are readily accessible with this equipment. Computer users also have available to them a broad range of information on virtually any subject, as well as untold thousands of individuals conversant with those subjects and ready to provide assistance.

Samples from CompuServe in this chapter are infinitesimal in comparison to what is available from just one of thousands of databases. With associated services such as the CompuServe executive service, through which practitioners can monitor current events on behalf of clients, they are becoming invaluable resources in public relations practice.

ADDITIONAL READING

Brody, E. W. *Public Relations Programming and Production*. New York: Praeger, 1988.

Castells, Manuel, ed. *High Technology, Space and Society*. Beverly Hills, CA: Sage, 1985.

Cohen, Paula Marantz. *A Public Relations Primer: Thinking and Writing in Context*. Englewood Cliffs, NJ: Prentice Hall, 1987.

Didsbury, Howard F., ed. *Communications and the Future: Prospects, Promises and Problems*. Washington, DC: World Future Society, 1982.

Dizard, Wilson P., Jr. *The Coming Information Age: An Overview of Technology, Economics and Politics*. 2d ed. New York: Longman, 1985.

Foundation for Public Relations Research and Education. *New Technology and Public Relations*. New York: Foundation for Public Relations Research and Education, 1986.

Glossbrenner, Alfred. *How to Look It Up Online*. New York: St. Martin's Press, 1987.

Gross, Lynne Schafer. *Telecommunications: An Introduction to Radio, Television and Other Electronic Media*. 2d ed. Dubuque, IA: Wm. C. Brown, 1986.

Hills, J. P. *Trends in Information Transfer*. Westport, CT: Greenwood Press, 1982.

Nager, Norman R., and T. Harrell Allen. *Public Relations Management by Objectives*. New York: Longman, 1984.

Phillips, Charles S. *Secrets of Successful Public Relations*. Englewood Cliffs, NJ: Prentice Hall, 1985.

Reilly, Robert T. *Public Relations in Action*. 2d ed. Englewood Cliffs, NJ: Prentice Hall, 1987.

Rogers, Everett M. *Communication Technology: The New Media in Society*. New York: Free Press, 1986.

Williams, Frederick. *Technology and Communication Behavior*. Belmont, CA: Wadsworth, 1987.

Part Two
Formal Research Methods

7 The Research Problem

Before going through the required steps of formal research, an overview of the entire process is necessary. Scientific method—the same basic process the natural sciences use in discovering answers to physical, chemical, and biological problems—provides the best starting point for public relations research. Prior to launching a project, and perhaps throughout the study, the public relations researcher is advised to consult with outside experts who can bring both resources and balance to the project. And, because this text is likely to be one of the earliest exposures to formal research a public relations professional receives, an attempt is made to point out the wide range of possible problems that might be solved through formal research methods.

SCIENTIFIC METHOD

Both the physical and social sciences share a common research process called the *scientific method*. It is an eight-step plan which, if followed with care, helps ensure the success of any formal research strategy. All of the steps are necessary, even if they may seem too rigid for day-to-day application. For example, we are taught to make a formal outline as preparation for writing English themes. Outlines are excellent exercises in thought organization and they are beneficial in a variety of complex writing tasks. But once a student becomes comfortable doing longer themes, the formal outline rarely is employed. The eight-step scientific method, on the other hand, must be used in every formal research procedure. Studies that do not rely on it—seat-of-the-pants research—are destined for difficulty or disaster. The steps are outlined in the following sections with an explanation for their necessity.

Stating the Problem

As obvious as it may appear, researchers begin by stating the problem at hand. The ''problem'' is some observed phenomenon that is not fully understood. It could be: ''Why are our employees considering joining a union?'' or ''If we build a new water reservoir in the suburbs, can we expect to get a rate increase for our water utility next year?'' The problem might be complex or multifaceted, in which case its separate component parts should be stated for clarity and simplicity. The purpose of the problem statement is to ensure that everyone associated with the investigation understands precisely what needs to be researched. Often, at this point, discussion can lead to improved agreement about what answers are needed from research: What is the expected goal of the research effort?

Stating the Hypotheses

This is one of those formal, rigid steps that is often ignored in research methodology. This is a mistake because formal hypotheses statements are critical to the success of any research project. An hypothesis is a concise, positive statement of what is thought to be the cause of a problem and its possible effect. In the above examples, hypotheses might be:

1. The interest in union activity is related to inequitable wages paid employees.
2. The interest in union activity is related to insufficient communication between employees and management.
3. Union activity is related to perceived unsafe work conditions.
4. Less-than-average industry benefits are associated with the current interest in unions at out plant.
5. Lack of overtime pay is related to union interest.

In the utility company example, an hypothesis might be: ''Utility commissioners will agree investing $3 million for a new reservoir is justification for a $1 per year water rate increase.''

The union problem in the first example provides additional insight into the purpose of stating hypotheses. The researcher's hypothesis does not have to be ''right.'' In fact, the example offers a series of conflicting hypotheses, each suggesting a possible cause for the observation that employees are thinking about starting a union. It may be that several of the statements will be supported, perhaps those dealing with wages and benefits, but not those dealing with safety and communication. It may be that none of the assumed ''causes'' is found to be related to the union activity. In this case, all of the hypotheses will be rejected. That, too, is certainly a justifiable outcome worthy of investing in a formal research project: We would find that interest in the union cannot be linked to wages, benefits, communication, or safety. The investigation might identify other explanations for this union interest (or it might not), but it will rule out those management might have considered the most likely possibilities.

Unless hypotheses are offered prior to beginning the investigation, the study is doomed to failure. How can we hope to find answers if we haven't identified what we're looking for?

Defining Key Words

The key words of the hypotheses must be operationalized—defined succinctly enough to be measured. This step is critical in focusing the research project and in forming the research procedures. What, exactly, are we studying and how are we going to measure it?

Returning to the union example's first hypothesis—"1. The interest in union activity is related to inequitable wages paid employees."—what are the key words that require operational definitions? They are: (1) "interest in union activity," (2) "inequitable wages," and (3) "employees." What do we mean by these terms and how should we measure them? The first is fairly easy. Interest in union activity is someone's probability of joining a union. "Interest" could be a variety of attitudes toward the union; it might be having heard about the union, having talked to a co-worker about the union, or attending a union interest group meeting. For our purposes, "interest" can be measured by a few answers on an anonymous questionnaire asking items such as: "Do you think unions benefit employees?" "Have you considered joining a union in the past month?" "If asked to join a union tomorrow, how likely might you be to actually join: very likely, somewhat likely, not sure, somewhat unlikely, or very unlikely?" The researchers might agree that the answer to the last question is the best measure of "interest in union activity." In fact, at this point the wording of the hypothesis might be altered to: "The likelihood of joining a union is related to inequitable wages paid employees."

Next we operationally define "inequitable wages." What does it mean and how should we measure it? A wide range of choices can be derived by comparing this firm's wages to those in similar types of businesses or in local businesses of similar sizes. But we might conclude that if workers believe their wages are inequitable, this is a suitable measure of the concept. Again, we might ask on an anonymous questionnaire, "How well does your current rate of pay match the work you do: Is it very much higher, much higher, a little bit higher, about right, a little bit lower, much lower or very much lower?"

The last operational definition needed is that for "employees." Depending on the company, there might be a variety of definitions, but for purposes of the inquiry, employees could be operationalized as all workers in lines that might be eligible for membership in this union. If it is a manufacturing plant, all workers on the floor up to foreman lines might be included, or another definition might be required instead. Identifying the groups eligible to join a union will be relatively easy and our research should be directed only at those workers. If we arbitrarily include all employees, the results we get will not provide valid estimates of employee interest in joining the union.

Determining Measurement Procedures

How will the data be gathered for this research project? Beyond the wide variety of informal research strategies presented in the first part of this text, the usual data-gathering procedures of formal research include the survey, the experiment, and content analysis. Each of these will be discussed in detail in later chapters, but the survey is likely to be the data-gathering procedure of choice for the union project being described here. Critical decisions will be needed in our approach. We should expect some hesitancy and suspicion when asking workers about such sensitive subjects as their interest in joining a union or about their pay. A survey research project will have to be carefully planned to assuage workers' fears of retribution and to increase the likelihood that their answers will be forthright. But if we want to assess reasons for their interest in joining a union, we'll have to ask them. Using an experiment might require bringing workers face-to-face with an interviewer, thus compromising workers' anonymity. It might be possible to analyze the printed handouts and speeches of union organizers to see what themes—rationales for joining—are being presented to workers. But the best possibility for data-gathering is a carefully structured survey that allows respondents to answer truthfully.

Collecting Data

Once the data-collection procedure has been determined, the data can be gathered. This is the process of deciding which worker groups should be included and administering the data gathering instrument, in this case an anonymous questionnaire.

Analyzing the Data

If the hypotheses have been stated and operationalized properly, data analysis follows easily. Researchers will have determined in advance which are the key questions designed to answer the hypotheses and which statistical tools will be used to determine if the hypotheses have been supported.

Reporting the Findings

After data analysis, discussion, and close scrutiny of the study's findings, it is time to write the report. For now, consider that the report will be directed to management. It will be an overview of the six previous steps of scientific method stating plainly what the problem is, the hypotheses, their operational definitions, the measurement and data-gathering procedures, and the findings. Additionally, it will include suggestions of how the findings might be used to solve the problem.

Relating Results to the Wider Body of Knowledge

It is not enough to provide this single study's answers with suggestions about how to use them. Researchers owe their clients a wider perspective of what the study has found and what it might mean, both for the immediate problem and for broad policy decisions that may come later. Surely other firms have faced the same problem. What did their studies show, and how do this study's findings confirm or conflict?

In this case, assuming perceived wage inequity was found to be most highly related to interest in joining a union, what should management know about how similar firms have reacted to wage increases when faced with union organizers? Have those policies been effective? How might they apply in this instance? Are there more effective strategies what might be warranted, based on this study's findings and on other examples?

No single study should be considered so unique that its findings can be used in a vacuum. Management decisions require supportive evidence, as much collateral information as is relevant and available. Providing a wider view of the study's outcomes is as much a part of the researcher's job as doing any single study.

OUTSIDE EXPERTISE

How much of the research project should a public relations professional be required to do? While practitioners should be able to direct the entire project, in practice they would be foolish to try. The experience may be likened to producing the company's annual report. The head of public relations is responsible for the entire report, from conceptualization through finished product. But this director must rely on a staff of reporters, writers, photographers, graphic artists, and production people, both inside and outside the firm. No practitioner would attempt to do the annual report single-handedly.

A research project can be more demanding than an annual report. Additionally, the required technical knowledge is immense and highly specialized. It would make little sense for a public relations director to attempt the project without the help of experts. As a practical matter, very few public relations directors do much more than advise management abut when to use formal research and then oversee the projects. Most hire research firms whose experience and expertise they trust. Hiring outside consultants reduces the work burden, the risk of making a serious mistake, and the time required to complete a project. Research firms usually have a team of project coordinators, survey interviewers, telephone banks, and computers programmed to do statistical analyses. Consultants also provide suggestions on the direction formal research might take.

In the union example, outside help is absolutely necessary. There is no possibility that workers will provide sensitive information about their union interest and wages if the company is asking the questions directly. Workers' anonymity will have to be guaranteed, and they must feel confident that the information they provide will not be used to their detriment. That will be a hard enough task for an outside firm to accomplish; impossible for the company.

In most other situations, however, the decision to rely on outside help makes good sense. The firm and its public relations personnel are likely to be too involved in the problem to do formal research objectively. An outside consultant can provide that objectivity.

Outside help should be called in at the earliest possible stage of a formal research project. Otherwise, valuable suggestions that might have improved the study will be lost, or the project might be too far along for the consultant to perform worthwhile services. Some projects can be done in-house. Perhaps a public relations director intends to use outside help only in the data analysis stage—to do a series of computer runs on the collected data. Even in such instances it is a good idea to bring in the research firm at the beginning. Data analysis can be quick and clean, or it can be tricky. If the consultant knows in advance what the format of the data is likely to be, the possibility of error is greatly reduced.

In summary, the public relations professional should plan to use outside help and should bring formal research experts in on the project as early as possible.

THE RANGE OF RESEARCH TOPICS

Although scientific research procedures were originally formulated by the Greeks in ancient times, the modern use of these tactics has come about only in the last two or three centuries. Public relations practitioners have relied on scientific method for less than 30 years, and many have earned degrees in public relations without any formal education in research. Still, once exposed to the procedures, a practitioner can usually think of hundreds of problems that might be solved by formal research. A working public relations professional may come up with a dozen projects related to his or her present job that are ripe for these research procedures. But a public relations student—who is not yet in the profession—may have difficulty imagining uses for formal research. This is unfortunate because the methods are widely applicable. Most public relations positions involve problems for which formal research is the best, and sometimes the only, hope for answers.

Consider the corporation. Its publics include employees, stockholders, customers, prospective customers, suppliers, residents in the community where the company is located, the wider region, and the nation. Each stakeholder group has opinions about the corporation, its products, and its management. Each of these publics may be at odds with others, and all of them (preferably working together) are essential to the firm's success. What are their views toward the corporation? What are they thinking about now, and what may be important to them during the next five years? Answers to these questions will affect the corporation's future. Reacting to them when a crisis occurs is a poor way to run any business. Instead, the company's decisions must be based at all times on knowledge about how it is viewed by its publics and what issues may be influencing public attitudes. These are the questions formal research can answer best.

Public agencies—law enforcement, educational, government—have the same general concerns. So do private charities, the churches, the mass media, and virtually every other organization. It may be obvious that a public utility needs to know how its subscribers view the services it provides. But it might be less obvious that every organization has the same informational needs. Let's look at just one example: the American Red Cross chapter in St. Paul, Minnesota.

Everyone is familiar with the Red Cross and its services. Imagine that you are the public relations director for a Red Cross chapter in a large city like St. Paul. What are your essential public relations duties? First, disaster relief and the associated public relations problems of dealing with the mass media during disasters such as floods, fires, and subzero freezes. Such emergencies may occur with relative frequency, perhaps as often as a dozen times a year. There are health-related problems, such as possible outbreaks of flu or measles, and a continuing program of first aid and CPR training, health education, and AIDS awareness. Just keeping up with the training programs requires a full-time public relations effort. There are the volunteers—maybe several hundred people in the community—who must be relied on to staff the training and emergency services Red Cross provides. There is the blood program, the donors and the drives, the bloodmobiles, and the blood banks. Finally, there is fund raising, which is likely to be a year-long program involving several phone solicitations, telethons, and letter writing campaigns. In all, the job of public relations director for a major Red Cross agency requires the full range of public relations activities including media relations, special events, advertising, and fund raising. Keeping up with these activities, even with a large support staff of public relations professionals, would seem to ensure a 60-hour work week with little time devoted to any long-range planning. Although there might be some possibilities for formal research, surely such projects would be relegated to the back burner while the public relations director deals with the more immediate and perpetual front-burner blazes.

Or is this true?

Public relations practitioners from the St. Paul Red Cross chapter say that, far from being a back-burner activity that is occasionally done when someone gets around to it, formal research is part of their week-in, week-out routine.* Research, they say, actually makes their worklife easier because they work

*David J. Therkelsen, director of public relations for the St. Paul Area Chapter and St. Paul Regional Blood Services of the American Red Cross, provided these examples of formal research in a letter to the authors, February 2, 1988. His words are used with his permission.

smarter; they work on real public relations issues, not just those they think might exist.

Here is a closer look at how this non-profit organization uses public opinion research to understand and communicate better with its key publics. Starting with that broad and elusive public, the general public, St. Paul Red Cross takes its pulse every three years by conducting a telephone survey of 300 randomly selected households in its service area. The agency has learned through these surveys that Red Cross is universally known and widely respected in its "backyard" of 700,000 citizens. The surveys show that a large proportion of local residents have actually used Red Cross services at one time or another but, somewhat disquieting, only about half of those using services immediately recognize them as being provided by Red Cross. That finding led to better identification at the "point of sale." For example, people who take a CPR (cardiopulmonary resuscitation) or first aid course get visual reminders that the course came from the Red Cross, not the school building where the training was offered.

Community-wide surveys have also established that most residents believe Red Cross has "about the right amount" or "not enough" funding, thus indicating support for additional fund raising. Those who believe Red Cross does not have enough funds say the agency should either raise user fees or have more fund drives, but overwhelmingly they say Red Cross should not cut back its services. In an uncertain fund-raising environment, these research findings give the agency confidence to move more aggressively than many others have.

One surprise that St. Paul Red Cross found in one of its community-wide surveys was the discovery that its eligibility policies for obtaining blood and blood products were well understood by nearly everyone except older people. Since older people receive blood transfusions in far greater proportion than the rest of the public, Red Cross realizes that it must do more to make senior citizens aware of a policy that affects them. Without the survey, the agency might not have recognized its problem until too late.

In obtaining support of all kinds—financial, volunteer leadership, program support—St. Paul Red Cross has learned there is a relatively small and identifiable group of community leaders who exercise disproportionate influence on what happens locally. These are the local opinion leaders, a key public identified by communication researchers as early as 1940 and the subject of continuing public opinion research for five decades. St. Paul Red Cross has adopted a strategy of targeting these community leaders and has supported that strategy through its own research. The overall strategy has been aimed at persuading community leaders that Red Cross is a financially strong, well-managed organization that can be trusted to handle critical community jobs ranging from procuring human organs and tissues to providing assistance to the hungry and the homeless. Research has demonstrated that the strategy is working. Targeted community leaders are more likely than others to believe St. Paul Red Cross is "well managed," and that it is "better managed" than many other non-profit organizations and for-profit businesses. These findings, in turn, justified continuing the strategy and fine-tuning some of its programs such as targeted publications.

In part because of the support it enjoys from community leaders, St. Paul Red Cross has been among the first of its counterparts nationally to adapt the medical and scientific expertise it has as a blood supplier and move into the field of human organ and tissue procurement: helping transplant centers obtain hearts, livers, kidneys, and tissues such as bone—even bone marrow.

But recruiting people to donate organs or their bone marrow is a very different proposition than asking them to give blood. So Red Cross entered these new fields carefully, guided by its own research. Surveys told the Red Cross, for example, that while most people favor organ donation, they have misconceptions about it. Many believe that by signing a donor card or a driver's license form they will automatically be considered as donors after their death. The reality, however, is that surviving family members make the crucial decisions about whether or not organs are donated. So Red Cross aimed its campaigns not at convincing people to become donors—most already were convinced—but at urging them to discuss their wishes with their family.

Opinion research influenced not only the content but the tone of communications about organ donation. Red Cross discovered those who were most likely to be in favor of organ donation, but least likely to have acted upon their belief, were people with a more "traditional" value system: They were relatively conservative, attended mainstream church denominations, and so forth. This finding led to creative decisions to emphasize organ transplantations not as experimental, high-tech medical procedures, but instead as routine procedures to treat ordinary people with a variety of diseases.

One disease that has dominated the social and political agenda in the 1980s is Acquired Immune Deficiency Syndrome (AIDS). Red Cross is involved with AIDS in two major ways: as a community health education resource and as the main steward of the nation's blood supply. St. Paul Red Cross has made extensive use of public opinion research, especially in its role of providing a safe and adequate supply of blood and blood products. Three of its research projects are described in the following examples:

When Red Cross began testing all units of donated blood for exposure to the AIDS virus, the St. Paul office wanted to know ahead of time the concerns its donor population might have about the new procedures. A series of focus groups helped provide the answers.

On-site and telephone surveys of blood donors were used to measure donor knowledge and attitudes about AIDS, and specifically to determine if donors held the mistaken belief that they could get AIDS by giving blood. While this belief apparently is prevalent in society as a whole, Red Cross found that almost all of its donors have a correct understanding on the point. Thus, the agency refrained from implementing a massive education effort, one that under the circumstances might have created more doubt than clarity.

St. Paul Red Cross also studied physicians' opinions to determine their level of understanding of the risks—and the benefits—to their patients of a blood transfusion.

St. Paul Red Cross and its public relations department have undertaken dozens of other opinion research studies. Sometimes they are used to plan programs—to find out in advance what key publics want or expect of Red Cross. Sometimes they are to test the content of form of intended communication vehicles. Sometimes they are to evaluate whether a campaign worked. The chapter is convinced that its programs and its communications are far more efficient and effective because it takes the time to study, systematically, the audiences that are important to it.

SURVEY PROJECT CASE PROBLEM

An attempt has been made to emphasize that there are thousands of practical situations in which formal research methods, such as survey research, can and should be applied. However, for instructional purposes, a single, imaginary example will serve as the case problem. Admittedly, the example is designed to facilitate learning survey research methods—it is unlikely anyone has actually been involved in a similar case. Here is the problem:

You are a public relations counselor who earns fees giving advice to corporations and agencies and assisting these clients in meeting their public relations needs. You have a very solid reputation in your community, a city of one million residents that is the dominant metro market in a 100-square-mile region composed primarily of rural farmland. The area is generally poor, constantly on the lookout for economic improvement and in dire need of additional revenue-producing businesses to help maintain the tax base for government services.

Within the past month, to the surprise of many, the state legislature approved local-option horse racing with pari-mutuel betting. Under the local-option plan, counties with more than 500,000 population may vote to allow horse racing in a referendum election if there is a majority vote favoring the measure. The legislature refused to consider this plan each time it was proposed during the last five legislative sessions because politicians were lobbied by conservatives and religious groups opposing the plan. The surprise was that the measure was approved during this session.

You are approached by a consortium of business leaders and other local citizens who have applied to the state for a charter to build and operate a horse racing track. The group intends to put the horse racing measure to a vote in this county in about six months and is now soliciting signatures on a referendum petition. The consortium is confident the state will approve its charter application. The group has about $50,000 it can spend to ensure voters will approve the referendum. Can you help?

First, you clarify that you cannot guarantee voters will approve the measure, but you assure the group's representatives that you can determine for them voters' current thinking about the horse racing proposal and you can help identify the main issues that are likely to influence voters' decision on the proposal.

The consortium representatives are pleased. They authorize you to go ahead with the project and to keep them informed of your progress on a weekly basis. They want a written proposal with anticipated expenses and completion date in the form of a letter. The sooner you can complete the project, they say, the better. They intend to use the information you provide to organize their campaign program materials, and they would like to have your completed report by the end of the month.

You talk with these representatives for another hour to gather as much background information as possible from their knowledge of the horse racing issue. You learn what publics have been involved in the issue, what the consortium believes are the main points of controversy and who the key players—both pro and con—in the debate are likely to be. This information will be your starting point for the initial phase of the project: the informal research stage in which you spend a couple of days on the phone with the sources they named and in the library with state and national newspapers.

From your informal research, you gain insights about horse racing in other states, including districts in which the issue was defeated. You read about the proposal's progress in your own state, including the reasons its was unsuccessful in the legislature for so many years and the people who favored and opposed it. You make several phone calls to many of the people named in the newspaper stories. By the second day, you have a good impression of the issues involved in the horse racing controversy from a variety of sources. You are ready to begin the formal stages of a survey research project.

SUMMARY

As an introduction to formal research, the eight steps of scientific method are presented with explanations and examples appropriate to public relations. The chapter conceded that practitioners will probably not be involved with formal research on a daily basis; hence advice from commercial research firms and consultants should be sought in most cases. When outside help is used, the public relations director should involve these experts at the project's initiation rather than later. But, the public relations professional is still the research project's director. He or she must know enough about formal research methodology to design and oversee projects, suggest projects, report the results to management, and take responsibility for each project's outcomes.

How great is the need for formal research in a public relations practitioner's daily operations? The extensive studies sponsored by the St. Paul Area chapter of the American Red Cross are used as an example of research projects that take public relations practice beyond its daily communication routine to a more sophisticated level. The example suggests formal research helps a practitioner understand an organization's present needs and plan for the future.

The chapter presents a proposed horse race track case problem that will serve as an example in the next few chapters on survey research procedures.

ADDITIONAL READING

Awad, Joseph F. *The Power of Public Relations*. New York: Praeger, 1985, pp. 53–60.

Finn, Peter. "In-House Research Becomes a Factor." *Public Relations Journal* (July 1984): 18–20.

Leahigh, Alan K. "If You Can't Count It, Does It Count?" *Public Relations Quarterly* 30:4 (1985–86): 23–27.

Pavlik, John V. *Public Relations: What Research Tells Us*. Sage Commtext Series, Vol. 16. Newbury Park, CA: Sage Publications, 1987.

Rubin, Rebecca B., Alan M. Rubin, and Linda J. Piele. *Communication Research: Strategies and Sources*. Belmont, CA: Wadsworth, 1986.

Simon, Raymond. *Public Relations: Concepts and Practices*. Grid Publishing, 1980, pp. 163–86.

Tichenor, Phillip J. "The Logic of Social and Behavioral Science." In *Research Methods in Mass Communication*, ed. Guido H. Stempel III and Bruce H. Westley. Englewood Cliffs, NJ: Prentice Hall, 1981, pp. 10–28.

Wimmer, Roger D., and Joseph R. Dominick. *Mass Media Research: An Introduction*, 2d ed. Belmont, CA: Wadsworth, 1987, pp. 18–41, 363–70.

8 Preliminary Research Considerations

The initial informational stage of the research project has been completed (see project description at the end of Chapter 7). It is now time to develop a formal research project.

DEFINING THE PROBLEM

The first formal phase of the research project, according to the scientific method, is to determine the problem. In the present example of measuring attitude on a horse race track, the problem is clearly defined. The client wants to know if the horse racing referendum will pass—specifically, if the referendum were being voted today, what percent of the voters would vote for the measure. Additionally, the client wants to identify what the main public issue concerns currently are, and what they are likely to be as the campaign progresses. Taking the problem to its most practical level, clients want to know which kinds of voters are likely to have which kinds of concerns about the race track. Knowing this information, the client will be able to target campaign messages to identified voter subgroups in the population.

While this may seem a heavy order to fill, it is no more challenging than most public issue questions a corporation or agency might face. In fact, this research problem has some easily identifiable goals and expected outcomes. Clarifying those goals is the next step in the process. Unfortunately, it is a step inexperienced practitioners either omit entirely or to which they pay too little attention. This criticism is not directed singularly at public relations research endeavors. Social science researchers, whose educational background emphasizes research methods, too frequently leap directly from a vaguely defined problem to data collection. Such enthusiasm invariably leads to regret or disaster. Formal research must be taken one step at a time, with each step being given the attention it deserves. Cutting corners at the early stages of the research design is certain to result in wasted energies at a later stage. It is imperative that the hypothesis stage receive proper attention before progressing further.

HYPOTHESES

An hypothesis is the guide to success in any research project. It narrows and focuses the research, making the project manageable. Additionally, stating formal hypotheses sets the goals for the study. Without hypotheses, researchers will be unable to determine if the study's outcomes accomplished the intended purposes. Hypotheses are similar to targets. A marksman in Olympic competition with rifle or bow must have a target on which to set sights and must be able to clearly see the target while going through the steps of positioning, loading, aiming, and firing. Without the target, there is no direction to the act and there is no way to measure victory. The same is true for research. If we don't know the intended outcome of the project, we cannot know if we have succeeded in reaching it.

Unfortunately, too many public relations projects are initiated on a whim. The CEO of a large company reads a report showing many of the firm's 3,000 employees are using the company's WATTS lines to make personal calls during business hours. The report includes an estimate that dollars spent in telephone line charges are $120,000 per year and the loss in worker hours amounts to another $240,000. The CEO is furious. Initial response may be to issue an ultimatum warning all employees that anyone caught using company WATTS lines for personal calls will be fired and prosecuted to the fullest extent of the law. Ideally, the CEO has a trusted vice-president of public relations (who may have prevented the CEO from diving headlong into catastrophe on more than one occasion), and the CEO seeks the public relations director's advice. The vice-president counsels that a threatening directive is likely to cause more harm than good. Instead, the public relations vice-president suggests a more subtle approach. Okay, says the CEO, but I want all the personal calls stopped within 30 days. They negotiate and settle on this goal: After 30 days the cost in unauthorized WATTS line use must drop to less than 25 percent of its current monthly figure. Today's figure is estimated at $10,000 per month. After the internal public relations campaign, that figure should be no more than $2,500 per month. A goal has been set. The hypothesis is: A friendly campaign designed to make employees aware of telephone WATTS line abuse will result in a savings in unauthorized line charges.

This statement has all the elements of an hypothesis: 1) It is a positive statement; 2) it links a supposed cause with an outcome; 3) it is specific; and 4) it is measurable. Of course, to be measured, the hypothesis requires *operational definitions*. Almost all hypotheses require definitions of words that might be vague or misunderstood. The WATTS line hypothesis requires two operational definitions. The first is "friendly campaign." Here the vice-president of public relations must define what is being proposed. What is meant by a "friendly campaign"? This operational definition should be a description of the public relations effort that will be undertaken. An example is a campaign by Jerry Daly, then vice-president of corporate public relations at Holiday Inn, Inc., in the early 1980s. An actor dressed as Sherlock Holmes gave shiny new dimes to employees and put stickers on company telephones reminding everyone that the WATTS lines were to be used for company calls only. The character, called "Sherlock Phones," was selected as a way to remind employees of the legendary detective's friend, Dr. Watts.

The other term needing definition is "savings." A reduction to 25 percent of current unauthorized WATTS line expenses was established as the benchmark, so the operational definition of "savings" is $7,500 (a reduction from $10,000 to $2,500 per month, measured in the same way the original report determined unauthorized line use was $10,000 per month). Operational definitions can be anything the researcher believes is appropriate (and the boss or client can accept). For example, another type of campaign might have been planned, and that would have become the operational definition of "friendly campaign." The operational definition of "savings" could have been any figure agreed upon, even if it was only a "drop" in unauthorized line charges (in which case any charges less than $9,999 per month would have been the agreed upon target for success).

Hypotheses with this kind of operational specificity are rarely practical in public relations projects. Frequently, dollar figures aren't appropriate for public relations outcomes. Sometimes achieving changes in people's attitudes, enhancing the image of a company or client, or merely educating a relevant public are the goals of public relations campaigns. Because these outcomes are more ephemeral, reducing the hypothesis to measurable definitions is more difficult. The horse race track example, a more typical public relations problem, provides a basis for further considerations about hypotheses.

One of the chief problems with stating hypotheses is that they are framed in terms that are too general; beginning researchers expect too much of their hypotheses. Imagine the following as a target for the horse race track project:

This county's voters will approve a pari-mutuel betting horse race track.

While this statement may be the crux of the client's interest (it is in fact the bottom line for the project), the statement is far too broad to serve as direction for the research effort. Instead, as in most research projects, the study requires a set of more specific hypotheses based on what is known or suspected about the problem derived from the initial information gathered. The initial phase in this study has included interviews with proponents and opponents of the race track and a search for the "literature." In this case, the literature consisted of newspaper articles and other printed information about proposed horse race tracks in other cities and the published pro and con arguments about the race track in this state as the measure was debated in the legislature. Based on this review of existing information, hypotheses for the study might be as follows:

Hypothesis Number 1. If the horse race track referendum were being voted in this county now, voters would approve the measure by a statistically significant margin.

Operational definitions are not needed for this major hypothesis because all of the terms are clear. It is known precisely what is meant by a horse race track referendum, what county is indicated, that "voters" means registered voters, and that approval of the measure will require a vote of at least 50.1 percent. (The "statistically significant margin" is also a measurable term, but it will be discussed later.)

Hypothesis Number 2. Voters' religious affiliation is the chief determinant of attitude in deciding how to vote on the race track proposal.

Hypothesis 2-A. Voters whose religious affiliation is more traditional will oppose the track; those whose religious affiliation is more liberal will favor the track.
Operational definitions. "Traditional" religious affiliation includes Protestant denominations of Baptist, Presbyterian and Methodist; "liberal" is all other religious denominations and people who say they have no religious affiliation.

Note that the definition of a "traditional" denomination depends on the researcher's best estimate of how churches in the county might approach the question of gambling. Making an error in distinguishing traditional from liberal denominations may destroy the outcome. For instance, if Baptist and Presbyterian denominations in the county generally oppose gambling, but Methodists generally do not, the findings may not support the hypothesis. Perhaps a majority of the Methodists, who are being inappropriately grouped with Baptists and Presbyterians, may favor the horse race track. If Methodists report that they do favor the track, the "traditional" denomination hypothesis may fail because the researcher erred in combining a non-traditional group with two traditional groups.

Supporting or rejecting hypotheses is the purpose of formal research. In fact, each hypothesis is stated in the positive for a reason. Positive statements are called *research hypotheses*. Each is assumed to have an unstated or *null hypothesis*, the antithesis of the research hypothesis. Some studies state both. This study's major hypothesis might be stated as H_1 (the research hypotheses): "If the horse race track referendum were being voted in this county now, voters would approve the measure by a statistically significant margin." Then, H_0 (the null hypothesis) is: "If the horse race track referendum were being voted in this county now, voters would *not* approve the measure by a statistically significant margin." Because each H_1 assumes an H_0, its exact opposite, the null hypothesis is usually unstated. Failure to find support for the research hypothesis results in accepting its antithesis, the null hypothesis.

Here are more hypotheses for the race track project:

Hypotheses Number 3. A voter's personal moral attitude on gambling is the chief determinant of attitude in deciding how to vote on the race track proposal.

This hypothesis raises a couple of points about the function of all hypotheses. First, it is in contrast, though not necessarily in direct contrast, with H_2, the second research hypothesis dealing with religious affiliation. The second hypothesis probes church membership, the third hypothesis probes moral attitude, not church membership. These two related hypotheses are offered to determine which aspect of a person's background—church membership or personal attitude—will be the greater influence in that person's voting decision on the race track. We can expect that some people who are not affiliated with any church but who oppose gambling on moral grounds will vote against the measure. We can also expect some church members do not subscribe personally to all aspects of their church's doctrine. If membership is the chief determinant in people's voting decisions, clergy will be extremely influential as the horse race campaign evolves; if personal moral attitude is the chief determinant, clergy will be less influential. Both aspects of voter decision are pertinent to the research project. So it is certainly possible to offer conflicting hypotheses in the same study. In fact, it is possible to offer a host of conflicting hypotheses because hypotheses are only targets, and the research will succeed if it hits one or more.

Researchers usually begin by listing a series of hypotheses that include all of the aspects to be investigated in the study. The objective is to try to identify and measure all the aspects and determine which of them bears on the major research question. When two hypotheses directly conflict, and one of them is accepted, the other will be rejected. If this seems self-defeating, remember that hypotheses are only targets. Hypotheses are never "right" or "wrong"—they are only "supported" (accepted) or "not supported" (rejected). It often happens that researchers develop a long list of hypotheses in an attempt to tap every possible relationship relevant to the study's objectives. Then they find that none of their hypotheses is supported; all are rejected. Although this may seem futile—a waste of time doing an invalid project—this is far from the truth. Instead the study has succeeded in eliminating a host of possible explanations. In this case, not hitting all the targets results in eliminating those targets from consideration. While the researcher may not have successfully identified the "cause," all suspected "causes" were tested as hypotheses, and all were rejected. Very often, eliminating suspected "causes" provides clients the information they need to know.

The other point demonstrated by this new hypothesis is that while H_2 is easy to measure, H_3 is difficult to measure. We can measure church affiliation in a straightforward manner by asking: "To which of the following religious denominations do you belong?" followed by a list of possibilities. A person may say he or she "belongs" to a particular denomination, and that will be accepted as "affiliation" whether or not the person is a current dues paying member.

Measuring moral attitude is more complex. It might require one or more questions dealing with the person's feelings about gambling as a general social issue or as a moral position each person holds toward gambling. Attitude measurements, particularly those on moral topics, require great care and sensitivity. So H_2 requires little in the way of operational definitions, but H_3 may require extensive operationalizing—perhaps a list of the two or three questions that will be used to measure a person's moral attitude on gambling. Without explaining how "moral attitude" will be measured, the hypothesis is vague. It does not serve well as a target.

Hypothesis Number 4. Female voters will tend to oppose the horse race track measure; male voters will tend to support it.

There's an assumption here that some of the background information (perhaps a newspaper or magazine article about the voting patterns on a race track issue in another city) led the researcher to believe females would be less likely than males to vote for the measure. However, if there was no previous evidence of this in the literature, but the researcher just suspects it is true, the hypothesis could be stated this way. It is better to base hypotheses on the implications from the reviewed literature, but it isn't always necessary to do so. There should, however, be some rationale behind the way hypotheses are stated.

The female versus male hypothesis requires no operational definitions, but it does state a specific expected outcome: More than half the females will oppose the track and more than half the males will support the track. If this hypothesis fails, the true voter expectations about the track will still be known, even if there is no difference in preference between the two sexes.

Hypothesis Number 5. Younger voters will tend to support the race track measure; older voters will tend to oppose it.

Hypothesis Number 6. Voters interested in sports will tend to support the race track measure; non-sports enthusiasts will tend to oppose it.

Another operational definition is needs in H_6. How will the research measure a "sports enthusiast"? Any reasonable procedure to discriminate between sports enthusiasts and non-enthusiasts is appropriate. The operational definition might be: Sports enthusiasts are those who say they enjoy sports "very much" or "somewhat" when asked, and who have attended at least one sports event in the past year. The two measures will be derived from items in the questionnaire.

Hypothesis Number 7. Voters who are most informed about the race track at the time of the study will tend to support the measure; those less informed will tend to oppose the measure.

Again, "informed" may be operationalized in any way the researcher believes will correctly discriminate informed from non-informed voters. It may be possible to make this distinction by asking a single question: "Does the current proposal about a horse race track provide funding: a) from taxpayer dollars, b) from interest-bearing loans, c) from anticipated proceeds at the track, or d) you're not sure about the funding proposal.'' A correct answer (let's say it is ''c'') to this question can be the operational definition of an informed voter.

The study might contain other hypotheses, depending on what is suspected from reviewing the literature about horse race track proposals. For purposes of explanation, however, the seven hypotheses are sufficient. The key aspect to remember about hypotheses is that they must be stated before undertaking any further steps of the research project. If an important aspect of the study is ignored at this point, it's unlikely that it will be remembered in time to be included on the survey form. Researchers frequently find during the data analysis stage— one of the last procedures in a research project—that a critical item was omitted, perhaps one that might have clarified unanticipated relationships in the outcomes.

For instance, there might be a relationship between a voter's age and zip code, and the voter's opposition to the race track. Older people, particularly older people who live in certain district, may be the staunchest opponents of the track. Had the study included years of residence in the county, possibly the key consideration in opposition, the relationship would be clear: More transient families (people who have lived in other places during the past ten years) are more likely to have been in areas where race tracks are common; hence they are more likely to favor a track than people who have lived in this community ten years or more. Finding the age/district relationship would help direct campaign messages to the right people in the right places, but the message might have been made more persuasive if it were known that length of residency is the real explanation for this target group's opposition. Obviously researchers can't anticipate every critical relationship at the outset, but taking enough time to state hypotheses is the best way to reduce the likelihood of forgetting something important.

DEFINING RELEVANT PUBLICS

After becoming familiar with the scope of a public relations problem, the next logical step is to define the relevant publics. What group or groups have a stake in the outcome of the campaign? In the horse race track problem, the relevant public for a public opinion survey consists of those persons who will vote on the referendum when it becomes a ballot issue. Because the state legislature's bill calls for a county-wide election to approve legalized horse racing and parimutuel betting, the specific relevant public for the project is limited to people in the county.

This stage of the survey research project is called *defining the universe. Universe* or *population* is everyone who qualifies for inclusion in the survey. Defining the universe is often a problem. For instance, if the project involved acceptance of automobile air safety bags—the plastic bags hidden under the car's dash that inflate instantly at the first impact with another car—the universe might be all drivers. All drivers might have an opinion about whether air safety bags are a good idea. But once the bags are installed in vehicles at the manufacturing plant, drivers' opinion doesn't matter. "Acceptance" of this new device is really of more interest to car manufacturers; it is part of the automobile purchase decision. If the manufacturers want to know if people are willing to pay a higher price for their automobile with the bags, the universe should be all automobile purchasers instead of all drivers. If Ford Motor Co. is doing the study to determine how Ford buyers feel about adding costs for the air bags, the universe is all current and potential buyers of Fords. Perhaps Ford Motor Co. assumes every car purchaser is a potential Ford product buyer. If that is the case, the survey universe is, again, all car buyers.

Moving from a marketing survey problem to one dealing with corporate employees, consider the case of a 10,000-employee company whose management wants to change normal working hours from the present 9 A.M.-to-5 P.M. day to a 7:30 A.M.-to-3:30 P.M. work day. Instead of mandating the change without considering employee feelings, the firm decides to survey its workers so they will have an opportunity to voice opinion on the change in work hours. The universe might be defined as all persons who work for the company. However, if the change is to apply only to workers who are paid on an hourly basis, the definition of the universe is the hourly paid workers. Managers, executives, and others who earn a monthly pay check, regardless of the hours they put in, are excluded from the definition of the universe. So are part-time employees, temporary employees, and contract workers, none of whom should have the same voice in the decision as full-time hourly employees.

If the survey project involves measuring what a community's opinion leaders think about the city's school system, the researcher will have to devise some definition of what constitutes an "opinion leader in this community." Excluding some people who are opinion leaders or including some who are not will adversely affect the outcome of the project. If the definition of an opinion leader is appropriate to the study's purposes, everyone who qualifies as a leader should be considered part of the universe.

If the project is a readership study of the city's daily newspaper, the universe— those people whose opinion about the content of the daily newspaper counts most—should be people who read the paper.

In the horse race track project, the definition of the universe is not quite right. To include persons who will make the decision on the race track, the definition of the universe should be all registered voters in the county. Registered voters are the only ones eligible to participate in the referendum.

CHOICE OF INTERVIEWING METHODS

Survey research is the preferred methodology to solve this public relations problem because it is the only way to assess the attitude of a broad spectrum of the general public. Although there are several methods for approximating or making an educated guess about what the public may be thinking on an issue, a public opinion survey is the only way to be certain. Executing a public opinion survey is both time consuming and expensive, but it is worth the effort and expense to be right.

There are three ways to conduct a public opinion survey with a questionnaire form: *personal interviews, telephone interviews,* or *mail interviews.* Each has its inherent advantages and disadvantages, and these must be weighed carefully in deciding which is the right approach to use.

Personal Interviews

These are face-to-face interviews done in the home or office. Advantages are that they allow the most time for the interview. Assuming an appointment is agreed upon, the interviewer may take up to two or three hours with the interviewee (although survey interviews seldom require that much time). There is no doubt about whether the right person is completing the form because the interviewer talks face-to-face with the subject. As people will generally agree to the personal interview—it can be an interesting break from their routine—participation is high.

Personal interviews also have the advantage of allowing complicated manipulations because the interviewer is present to explain any misunderstandings in procedure. For example, the study may require looking at a set of four color photographs and completing the table in Figure 8.1 of viewer impressions of the questionnaire form: The subject may be unable to perform the task, even if the pictures could be sent through the mail, without procedural assistance from the interviewer. Explanations are likely to be necessary about how many checks can go in each column or each row. It may be necessary to show only one picture at a time or to show the pictures in a specified order. These tasks can be performed only in a personal interview.

But there are disadvantages to the personal interview. It takes at least two weeks to complete a survey of, say 600 people, because appointments will have to be made in advance and because travel to homes or offices will be time consuming. Appointments will be broken or rescheduled. Such a study might require a month or more. But the major disadvantage of the personal interview is cost. It is by far the most expensive interviewing method, costing from $10 to $125 per completed interview, depending on the survey. Interviewers must be extensively trained and paid appropriately for their time and skill; there is appointment time and travel time to be considered, and the interview itself is likely to be extensive.

Telephone Interviews

The single main advantage of doing a telephone survey is speed. With a group of trained interviewers and a bank of telephones, a survey can be completed overnight. Results for many political surveys require this kind of turnaround

Figure 8.1
Example of Complicated Questionnaire Item

	Land-scape	House	Sky-scraper	Sea-shore	Tree
Peaceful					
Vibrant					
Safe					
Fun					
Frightening					
Lonesome					

Instructions: For each of the pictures, determine which
of the moods most closely matches how you
felt when you first saw the picture. Some
of the pictures may not be placed in the
the listed mood categories where the
column box is filled in. Each picture
should be checked in as many of the blanks
as correctly indicate the mood you first
felt when you looked at the picture. For
instance, if you felt "lonesome" when you
looked at the landscape and the seashore
pictures, check each one in the "lonesome"
row.

time, and speed (although not necessarily overnight) is often a primary consideration for public relations studies done for businesses. Other advantages are relatively low costs, perhaps between $2 and $5 per completed survey, depending on how extensive the questionnaire is and how long the phone call takes to complete the form. Surprisingly, people will remain on the telephone for as long as 45 minutes to complete a survey, if they are interested in the topic. Most telephone interviews, however, are held to less than 15 minutes, and researchers should expect refusal rates to climb as the length of time needed exceeds 10 minutes.

Participation for telephone interviews is relatively high. Depending on the topic and the time, a 75- to 90-percent completion rate is possible if care is taken to explain the importance of the study at the beginning of the call. Despite the growing adverse reputation of telephone surveys—due to computer-generated calls and telephone sales solicitations disguised as surveys—most people will still agree to participate if they believe the survey call is legitimate.

Mail Interviews

The primary advantage of a mail survey is its low cost. Questionnaire forms can be printed and sent with a cover letter in a bulk mailing with a business reply envelope for less than 50 cents in postage per returned questionnaire. A survey of 600 can be completed for less than $300, making mail "interviews" by far the most cost-efficient form of doing a survey. Another advantage of a mail survey is that it reduces *prestige bias*, or having the respondent fell pressure to "slant" answers to create a better social impression. For example, a television viewership survey done by telephone interviews might inquire, "What station was your television tuned to when you received this call?" Many respondents who were watching situation comedies on network television are likely to say they were watching the Public Broadcasting System (PBS). Quite a few telephone surveys have reported much heavier viewing of PBS than was documented by in-home diary studies (where one person in the home keeps logs of daily viewing) done during the same week the telephone survey was made. Respondents have a tendency to give what they consider the most socially acceptable answer if they are face-to-face with an interviewer or speaking to one over the telephone. Respondents feel more comfortable with the anonymity of mail surveys and will generally be more forthright in providing answers through the mail. The anonymity of mail surveys can be a real advantage in public relations. If a corporation is doing a survey on its employees' views of management, workers may not provide truthful answers in face-to-face or telephone interviews—particularly if the management situation is bad—because employees may fear retribution if they report managerial problems. Mail surveys may offer workers a better opportunity to pinpoint difficulties openly.

But mail surveys have some significant disadvantages. Foremost is the return rate, which is usually far lower than for either personal or telephone interviews. A 50 percent response rate to a mail survey is a very good response rate. More usual is a 10- to 30-percent response rate, which raises questions about the validity of the study. Another disadvantage of mail surveys is that it takes a long time to complete the study, sometimes as long as six weeks to get the majority of returns (those that will be returned) through the mail.

The mail survey must be short. It is probably unreasonable to expect a respondent to spend more than 10 minutes completing a mail survey, and the longer it takes to complete the form, the more likely the questionnaire will end up in the trash with people's junk mail. Finally, instructions on a mail survey must be simple. Respondents can't be expected to pore over the form trying to

Table 8.1
Interviewing Methods Compared

	Personal Interviews	*Mail*	*Telephone*
How long can the "interview" session take?	2 hours	15 minutes	30 minutes
How complicated can questionnaire items be?	extremely complicated	must be simple	between the two
What inter-view view costs are involved?	very expensive ($10-$125)	very cheap	fairly cheap
What is the likely response rate?	very high	very low	fairly high
How quickly is information needed?	takes two weeks	may take six weeks	over-night
How certain can we be that the right interviewee is answering items?	absolutely certain	no way of knowing	pretty certain
What is the likely-hood of prestige bias?	very high	very low	between the two

figure out how to complete it. The questions must be straightforward, and the instructions must be brief and clear.

Table 8.1 provides the guidelines for making decisions about which interviewing method to use. It indicates—as is in fact the case—that telephone interviews are the method of choice in most instances because they have more of the advantages and fewer of the disadvantages of the other two methods.

One other crucial point about the interview choice is that the study's purpose should determine which interviewing method to use. Most studies include at least one key decision point that supersedes other considerations. For instance, cost is a key factor in most studies, and cost often rules out the personal interview method. But speed may be more important than cost. If a decision based on the study's results must be made in time for the annual board meeting next week, telephone interviewing is the only way to get the results in time. If the study's purpose demands that the respondent complete some complicated questionnaire procedures, personal interviewing is the only way to do the survey. Each study will have its unique requirements, and these crucial needs should determine which interviewing method is used in the study.

SECURING A ROSTER

A *roster* is a list of everyone in the defined universe. Securing a roster is often relatively easy. In the brief example used earlier in this chapter in the section "Defining Relevant Publics," a large corporation's hourly paid workers were being surveyed about changing work hours. Procuring a roster of hourly paid employees is merely a matter of having the payroll department provide a list of the company's full-time, permanent, hourly paid workers. But many survey situations virtually defy securing a roster. For instance, union organizers would have difficulty securing the same hourly paid worker list from the company. Legal constraints would prevent securing a roster of hospital patients.

A host of survey projects must be carried out in situations where it is impossible to obtain a roster. Even in instances where it is possible to get a roster, the list itself may be invalid. It may be out-of-date or inaccurate. However, in many public opinion survey research situations, lack of a valid roster is a problem that can be overcome. It will have to be overcome in the present study dealing with the horse race track referendum. Instead of using a roster, researchers can reach members of a defined universe through more sophisticated sampling techniques.

Sampling technique is an important—but slightly more advanced—aspect of preliminary decision making for survey research to be discussed in the next chapter.

SUMMARY

The preliminary decision-making process in survey research has been presented using the first few stages of the scientific method with examples based on the primary research study under consideration—the horse race track. Additional examples related to formal public relations research projects were presented along with some terms and definitions common to social science research. Preliminary decision-making procedures include: 1) defining the problem, 2) stating hypotheses, 3) defining relevant publics, 4) choosing an interviewing method, and 5) securing a roster.

ADDITIONAL READING

Blalock, Herbert M., Jr. *Conceptualization and Measurement in the Social Sciences.* Newbury Park, CA: Sage, 1984.

Fink, Arlene, and Jacqueline Kosecoff. *How to Conduct Surveys: A Step-by-Step Guide.* Newbury Park, CA: Sage, 1985.

Gilreath, Charles L. *Computerized Literature Searching: Research Strategies and Databases.* Boulder, CO: Westview, 1984.

Hsia, H. J. *Mass Communication Research Methods: A Step-by-Step Approach*. Hillsdale, NJ: Lawrence Erlbaum Associates, 1988.

Kerlinger, Fred Nichols. *Behavioral Research: A Conceptual Approach*. 2d ed. New York: Holt, Rinehart and Winston, 1979.

Lovell, Ronald P. *Inside Public Relations*. Boston: Allyn & Bacon, 1982.

Robinson, Edward J. *Public Relations and Survey Research*. New York: Appleton-Century-Crofts, 1969.

Rubin, Rebecca B., Alan M. Rubin, and Linda J. Piele. *Communication Research: Strategies and Sources*. Belmont, CA: Wadsworth, 1986, pp. 13–27.

Tucker, Raymond K., Richard L. Weaver II, and Cynthia Berryman-Fink. *Research in Speech Communication*. Englewood Cliffs, NJ: Prentice Hall, 1981, pp. 24–40.

Williams, Martha E. *Computer-Readable Databases: A Directory and Data Sourcebook*. Chicago: American Library Association, 1984.

Wimmer, Roger D., and Joseph R. Dominick. *Mass Media Research: An Introduction*. 2d ed. Belmont, CA: Wadsworth, 1987, pp. 102–34.

9 Intermediate Research Considerations

The early stages of formal research decision making involve a clarification process that takes place in the conference room or in the researcher's mind. Projects are considered from the standpoint of purpose: What information is needed and what is the best way to obtain it? When purpose and direction have been established, the intermediate steps should be a logical progression involving the application of the right research techniques. Using the horse race track as an example, the project can be continued with focus on these intermediate research techniques. We are at the fourth point in the scientific method discussed in Chapter 7: determining measurement procedures. Needed now are a decision on a sampling plan, the choice of interviewing method, and construction of a questionnaire.

SAMPLES

One of the chief strategy decisions in planning a public relations campaign is to define relevant publics—to decide what group or groups have a stake in policy decisions a company or agency might make. Social science research projects also define relevant groups—the universe or population—as discussed in Chapter 8. A *census* is a survey that includes every member of the defined universe. For example, if a state tourism agency wanted to know how well its publicists were doing in their media relations efforts, one strategy would be to contact editors of the state's news media. To make the study manageable, the agency might start with the tourism writers of the state's major daily newspapers asking these writers if they received news releases from the agency and, if so, was one of the releases used as a basis for a story in their own paper in the past month. If there are 25 daily newspapers, and if one individual could be identified as the tourism writer for each daily paper, it would be possible to include all 25 in the survey. This would be a census, and it would be the right approach for finding out how effective the agency's publicists are, at least in providing story tips for the state's daily newspapers. In this case, the census is not only manageable, but it has the advantage of including every daily paper in the state.

A sample is asking anything less than the entire population under study. If only 24 papers could be contacted, the study would be based on a *sample* of the state's 25 daily newspapers, albeit a sample that was nearly a census. Still, if the writer who didn't respond wrote for the state's largest daily, with one-third of the state's total daily circulation, the sample of 24 papers might provide a less-than-complete picture of the agency's impact in reaching the newspaper reading audience. But this example is the exception. More often a media impact study would include all news media in the state, including daily newspapers and weeklies, radio and television stations, business publications, newsletters, etc. The list of news outlets might include 1,500 publications and stations. Asking each would be costly and cumbersome, at best, so the agency would rely instead on a sample of news media outlets. The same is true for virtually all public opinion surveys and most other social science research studies, even if they are limited to measuring attitude among hourly employees in a company's workforce.

Two types of samples are possible in social science research, *non-probability* samples and *probability* samples. Each has a purpose and a variety of approaches, and all can be used in public relations research projects, depending on the study's purpose. The difference between the two is that a probability sample can be used to extrapolate findings from the sample to the population. Statistical formulas can be applied to probability samples, but not to non-probability samples.

Non-Probability Samples

The most common type of sample is called an *available* sample—using subjects who are easily accessible. Much of the published academic research during the past 50 years has been the result of studies done on samples of sophomores in college classes. In political science, sociology, psychology, communication, and even public relations, the literature is replete with sophomore samples because such students, in their introductory courses in the major, provide a large, convenient pool of subjects.

Similarly, marketing studies involving shoppers at malls also use available samples of people. Handing out questionnaires to company employees in the lunch room is another example of using an available sample. While the procedure has the advantage of being cost-effective and quick, it has the distinct drawback of being unrepresentative. Sophomores in college are certainly not representative of any other kind of group, nor are the shoppers representative even of other shoppers. If the marketing "intercept study" booth in the mall is positioned near an expensive department store, those shoppers probably differ from shoppers who might be interviewed in front of a mall drug store or teen clothing store.

Employees who eat in the company lunch room are likely to differ from those who don't eat there.

However, researchers who use available samples are making as assumption that available groups of people will respond to the survey in ways similar to those that might be found among other groups. Sophomores are, after all, people too, and their reactions or answers to a questionnaire might be exactly the same as those found in the entire population on a wide variety of topics including politics, visual perception, or family life (but probably not on beer consumption. legalization of marijuana, or sex).

If the product being tested in the mall marketing study is expensive perfume, a case might be made that an available sample taken in front of an expensive department store is precisely the right group of potential buyers to interview. And, while employees who eat in the company lunch room may differ from employees who don't eat there, they may also be similar, or similar enough, to all company employees for the intended purpose of the study.

Answers obtained from available samples are not invalid per se, but using such results for decision making can be deceptive, and the researcher will never know in which instance the outcomes should be believed. Still, such studies provide tremendous convenience and offer the kind of tentative results that might be used effectively in *exploratory* research. Exploratory research consists of preliminary investigations that are usually designed to rule out further need for study. For instance, if a psychologist wants to learn whether young people have a favorite color, an available sample of college sophomores might be appropriate. If color slides are flashed on a large screen in a class of 200 students, and the result is that the group has no single color preference, the research might stop at this point without further expenditure of resources on a more representative sample of young people.

Another type of non-probability sample is the *purposive* sample. Here subjects are chosen specifically because they possess a certain characteristic or some knowledge the researcher is interested in. Public relations practitioners who do periodic image studies are frequently more concerned about how their firm is viewed not by the general public but by opinion leaders in the community. If community leaders think the company is well managed, that is a sufficient measure of success and possibly better than asking the general public, many of whom are not likely to know enough about the company—or about corporate management—to offer a valid opinion. Such an image study would use a purposive sample of community leaders or possibly only corporate leaders in the community.

A wide variety of public relations studies require a purposive sample rather than a probability sample, and frequently the purposive sample is both small and specialized. For instance, a firm might want to know if its wholesale buyers are satisfied with its distribution system, or if doctors at a medical center are familiar with the provisions of a new retirement plan the center is offering. Why did people who purchased an import passenger car in the past three years make that decision? What would influence them to purchase a domestic brand the next time they buy a car?

Although these samples are considered purposive, the studies are really only defining the universe with greater than normal precision. To qualify in the medical center example, the subject has to be a doctor who works at the center and is eligible to participate in the retirement plan. For the foreign versus domestic car study, a person must have purchased an import car in the past three years. Not everyone in the United States who did so will necessarily be included in the study. Instead, from the defined universe of past-three-years import car buyers, possibly a million purchasers, a sample of perhaps 1,500 will be selected. The smaller sample might be a probability sample, but it would represent only the universe of those who were purposively selected for study.

A *quota* sample is similar to the purposive sample in that its constituents are predetermined by the researcher based on some known property of the universe. In a quota sample, an effort is made to ensure that a necessary subgroup is represented at its proper level of existence in the population. For example, the city council wants to know if its bus franchise is providing adequate service to residents. However, based on collected data from the transit authority, it is known that only 20 percent of the city's residents regularly use the public bus system while the other 80 percent use it infrequently, if at all. Twenty percent of the sample for such a research project should be composed of frequent bus riders. A random sample of city residents selected from the residential telephone directory may not yield the 20 percent frequent rider figure, particularly if the lowest income city residents are known to rely most heavily on bus transportation and these residents are least likely to have a telephone. If telephone interviewing is required for the survey (perhaps the results are needed by next week), it will be necessary to ask respondents if they ride city buses frequently. The screening question might be, "Did you rise a city bus yesterday?" In a total sample of 700, the researcher would supervise phone interviews to ensure that at least 140 "yes" persons, or 20 percent of the final sample, are included in the sample.

The main problem with a quota sample is that it provides a disproportionate chance for a certain segment of the population to be represented in the sample. The bus example is actually one of the least intrusive quota sampling methods because a random phone sample would probably net at least 15 percent bus riders regardless of their likelihood of having a telephone. If a study's purpose is to compare the attitude of native Americans with others, and the city's population of native Americans is only 2 percent, a special sampling approach would be needed to include enough native Americans. In fact, if the study's purpose is this specific comparison, native Americans would have to be oversampled. The research design might require including 25 percent native Americans or 175 in a 700-subject sample, enough to have some confidence in their attitude responses. Oversampling native Americans skews the sample because it represents them at more than ten times their actual proportion in the population.

The final non-probability sample is called a *volunteer* sample. This design relies on people who willingly participate with little or no urging. For instance, a common mistake made in newspaper, magazine, and newsletter readership studies is to print the questionnaire in the publication and offer an incentive (a free month's subscription or other prize) to those who clip the questionnaire, complete it, and return it. Printing the questionnaire in the publication is an extremely efficient way to collect survey data, but it is not an effective research method. If the publication has 20,000 subscribers, 600 might return the questionnaire. But these volunteers are likely to differ from the 19,400 subscribers who decided not to complete the form. The researcher should assume these volunteers are either the most loyal readers, or those who have a bone to pick with the editors, or those who want the prize. In any case, the volunteers have some reason for agreeing to participate in the study when the vast majority declined.

In the mid–1970s, *Cosmopolitan* magazine, an early and leading proponent of the women's movement, published a questionnaire on changes in sexual liberation. More than 30,000 subscribers returned the forms, and stories were published based on the results of this large sample. The findings were startling, indicating women in the '70s were far more sexually liberated than even *Cosmopolitan's* editors might have imagined. Such outcomes should not have been surprising because the volunteer sample, regardless of its impressive size, was likely to be composed of women subscribers who were sexually liberated enough to have something to say and not embarrassed to report it.

Volunteer samples—in virtually every research study—should be avoided because there is usually some reason why these individuals want to participate. Researchers have no way of knowing what motivates volunteers, so there is no way to assess how the non-volunteers might differ in attitude or demographics. All studies do rely on "volunteers," if volunteers are defined as those who agreed to participate in the study. But when the response rate is lower than 50 percent of those sampled, it is probably true that respondents differ in some significant way from non-respondents. A low response rate should always make the survey findings suspect.

Probability Samples

There is only one single difference between probability and non-probability samples, In a probability sample, everyone in the defined population must have an *equal chance* of being selected for the sample. Regardless of the method for selection—tossing dice, using a list of random numbers, or allowing a computer to generate a sample—each member of the defined universe must have the same chance as every other member to be selected for the sample. If a sample is selected in this manner, it will represent the population, and findings from the sample can be generalized to the population through the application of statistical techniques. If the sample is large enough, perhaps 1,200 or more, any known

Table 9.1
Brand of Automobile Owned by Families in the United States (fictional data)

	U.S. Population	Sample Of At Least 1,200
Chevrolet	18.1%	17.8%
Ford	15.5	15.4
Oldmobile	10.9	11.0
Buick	8.0	8.3
Pontiac	6.7	6.7
Chrysler	5.2	4.9
Toyota	4.4	4.5
Nissan	3.9	3.8
All other	27.3	27.6
Total	100.0%	100.0%

characteristic of the entire population should be found in the sample at about the same percentage as it is found in the population.

Table 9.1 provides fictional data of known population parameters (the brand of automobile a family owns) and this parameter in a sample. If there is an equal chance of selection from the population to the sample, researchers should expect a close match on all of the known parameters, indicating that the sample is representative of the population.

The most frequently used type of non-probability sample is called a simple *random* sample. This type of sample assumes there is a list or roster of the population, although a list is not essential if there is some other acceptable method of contacting members of the defined population. With a current and accurate list of names of everyone in the population, sampling is a straightforward and relatively simple task, although it can be time consuming. If a service organization has a current list of its membership, the researcher can number the members consecutively and can use a table or random numbers to select the sample. With a list of 3,500 members numbered consecutively from 0001 to 3500, the table of random numbers is entered enough times to draw a sample of the size required for the research project. Table 9.2 is an example of a list of random numbers. Closing one's eyes and pointing a pencil to the list, then accepting any four-digit number to the right of the pencil point that falls between 0000 and 3501, is an acceptable procedure. The pencil point indicated on the table would yield subject 2037 on the numbered membership list.

Another simple random sample selection procedure used frequently today is

Table 9.2
Example of a Partial List of Random Numbers

```
7 0 3 6 0 9 1 9 8 0 2 4 5 5 1 4 6 7 9 2 1 0 9 9 7 2 4 3 5 1 8

4 7 8 4 3 4 2 8 4 5 6 0 4 3 0 8 7 1 3 5 9 6 0 2 0 8 1 5 3 9 6

0 5 7 7 0 8 4 5 3 9 8 0 1 5 7 9 0 4 8 1 0 2 7 4 9 2 4 6 4 2 0

9 4 2 5 7 8 2 3 9 7 2 5 4·2 0 3 7 0 6 4 4 4 8 3 5 1 5 9 0 3 7

2 8 8 5 4 2 8 0 7 5 9 6 6 3 9 2 1 7 5 8 2 4 0 9 5 1 3 6 8 5 1

8 3 7 3 3 5 9 2 4 6 0 8 2 7 4 5 9 6 2 8 3 7 8 4 1 3 7 5 4 9 2

3 0 2 5 4 7 7 9 2 5 3 9 1 6 2 6 8 4 9 3 0 4 8 2 7 5 0 8 1 3 6

1 6 8 8 3 5 0 2 8 0 4 2 7 7 6 0 3 8 2 5 1 0 9 4 2 6 3 6 9 1 7
```

based on telephone directory selection. While it is not the best method for ensuring that every person in the directory's listing area has an equal chance of being selected for the sample—some people don't have telephones and some have unlisted numbers—the directory is often the only way to select a sample for a limited-budget public opinion survey. The assumption is that almost everyone has a telephone today, so the sample is not damaged appreciably by excluding those without a phone. But the main sampling problem using a telephone directory is those who have moved into the area since the directory was published, those whose numbers have been changed, and those who have unlisted telephone numbers.

One way to circumvent this difficulty is *random digit dialing* with *replacement* digits. True random digit dialing would be done by generating seven-digit phone numbers from a computer or other totally random method. However, probably fewer than one-third of the numbers generated this way will actually be working phone numbers. There's a better way to select a random sample of residences with phones.

Telephone companies issue prefix numbers (the first three digits of a seven-digit number such as 754–) based on population concentration in a geographic area. A city might have from 50 to 100 prefix numbers with the last four digits assigned in ways that facilitate frequent number changes. Because the prefix numbers are related to population concentration, selecting a number from the telephone directory can result in a good random sample if the last one or two digits of a listed number are dropped and replaced with other digits that are also selected in a random manner. The number 754–4324 might be an actual listing selected randomly from the directory. By subtracting "1" from the last digit, the researcher produces the number 754–3423. There is probably a 75 percent chance that if 754–3424 is a listed number, 754–3423 is also a working number, although it might be a business, a new resident, or an unlisted number. So random digit dialing with replacement includes listings that are more recent than the printed directory, and it includes unlisted numbers.

Systematic sampling is similar to a simple random sampling method, but it requires having a list of the population arranged in some numerical order (or the researcher can number the list). There are many instances in which public relations researchers do have access to such a list.

For example, a readership study of a company's monthly employee newsletter could begin with a roster of every employee in the firm who receives the newsletter. Some firms mail the newsletter to employees' home addresses so its contents can be shared with other members of the family. In such cases, the newsletter's mailing list would be the roster for a sample. Most mailing lists are stored on computer and are coded so subgroups of employees can be identified (420001 might indicate an hourly paid worker, code "42," and "0001" would be the first individual member, perhaps Alice Abernathy).

The researcher first determines how large a sample is needed and how many *elements* or subjects are on the roster. If the company's newsletter mailing list has 10,000 names, and if the researcher needs a sample of 1,000, the *sampling interval* would be 10. Every *n*th (in this case tenth) name on the list would be included in the sample once an *entry point* is randomly selected. If the entry point to the list is name number 6,758, the next name chosen would be 6,768 and so forth until a sample of 1,000 names is obtained from the list. Most computers can be programmed to randomly select an entry point and to select every next fifth or tenth name on the list after that point. Because the procedure is so close to a simple random sampling method, most researchers consider the two equally effective.

While the systematic random sample can be drawn in an extremely efficient manner, its one drawback is periodicity, or the danger that a list will be arranged in some manner that might bias the sample. A conceivable bias in the newsletter mailing list might be that the list is arranged so every tenth name is that of a supervisor. A systematic sample of the list might exclude all supervisors, or it might include *only* supervisors. While this possibility is unlikely, list arrangements should be scanned to ensure they are not constructed in a manner that might yield a biased sample.

The other types of samples are more complex and should be considered only if there is no list or if some aspect of the research design demands their use. *Stratified* sampling is used if the project requires including segments of the population that might not be included at sufficient levels in a random sampling procedure. In the company newsletter example, the purpose of the study might be to contrast supervisor versus non-supervisor opinion about the newsletter. If the total sample size is to be 1,000, the sampling interval of the list of 10,000 employees will be 10. But if there are only 1,000 employees on the list whose job designation is supervisor or higher (their *incidence* in the population of 10,000 is 10 percent) a systematic or simple random sample of the list might not yield the full complement of 100 supervisors. *Stratified* sampling will have to be employed to ensure getting 100 supervisors in the sample. This is usually done by selecting subjects for the sample one at a time and filling the required number of supervisors first, then sampling the other 900 employees from the list randomly.

If there is no list or list substitute, the sampling procedure choice should be a *cluster* sample. If a hospital is interested in comparing its patients' impressions of its services with those of other hospitals' patients, sampling becomes a problem. There is probably no way to secure a list of people who have been in the city's hospitals during the past year. A telephone survey on such a potentially sensitive topic might be inappropriate so personal interviews might be necessary. The hospital's public relations director might decide to cluster sample using zip codes in the city since zip codes are also designated by population concentrations. If there are 25 different zip codes in the city, groups of people might be selected proportionately by zip code categories. Care must be taken to divide the zip code clusters into small groups using as many of the 25 different codes as possible. If the zip codes are sampled to include only 8 of the 25, there is a danger of selecting a portion of town in which older people are concentrated. This might bias the sample by overrepresenting older hospital patients.

The last type of sample is called a *multi-stage* sampling design. Again, it is used where there is no roster and primarily where personal interviewing is determined to be the appropriate data-gathering method. A multi-stage design uses a funneling effect beginning at the largest sampling level and ending at the individual to be interviewed. For instance, in the hospital example, sampling of the city might begin at the city-and-suburbs stage and continue through the following steps.

First Stage

If the city has a population of 500,000 and there are 20 suburban areas with another 500,000 total population, a design might begin with placing slips of paper in a hat. Because the suburbs aren't equal in population, the smallest, with only 10,000 population, has one slip in the hat. A suburb with 50,000 population is represented by five slips of paper and so forth. The city, with 500,000 population, is written on 50 slips. Each slip represents 10,000 people and there are 100 slips of paper in the hat to be drawn randomly. If the final sample is to be 1,000, a slip will be drawn, recorded, and replaced in the hat so it can be included a second time. A total of 1,000 slips will be taken from the hat and recorded.

Second Stage

The next geographic level might be districts or wards in each municipality. A map of districts with their population levels can be used, and slips of paper representing districts can be placed in the hat. A suburb of 100,000 population might have 12 districts, 2 with 25,000 population each and the others with only 5,000 population. The name of each 5,000-population district is written on slips;

the two 25,000-population districts are included on 5 slips each. If this suburb has been selected for the sample nine times in the first sampling stage, nine slips will be drawn (with replacement) for this suburb. All the other suburbs and the central city will be treated in the same manner until 1,000 districts have been selected.

Third Stage

The next geographic dimension might be street blocks selected from the districts using city maps. According to their residential population concentration, 1,000 blocks would be chosen from the selected districts.

Fourth Stage

Streets would be selected from the blocks chosen in the third stage.

Fifth Stage

Houses would be selected from the streets included in the fourth stage.

Sixth Stage

Individuals would be selected from the chosen houses. In this stage, a random selection would be made between male and female, and between adult or child, if the research design includes residents under age 18.

These are the most common types of non-probability and probability samples. Which type is most appropriate for the horse race track research project used here as the survey research example?

It should be obvious that the race track example will require a probability sample. The client will expect survey results to be generalizable from the sample to the population of voters on the referendum measure. There are two possibilities, and the choice between these two depends, as it should, on the special information requirements of the race track project.

One choice is a systematic sample of voter registration rosters because it is possible to secure lists of registered voters in the county. If there are 500,000 registered voters, a sample of 1,000 could be obtained by accessing the voter lists through a random method to obtain an entry point and selecting every 500th name on the list (the sampling interval would be 500). Little concern needs to be taken with periodicity because the list should not be ordered in any special way. Depending on how sophisticated the voter list storage system is, it might be possible to derive a systematic sample of voters by accessing stored computer lists.

The efficiency of using the lists is attractive, but this procedure has a critical flaw. The problem is that a race track referendum including pari-mutuel betting is likely to be a controversial issue, particularly in a state that has not previously allowed race tracks and the associated gambling. Preliminary investigation by the researcher has already documented that the race track issue is divided along moral and religious lines. Because the client wants an early measurement of the referendum's success potential—in plenty of time to prepare campaign materials addressing voters' concerns—there is enough time for opponents to mount a massive voter registration campaign. The researcher should anticipate that voter rolls for the race track referendum will swell. Even if the number of registered voters increases by only five percent, newly registered voters are likely to be opponents of the measure, and they are more certain to actually cast a vote on the measure. Ignoring this probable alteration in voter rolls would exclude an important segment of what will probably be the actual votes cast in the referendum.

The second choice, and the right decision for this project's sampling plan, is a simple random sample of the population by random digit telephone dialing. Obtaining a sample by using telephone directories of cities in the county may be more efficient than using the voter registration lists, and the sample of respondents selected in this manner will include very person of voting age in the county who lives in a residence with a telephone—probably more than 97 percent of the adults currently residing in the county. Every adult of voting age will have an equal opportunity to be included in the sample, and through a series of screening questions interviewers will be able to ascertain respondents' current voter registration status, their interest in the race track issue, and their probability of voting in the referendum. This sampling strategy includes both the currently registered and those who might be part of a coming registration campaign designed to defeat (or support) the race track.

There are several ways to access listings in telephone directories to secure a random sample of county residences with telephones. Replacing the last two digits with random numbers ensures that new residents will be included along with unlisted numbers. The procedure is likely to be as efficient as using the voter registration lists, and it has the advantage of including people who may actually vote in the referendum but who are not yet registered to do so. It will probably be necessary to collect 1,300 names to ensure having a completed sample of 1,000 because some of the random numbers will be businesses, some will be non-working numbers, and some will be refusals.

SAMPLE SIZE CONSIDERATIONS

Several considerations should be used to determine the size of a survey sample. In general, the larger the sample, the better. But it is also true that costs increase with every increase in sample size, so the most efficient study is one with only a large enough sample to provide accurate answers. Fortunately, accuracy—or the margin of error—is closely related to sample size. *Margin of error* is how well the measurements taken on the sample can be generalized to the population under study. This is expressed as a percentage range. For example, if the margin of error is ±3.5 percent (read plus or minus 3.5 percent), we know that any parameter found in the sample will be within 3.5 percentage points of the same parameter found in the population. If the sample is 62 percent female, the

Table 9.3
Sample Size and Margin of Error

Sample Size	Margin of Error
25	±20%
50	±14.2%
100	±10%
200	±7.1%
400	±5%
800	±3.5%
1,600	±2.5%

percentage of the population that is female might be as low as 58.5 percent or as high as 65.5 percent. If the sample were asked if they are opposed to a race track and 44 percent say yes, with a margin of error of ±3.5 percent we know the answer to that question—had the entire population been asked—would have been as low as 40.5 percent yes or as high as 47.5 percent yes.

Table 9.3 shows sample sizes and their associated margin of error. For virtually all purposes, these never change, regardless of how large the population might be. Public opinion polls for national elections are based on samples of 1,200 to 1,600 voters, although the total number of registered voters in the United States is more than 75 million. The margin of error for such surveys is about ±3 percent. If a public relations director does a survey of 10,000 company employees and the sample is about 1,200 employees selected randomly from the 10,000, the margin of error is still about ±3 percent.

Table 9.3 demonstrates something very important about sample size and accuracy. With increases in sample size, there are decreases in error (or increases in accuracy), but the accuracy improvement increases at a diminishing rate. When the sample size doubles from 50 to 100, there is a 4.2 percent gain in accuracy, but when the sample size doubles again from 100 to 200, there is only a 2.9 percent gain in accuracy. When the sample doubles from 200 to 400, the accuracy gain is 2.1 percent; when it doubles from 400 to 800, accuracy improves only 1.5 percent. The larger the sample, the *more* gain in accuracy, but it takes much larger samples to produce smaller gains in accuracy. If sample size goes from 2,000 respondents (with a margin of error of ±2.2 percent) to 5,000 respondents, the margin of error at this sample level is 1.4 percent. Costs for increasing the sample from 2,000 to 5,000 have increased by 150 percent, but the accuracy has decreased less than 1 percent. Obviously, that additional 1 percent accuracy would have to be a critical factor before a researcher would decide to increase costs 150 percent to achieve it. There are few if any instances in which accuracy is so critical that sample parameters must be within 3 percentage points of the population parameter, hence there are virtually no conditions under which a sample of more than 1,600 is required.

In public relations research, for most purposes, a margin of error of ±3 percent is more accuracy than required. Election predictions are probably the most critical survey situations, but public relations practitioners seldom engage in election prediction studies. A case can be made for allowing much more margin of error in most public relations survey measurement procedures. In fact, for opinion testing, a margin of error of ±5 percent is probably sufficient. Table 9.3 shows that ±5 percent margin of error can be gained with a sample of only 400. A sample of 600 produces a margin of error of ±4.1 percent; a sample of 800 produces a margin of error of ±3.5 percent. Considering that costs double with each doubling of sample size, most public relations researchers can achieve their survey measurement needs with a sample of only 600 or even 400. Having a larger sample is simply not cost-efficient.

How much accuracy is required in the horse race track survey project? This is one of those few situations in which a public relations practitioner *is* trying to predict an election outcome. However, the objective here is not to write a news release for the Sunday paper before the Tuesday election. The clients want an accurate estimation of the current voter feeling about the coming referendum on the race track, but the election is still several months away. Prediction of the final outcome is not essential at this point because the intent behind this survey is to identify current concerns on the issue and to use that information to design campaign messages. The researcher should determine sample size by considering the lowest sample size that will provide enough accuracy for the client's needs.

It is possible to use a sample of 400 and to accept a margin of error of ±5 percent, but there is another consideration about sample size that should be included in this decision. That consideration is the number of respondents who are likely to be included in any critical segment of the sample. For instance, age is expected to be a critical factor in voters' decision about the race track. It would be beneficial to the study if the sample includes enough people in all the following age categories: (1) 18 to 29, (2) 30 to 39, (3) 40 to 49, (4) 50 to 59, and (5) 60 and older. A sample size of 400 might include fewer than 40 individuals in one of these age categories, and if sex and age become mutually critical factors, the problem of a small sample will be intensified if there are only 16 males in the 18-to–29 age category. The opinions of 16 people offer scant assurance that the sample will correctly measure the opinion of 20,000 young males who might vote on the referendum.

This secondary consideration about having enough respondents in any critical category suggests increasing the sample size, not because the researcher wants to reduce margin of error but to have more subjects represented in what are likely to be important subsections of the analysis. Instead of a sample of 400, the size should be increased to 600 or 800 subjects. Costs will increase, but the likelihood of having begun with too few subjects for complete measurement will decrease. The researcher should attempt to complete a sample of 800 respondents and might be content if those expectations result in a final sample of between 600 and 700.

SUMMARY

Using the horse race track as a continuing example, the chapter presents intermediate research considerations. The most important of these is sampling, and a discussion of both non-probability and probability sample designs is offered. The strengths and weaknesses of each design are indicated along with implications for public relations research studies. Another critical intermediate research decision is sample size. The chapter presents the concept of margin of error, and the public relations researcher is reminded that many studies in this field will yield worthwhile findings using samples of far less than 1,000 subjects.

ADDITIONAL READING

Babbie, Earl R. *The Practice of Social Research*, 4th ed. Belmont, CA: Wadsworth, 1986.

Bailey, Kenneth D. *Methods of Social Research*, 2d ed. New York: Free Press, 1982, pp. 83–107.

Cochran, William G. *Sampling Techniques*. 3d ed. New York: John Wiley, 1977.

Kalton, Graham. *Introduction to Survey Sampling*. Newbury Park, CA: Sage, 1983.

Kidder, Louise H. *Selltiz, Wrightsman and Cook's Research Methods in Social Relations*. 4th ed. New York: Holt, Rinehart and Winston, 1981.

Lake, Celinda C., and Pat Callbeck. *Public Opinion Polling*. Covelo, CA: Island Press, 1988, pp. 67–94.

Lavrakas, Paul J. *Telephone Survey Methods: Sampling, Selection, and Supervision*. Beverly Hills, CA: Sage, 1987.

Williams, Bill. *A Sampler on Sampling*. New York: John Wiley, 1978.

Wimmer, Roger D., and Joseph R. Dominick. *Mass Media Research: An Introduction*. 2d ed. Belmont, CA: Wadsworth, 1987, pp. 69–86.

10 Survey Questionnaires

Sampling method and questionnaire preparation are the two most important aspects of survey research. Samples are critical because if the project demands asking opinions of a random sample–and if the sample is not random—researchers will invariably report inaccurate conclusions. Findings from a biased sample are usually worthless. Similarly, a poorly executed questionnaire results in inaccurate conclusions. Survey research answers will never be any better than the questions asked, and constructing a viable questionnaire that accurately taps opinion and provides believable answers is an art form. Although it is an art, questionnaire construction can be simplified by using common sense and by learning some general guidelines (the lessons of countless surveys destroyed at this stage of the research process).

THE SURVEY AUDIENCE

Begin by remembering who the audience of the survey will be. Normally, the researcher will know what types of people will be answering the questions, but frequently this important consideration is ignored. If the sample population is general, the questionnaire items must be relatively simple and the time required to complete it should be kept as short as possible. If the sample is more specific, perhaps company employees, researchers can make some assumptions about motivation to participate and about how much knowledge the audience will possess. For example, company employees might be asked about the firm's health insurance plan and may be expected to have some knowledge about its specific benefits and limitations. They can relate recent experiences they have had in filing forms, and they can say whether they or their physicians were paid promptly by the insurance company. A questionnaire designed to assess the readership of church publications by church members can be quite specific about publication content. The researcher can assume church members will cooperate if the survey is sponsored by the church, and respondents will be at least somewhat familiar with the church publications.

A basic rule is that audiences who have a stake in the survey topic will be more knowledgeable and more cooperative. If they are interested in the topic, more of those sampled will agree to participate, will stay on the phone longer, and will possess some insights (or have had some forethought) about the specific questions to be asked. Samples taken from more general populations should be expected to possess neither extensive forethought on the topic nor commitment. It is often deflating to discover how hesitant these sample members are, how skeptical of the researcher's intent, and how poorly informed they are on the topic.

Still, survey research is carried out at an increasing rate and most of it is being done successfully. Regardless of an audience's reluctance to participate, response rates remain adequately high and valuable information is being collected. Professional research firms are able to keep respondents on the phone for up to 45 minutes and can complete two- and three-hour in-home interviews. It can be done by careful planning, particularly in the questionnaire construction stage.

QUESTIONNAIRE COMPONENTS

A questionnaire has three discrete sections: the introduction, the body and the ending.

Introduction

The introduction should be the most carefully worded portion of the form, regardless of whether it is a telephone, mail or in-person interview. Questionnaire introductions should be simple and friendly and provide certain crucial elements of information. These include:

1. Interviewer's name;
2. Sponsor's name;
3. How the interviewee was chosen;
4. Purpose of the study;
5. Anticipated length of the interview;
6. Confidentiality of the answers;
7. How the answers will be used;
8. A brief "thank you" in advance for participating.

While it may seem impossible to provide all of the information in a single, short paragraph, some of the points may be implied rather than actually stated. An introduction that includes all of the points might be:

Hello, my name is John Smith and I'm a student at State University. Our class is doing a survey for the business department on people's shopping habits. Your name was selected randomly from the telephone directory to provide confidential answers that will help decide the location of a new shopping center in town. I'd appreciate about ten minutes of your time now to complete my homework assignment for this class.

First, can you tell me. . . .

A more formal introduction might be:

Hello. This is Mary Jones with Consolidated Industries. We're surveying factory workers at our plant whose telephone numbers were selected by computer from employment lists. Am I speaking with a Consolidated Industries factory worker now? Good. Don't tell me your name, but if you can give me 5 minutes of your time, I'd like to ask you 20 questions about the recent injuries at the plant. We think your answers can help make Consolidated a safer place to work.

Did you hear about the two accidents this week in the loading dock area?

Careful editing of the wording might improve the impact and brevity of these two introductions while retaining all of the necessary information the respondents should have. Researchers are bound by ethics to be honest with their subjects and to provide full disclosure about how and why the survey is being done. While being as informative as possible, introductions should also be as compelling as they can legitimately be. One other point should be noted: Don't pause for a response between the introduction and the first question. A pause is an invitation for the person on the other end of the phone to refuse to participate. If the person is going to refuse, he or she will do so without an invitation from the caller. Instead, write the first question immediately after the introduction or write ''(don't pause)'' after that section.

Body

The first question begins the body of the questionnaire. It should be general enough so the respondents can answer it without feeling challenged to devise a hasty reply. In fact, a general question on the topic that can be answered by a simple yes or no will suffice. This first question might be a screening or *filter* question that is designed to qualify the respondent for the next series of questions or for participating further in the study.

In the second example above, asking if the person is a Consolidated factory worker gets the right person on the line. But the first question in the body of the questionnaire might be a filter question. The purpose of the study could be to find out about factory accident concerns from only those workers who are aware of the two recent accidents. If a respondent says no to the first question, the interviewer might terminate the survey, or the interviewer might be instructed on the questionnaire to skip from a no answer on item no. 1 to item no. 18, asking how long the worker has been with the company. Certain answers to filter questions, then, can eliminate respondents entirely or cause the interviewer to skip over one or more items on the form. If the factory worker doesn't know about the accidents, the worker can't be expected to answer any more questions about those accidents.

The body of a questionnaire should flow logically from general to progressively more specific questions. Qualifying or filter questions should be used so respondents who have no knowledge about an area won't be asked progressively more specific questions about that area. If the survey is a readership study about the agency's monthly magazine, the most general question might be: "Are you familiar with *The Insider*, the agency's monthly magazine?" A yes answer brings the next question: "How often did you usually read *The Insider*: (a) hardly ever, (b) a few times a year, (c) nearly every issue." A respondent who answers "hardly ever" will probably not be asked any of the next dozen questions dealing with content and graphic appearance of the magazine. Asking that series of items would be a chore for both the interviewer and respondent, and the information gained from a person who hardly ever reads the publication is questionable at best.

However, a person who answers "hardly ever" might be directed to a series of questions about why the person doesn't read the publication. These answers would be valuable for the agency editors to know, and a "hardly ever" reader is the best one to provide these insights. But filter questions must be designed with care so it is clear to the interviewer which answers prompt skips and so respondents who have just said they don't have information about a topic aren't asked more questions about that topic.

Flow from general to specific in the questionnaire body is most important, but the logical grouping of similar topic items also is necessary. A questionnaire should have consistency; otherwise it reads or sounds as if the researcher wasn't careful or isn't very knowledgeable about the subject matter. Inconsistent scattering of items throughout the questionnaire confuses respondents, and they terminate when they become confused. With logical grouping of similar content and adept transitions from one topic to the next, it is possible to cover a variety of survey interests in one questionnaire.

For example, a public opinion study of "news events" in a city was sponsored by three separate clients. The first section included 12 questions about people's attitudes on traffic congestion, a topic that had been in the news. At the end of that section the interviewer said, "Now let's turn to the downtown area of our city." This section was sponsored by apartment developers and contained 15 items about respondents' views on living in the downtown area of the city, another prominent news item. On completion of this section, interviewers said, "Finally, we'd like to ask your opinion about this city's daily newspaper." This section contained about 20 more questions about the newspaper. The final few questions dealt with respondents' income, education, race and sex. Each of the three sections was on a different topic, but the items in each section were arranged from the most general to the most specific question on the topic. Because all of the sections were loosely related to recent news in the city, it was possible to include them in one questionnaire merely by using transitional statements between sections.

Even the decision of which section to place first, second, and third on the questionnaire was based on common sense. The first section on traffic congestion was the most prominent news item in the city and it was something everyone could relate to personally. It made sense to use that topic to attune respondents to the questionnaire quickly. The middle section on downtown housing followed logically, at least in moving from traffic to the downtown area of the city. It was the least personal section because very few people actually lived downtown or had ever considered it, so that section would have been painfully slow if it had been placed at the end of the survey. The section on the city's newspaper made a perfect ending section because everyone had an opinion about the newspaper and most were quite outspoken in their remarks. Placing it at the end held respondents' attention through the last five minutes of the 15-minute telephone interview.

The last few items in the questionnaire are usually *demographic* or attribute questions including items such as age, education, race, sex, number of members in the family, own or rent, and income. Logic in questionnaire construction suggests that these more personal items be placed at the end of the survey form because a respondent who has invested time in going through the interview will be more likely to complete the survey by answering these questions. From the researcher's point of view, putting the more personal questions at the end provides all the information up to that point. Most studies aren't dependent on knowing the respondent's income, so the interviewer can obtain almost all the needed information before the end of the questionnaire without running the risk that a respondent will terminate on the income question (which seldom happens). Also, the interviewer has already established some rapport with the subject and may feel less threatened by the end of the interview.

There might be an occasion in which a questionnaire begins with a personal question such as income. In these few instances the logic is that a person who refuses to answer that question will probably not answer many of the other items in the survey. Another consideration is that income level may be a necessary screening question. If the study is designed to gather information from only members of families earning more than $50,000 per year, it would be a waste of time to wait until the end of the survey to ask this question.

Before asking demographic items at the end of the questionnaire form, it is customary to introduce them in a manner such as:

The last few questions are needed to obtain a description of the people who have participated in the study.
Counting yourself, how many people are currently living in your household?

Telling the respondent the survey is almost over promotes continued participation. Explaining that these last questions are only to "describe" the whole group of respondents helps to impersonalize the demographic items.

Interviewing Tactics

Novice interviewers are wary about asking personal questions, particularly questions about age and income, but they shouldn't be. The vast majority of respondents (probably 85 percent or more) will provide information about income and age if these questions are asked in a professional manner, denoting they are merely the next questions in a survey assignment. In fact, almost any question that is written briefly and clearly enough will be answered. Interviewers get into trouble only if they are hesitant or apologetic. When there is fear or embarrassment in the interviewer's voice, the respondent will be skeptical. But if the questions are asked in precisely the way they are written on the form, in the same order, and with the exact wording each time, answers will be easy to obtain.

Asking the questions in exactly the same way increases reliability of the results. Supervisors should warn interviewers not to "edit" the questions or emphasize certain words with voice inflections. The interview should be friendly but flawlessly professional. There is no need to worry about refusals. If the respondent doesn't intend to answer a question, he or she will say so.

The best method to train interviewers is to hold an intensive practice session during which those who will be making the calls or visiting respondents in person can go through the interview process several times with a supervisor. Training sessions should last long enough so that each interviewer is thoroughly familiar with the questionnaire form and has achieved a level of comfort and professionalism to instill confidence in the respondent. The first several calls or visits should be supervised with a critique following each interview. To prevent the interviewer's becoming lax on later renditions of the survey, periodic monitoring is necessary. Finally, it is a good idea to tell interviewers in advance that a sample of their respondents will be contacted after the questionnaire forms are turned in. Unfortunately, experience indicates there is tremendous temptation for interviewers to take short cuts or even to complete the forms themselves. Ensuring the reliability of interviews is a chore, but it is one of the researcher's primary responsibilities to the client.

Endings

The best ending for a questionnaire is usually the shortest. When the final question is answered the interviewer should tell the respondent the survey is complete, thank the respondent for participating, and say good-bye.

That ends our survey. I appreciate your help in talking with me. You've been very kind. Good-bye.

Normally, the questionnaire contains a final item in which the interviewer records the respondent's sex after the interview is completed (it's a needless question to ask). There is usually a signature blank on the form in which the interviewer signs his or her name and records the time and date of the interview. Often the interviewer signs a statement attesting to reliability:

I hereby guarantee that this form was completed with the authorized respondent and that the questions were asked in the stated order using wording exactly as printed, to the best of my ability.

Signing such a statement will not antagonize a professional interviewer. Non-professionals (those in-house staff members and clerks the public relations director might rely on for assistance and who may be making such calls for the first time) should accept the statement for what is intended: a reminder to interviewers that the questionnaire form must remain a precise guide for each interview.

QUESTIONNAIRE LENGTH

While the point has been made that telephone interviews can last up to 45 minutes and in-house interviews can take two hours, these are extremes. Most surveys do not have to be that long. Careful selection of questions can reduce the amount of time needed to gather the necessary information, and the shorter the survey, the better—in almost every way. Costs go up with each additional question asked. It takes longer to do the interviews, the coding, and the analysis. Also, the longer the questionnaire, the higher the refusal rate. Imagine being asked to spend half an hour on the telephone with a survey interviewer! And since researchers are ethically bound to be honest with their subjects, they must be told in advance how long the survey will last. It is a little easier to convince a subject to do an hour-long personal interview in the home, but the expense of in-person surveys is usually prohibitive anyway. A mail survey should take less than 15 minutes to complete or the response rate will be even lower than the dismal rate expected. The right approach, regardless of the interviewing method, is to make the questionnaire as short as possible. A mail survey should fit on one page, front and back, unless the researcher has some reason to believe the respondent will be committed to the topic (perhaps a survey of college graduates sent by the alma mater's alumni association).

Because telephone surveys are the most practical, and hence the most frequently used interviewing method, questionnaire length is critical. It is possible to ask up to 80 questions in a 15-minute phone interview, but most surveys shouldn't require 80 bits of information. Questionnaires do, however, have a way of expanding during the initial writing stage in spite of the researcher's efforts to keep length to a minimum. The recommendation is to write the first draft to include all of the information the client might need to answer all critical issues. When the first draft is complete, editing begins. Here the researcher culls questions that aren't critical and rewrites all questions to make them more compact. This process might reduce the questionnaire to one-third of the original draft's length. But there are additional tactics to reduce length that should also be used. These relate to the whole process of deciding questionnaire content.

CONTENT STRATEGIES

Earlier chapters have discussed the basics of deciding what items should be on the questionnaire form. For instance, the client (or boss) has some information needs that will be expressed and that will usually be specific enough to suggest the major hypothesis for the study. In the horse race track project, the client needs to know (1) what portion of the potential voters currently favor the track and (2) what are some of the major decision points expressed by voters that might be incorporated into a successful campaign. Most formal research projects are undertaken to answer very practical and very specific questions: Will employees vote for the union? What is the image of our organization in the community and how can we improve it? Do our stockholders approve a controversial plan to prevent the corporation's being threatened by unfriendly takeover attempts? If the client's information needs are not stated in specific enough terms to form hypotheses, continued client-researcher conversation will usually clarify exactly what the problem area is. A public relations research project shouldn't begin until the practitioner has provided the sponsor with a list of the hypotheses for the study, and the sponsor has signed approval to the list.

However, the primary hypotheses form only the skeleton of the questionnaire's objectives. Informal research provides the layer of muscle based on a literature review of results from past studies on the topic, interviews with authorities and a variety of similar information-gathering tactics that identify associated questions relating to the topic. These support the primary hypotheses and suggest germane items for the questionnaire form. In the race track topic, informal research identified religious and moral issues associated with gambling, possible concerns about organized crime, and interest in sports as some of the key concerns that have been the basis for horse race track campaigns in other regions and that are likely to be referendum campaign issues in this county. Now the researcher has a list of specific questions the client wants answered and many of the supporting questions expected to be associated with voters' decisions during the campaign.

The next step should be a discussion with the public relations professional staff. No individual should attempt to compile a questionnaire in a closed office and expect it to be a viable measurement instrument. The process requires input from other people, and public relations staff members are among the best counselors available because their daily routine involves tapping into communications networks. They are in constant contact with a variety of publics, keep informed about news events and general social trends, and have a feel for constituent concerns that is bound to affect the outcome of any public relations research project. A staff meeting—or several—should be held to flesh out the questionnaire form and to discuss items (and their exact wording) that ought to be on the form. Even those public relations staffers who are unfamiliar with formal survey research should be able to make valuable suggestions derived from knowing their contact publics. The newsletter editor can offer suggestions from both the employees' and management's perspectives; the publicity specialist knows the region's mass media and stays abreast of public issues. A questionnaire has the best chance of touching all the critical topic aspects if it is constructed through a group discussion process.

One other resource should be used in developing the questionnaire: a focus group session to which people who are among the survey population are invited to meet and discuss the topic. Focus groups are explained in Chapter 16, but their purpose in questionnaire construction is to ensure that the questionnaire items are not devised by "experts" in a vacuum removed from reality. That's a polite way of saying that clients and researchers may be too close to the topic—unable to see the forest for the trees. If the final form is derived by those who are most informed on the topic, there's a chance that it will not address the real interests of a less informed public, precisely the one that is intended to answer the questions. In the race track issue, despite all the informal research and interviewing of authorities, it is possible that some significant issues will be missed. These might be the issues voters really care about, but which won't even be addressed if voters aren't consulted before the questionnaire is complete.

The researcher should invite a group of six to ten county voters to meet at a convenient location and time. A few public relations staff members should be present to lead a loosely structured give-and-take discussion about the horse race track referendum. The invited voters don't have to be representative of the whole population of voters. This kind of focus group session isn't designed to provide answers on which campaign decisions can be made. Its purpose is to ensure that questionnaire topics include the spectrum of concerns this county's voters will have. It is better if those invited reflect a range of known demographics among voters—that there are older persons and younger ones; that the group is somewhat balanced by sex, race, and geographic location in the county; that members include a couple of high income and low income residents, etc. This diversity should improve the likelihood that certain subgroup opinions will be included, but the main purpose of the questionnaire focus group is to discover if there is some key concern the researcher, the client, or the informal data-gathering has omitted. It might be that past studies were done in more cosmopolitan areas, but this county's voters are most concerned about the nightclubs and striptease bars that might be built near a race track.

A side benefit of the questionnaire focus group is to help the survey project directors understand who will actually be answering the survey. The focus group conversation will indicate the depth to which this population is knowledgeable on the topic. Often the scope of the questionnaire has to be adjusted to be far less specific than researchers might have wished it to be. For instance, the focus group might indicate that county voters haven't even heard of the horse race track referendum; then the questionnaire must approach the topic by giving far more background information than researchers had intended. This might also mean that the questionnaire can't be as specific as the client might prefer because many potential voters won't have given the issue any thought prior to being called for the survey.

In the brief example on surveying factory workers about accidents in the loading dock, a focus group composed of employees might reveal that only two workers of the eight invited had heard about the recent accidents. Reporting that fact to management could result in the project's termination, or it would certainly suggest an entirely different approach to an employee survey on safety concerns. Of course, it is better to identify such differences between researcher expectations and reality before spending time hammering out a questionnaire.

TYPES OF VARIABLES

Questions on a questionnaire are considered *variables*. The assumption is that items on the form will derive different answers by at least some of the respondents, so the answers will vary. There are three general types of variables: *independent, dependent*, and *intervening*. A dependent variable is considered an outcome variable; an independent variable is considered a predictor variable. Although researchers don't actually talk in terms of "cause and effect"—it is extremely difficult in social science research to determine what is the cause and what is the effect—nonetheless independent (predictor) variables are treated as cause variables and dependent (outcome) variables are treated as effect variables. In the horse race track study, the main dependent variable is the yes, no, or don't know vote respondents report they intend to make on the coming referendum. Most of the other variables or items on the questionnaire will be independent variables, those the researcher expects to predict the way the voting decision will be made.

For example, the respondent's sex (a *demographic* variable being treated as an independent variable) is expected to influence how the respondent will vote on the race track. Past studies suggest males will be more likely to vote for the track and females will be more likely to vote against it. But there are several independent variables in the study that are expected to influence the voter preference variable: interest in sports, moral and religious beliefs, length of residence in the community, etc. The objective of the study is to identify which of the independent variables predict the voter decision on the race track, and it is likely that several of the independent variables will act both singly and in unison to predict the dependent variable. The client wants to know the outcome and the variables that will influence it.

In survey research, discriminating between independent and dependent variables can be confusing. It helps to think in terms of which variables might be antecedents or might precede the outcome. A person's belief that gambling is morally wrong should be viewed as an antecedent. Knowing a person holds that belief should lead researchers to expect the person will be inclined to vote against the race track because having a race track means betting. Level of concern about the county's economy and tax base should be associated with favoring the race track because the track will mean increased county tax revenues. The higher a respondent's concern about the economy and the lower his or her concern about gambling, the more likely the person should favor the race track.

However, these independent measures may not predict voter preference on the track. An intervening variable (one that "gets in the way" of the direct relationship between predictor and outcome) may be noted. Level of concern for the county's economy may not be a direct predictor of voting preference. Number of school-aged children might be an intervening variable. The rationale could be that the more children a person has in school, the more interested the person may be in having higher county revenues. County tax income is based on revenues, and half of the county taxes raised go to the school system. If the respondent has children in school, interest in the economy should be higher; those with no children in school may be less interested in the revenue and tax implications of the horse race measure. So, in fact, the reported direct association between interest in the economy and voter preference actually may not be direct at all. Voter preference really depends on how many school-aged children there are in the respondent's household. But if the researcher doesn't ask a question about school-aged children, that intervening variable will never be discovered. The assumption will be that there is a direct link between interest in the economy and the intention to vote for the horse race track. The researcher may recommend to the client that the way to campaign for passage of the race track measure is to raise voters' sensitivities about the county's economy. Actually, had the questionnaire form included an item about number of school-aged children at home, and the study had found a strong positive relationship between number of children and voter preference, the recommendation to the client would have been to focus the campaign specifically on benefits to the county's education system, not the economy in general.

Intervening variables interfere with the supposed direct relationship between independent and dependent variables. If all possible intervening variables could be anticipated in advance and included in the survey, their inclusion would eliminate the possibility of intervening variables. Analysis would identify which independent variables in the study are the strongest direct predictors. Unfortunately, the most carefully devised studies and the most wide-ranging questionnaire forms still provide no guarantee that an important intervening variable won't be omitted. The best any researcher can do is try to include as many items as have been identified as critical to the central issue of the study.

TYPES OF QUESTIONS

There are two distinct types of questions on a questionnaire form: *open-ended* and *closed-ended*.

Open-ended questions call for the respondent to provide an answer in his or her own words: "What is your opinion about betting on sporting events such as football games, horse races, or boxing matches?" Placed on a questionnaire form, this item requires the respondent to formulate a response that the interviewer then records, capturing as closely as possible the exact words the respondent gave. There are advantages and disadvantages to open-ended questions. A plus is that these items allow the respondent an opportunity for self-expression. Not only does the interviewee get to say what's on his or her mind, but the diversity of responses captures the extent of attitude on the topic and, sometimes, the richness of responses offers interesting insights the client may not have expected.

Open-ended questions are used for items that may require a very wide range of responses. Answers to the question on betting could range from "a tool of the devil" to "the U.S. Constitution allows personal freedom of choice in these matters." There might be several dozen subtle shades of answers between the two extremes. If the information is deemed important enough, and if it is expected to produce a wide range of responses, the item must be open-ended.

There are instances in which the researcher doesn't know the possible range of responses. The betting question serves as an example here, too. It will be possible (from questionnaire focus groups or pretests) to identify several likely responses to the betting question, but it will be obvious that almost every time another person is asked the question, a different type of response may be obtained. There may be 20 or 30 separate categories of response to the betting item, far too many to list on the questionnaire form or read to the interviewee. In such instances, an open-ended question is necessary.

Finally, the open-ended responses provide quotable material that can be included in the finished report. This material helps the client understand outcomes (which are usually reported in percentages and statistically significant differences) in human terms. Many studies—particularly those that might result in a news report to the media—include the open-ended questions just to have the quotes for the completed report.

With all these pluses going for open-ended questions, only one or two usually appear on a questionnaire. The primary reason for infrequent use is that responses to open-ended questions are difficult to quantify. Faced with 32 separate responses to an item, coders will have to reduce them to a manageable few, perhaps half a dozen or so. Deriving categories for the responses takes great care and opens the research to reliability problems: One coder may place a response in category three; another will decide a similar response belongs in category five. Coding open-ended responses is time consuming and raises the project's costs.

Open-ended questions require more time to ask and answer. This can stretch the "length" of the questionnaire—the time required for the respondent to complete the form. Having to write in or provide an answer verbally can be awkward for respondents. Many believe there is a "right" answer they should be giving; others worry about their writing prowess or their speech. Often their concern about self-expression results in simply saying they don't know, even if they do have an opinion on the item. They would be willing to answer if they were given a choice of categories from which to choose.

But a major disadvantage of open-ended questions is that the respondent is being expected to formulate an answer on a topic he or she may not have thought much about. Forcing respondents to give a top-of-the-head answer creates research validity problems. The first statement a respondent makes may not actually be what he or she believes or would say again if given the chance. Still, it will be what the interviewer records.

For all of these reasons, open-ended questions are used in instances where a questionnaire item can't be "closed." Closed-ended items are those for which the researcher has provided all the possible categories of answers in advance and the respondent has only to select the one that applies. An open-ended item to determine a respondent's religion would be : "What is your religious affiliation?" Closing that question would be: "Which of the following best describes your religious affiliation: (a) Protestant, (b) Catholic, (c) Jewish, (d) other denomination, (e) none."

Conceptual questions can also be closed, although it is best to provide the answers suggested by questionnaire focus groups or during pretests. If your were asked, "What is your chief goal in going to college?" a wide variety of responses is possible. But the majority of likely answers can be listed in this close-ended question:

Which of the following reasons best explains why you decided to go to college:

a. to get a job

b. to get a degree

c. to get a promotion or change jobs

d. to learn more about subjects that interest me

e. to become a more well-rounded individual

f. because my friends or family urged me to go

g. to prove I could do it

h. for social contact

i. for some other reason not mentioned above

This example contains one of the pitfalls of asking a conceptual question—respondents may not have thought about exactly why they decided to go to college—but it also shows that closing a conceptual question makes answering it easier for the respondent. Given the list of choices, most respondents will be able to select the one that best applies to their personal decision. The list of reasons will offer a more reasonable choice if some current college students are asked the question and their answers are used to guide the researcher in deciding what choices to include to close the question.

Close-ended question choices (possible answers structured in advance) must be *all-inclusive* and *mutually exclusive*. All-inclusive means they must cover the entire range of possible answers. Asking religion and offering only choices of Protestant and Catholic is not all-inclusive because it omits the possibility that a respondent will be Jewish, Mormon, Hindu, or Buddhist (or a variety of other faiths). If the entire range of possible responses is not known, use of "Other" as a choice can make the list all-inclusive, although it may leave a sizeable subcategory in the "Other" category. Mutually exclusive means that a respondent must not be faced with deciding between two categories, both of which apply. For instance, religion with the categories of Protestant, Baptist, Catholic, Jewish and Other, is not mutually exclusive because a respondent who is a Baptist is also a Protestant. If the income categories provided are: (a) under $10,000, (b) $10,000 to $20,000, (c) $20,000 to $30,000, (d) over $30,000, the choices are not mutually exclusive. A person whose income is roughly $20,000 may accurately answer in both category "b" and category "c." Mutual exclusivity would be achieved in categories of: (a) under $10,000, (b) $10,000 to $19,999, (c) $20,000 to $30,000, (d) over $30,000. The principles of all-inclusive and mutually exclusive must apply to every close-ended question in the study, but the concepts require only care; they are not difficult decisions.

In most instances, the vast majority of questionnaire items will be close-ended with only a few open-ended questions on the form. Deciding to use an open-ended question should be based on the several considerations this section offers, but the general rule is to use this type of question sparingly.

QUESTIONNAIRE SCALES

Perhaps the most difficult concept to master about items on a questionnaire is that of scale construction. A *scale* is a group (two or more) of items on the questionnaire that will be combined in some manner during the later data analysis process. Scales are usually used to measure more complicated concepts: those with a variety of dimensions for which the research goal requires subtle differentiation.

In the earlier example about factory worker accidents in the loading dock, the public relations researcher will want to discriminate among levels of knowledge about the two accidents. The first item respondents might be asked is: "Have you heard about the two recent accidents in the loading dock?" A no response will result in the interviewer skipping the next series of questions, but a yes response will prompt asking the rest of this series of questions:

Do you know the two people who were injured?
Do they work in the same building you do?
Did you witness the accident or its aftermath?

The series is not cumulative. For instance, a worker who witnessed the event might not know the names of the two injured workers, but might answer yes to all the other questions. Or if the respondent knew the two individuals but did not work in the same building, two of the four items would be given a yes answer. In any case, the researcher could justifiably assume the more yes answers given by the respondent on the four items, the more aware he or she is of the accidents: A person with a score of 3 is more aware than a person who scores 1 or 2 on the scale. Awareness of the recent accidents is likely to be related to other measures the questionnaire is designed to tap, such as concern about safety in the plant (probably the primary hypothesis for the study). The scale is composed of four discrete questions designed to be combined into a single measure of accident awareness.

Questionnaires can contain several traditional types of scales. Texts on questionnaire construction provide more details for designing these scales, but a brief description of each is offered here.

Likert-type scales can be either graphic (for mail or in-person surveys) or verbal (for telephone surveys). They are constructed as agree-disagree items with ranges of agreement provided on the questionnaire. A mail questionnaire might ask:

```
Acme Industries is a good place to work (please check
the blank that indicates your opinion):"

/_____/_____/_____/_____/_____/
strongly   agree    neutral  disagree  strongly
agree                                  disagree
  (1)       (2)       (3)      (4)       (5)
```

The same type of scale in a telephone survey would be: "What is your opinion about Acme Industries being a good place to work? Would you say: (1) strongly agree, (2) agree, (3) you are neutral, (4) you disagree, or (5) you strongly disagree with that statement?"

While the baseline is probably not equal—some respondents' opinion of a "good place to work" will be different than others—the assumption is that all respondents will generally have the same idea of what a good place to work means. A "1" response to the item is assumed a more positive opinion toward Acme than a "2" response.

It is certainly possible to arrange many questionnaire items in this manner, although there are several decisions the researcher may have to make about constructing the scales. If it is believed most respondents will rate the company favorably (a "2" response), the item might be constructed as a seven-point scale to better differentiate among the levels of favorable opinion:

```
/_____/_____/_____/_____/_____/_____/_____/
  very   strongly   agree   neutral  disagree strongly   very
strongly  agree                               disagree strongly
 agree                                                  disagree
```

The popularity of Likert-type scales is wide enough to make this form of questionnaire item worth considering, although further reading about its use is recommended.

Semantic differential scales are similar to Likert-type scales, but they can be used only on forms the respondent can view (mail and in-person surveys). Instead of an agree-disagree continuum, the scales use polar adjectives at each end of a non-labeled continuum in the following manner:

```
powerful /_____/_____/_____/_____/_____/ weak
```

In its most frequently used form, the semantic differential follows a concept that is rated on a series of polar adjective scales. The concept may be an attitude dimension such as:

```
        How would you rate the way our organization has dealt
   with the problem of hazardous waste disposal:

      effective /_____/_____/_____/_____/_____/ ineffective

          weak /_____/_____/_____/_____/_____/ strong

 comprehensive /_____/_____/_____/_____/_____/ partial
```

But the concept is more frequently just a label such as:

```
        Acme's newsletter, The Mast

      complete /_____/_____/_____/_____/_____/ incomplete

       passive /_____/_____/_____/_____/_____/ active

   interesting /_____/_____/_____/_____/_____/ dull

      untimely /_____/_____/_____/_____/_____/ current

      accurate /_____/_____/_____/_____/_____/ inaccurate
```

People can be rated on the semantic differential, and the scale can be an effective way of analyzing how those people (perhaps the officers of the corporation) are viewed by their constituent audiences in a richness of discrimination only the semantic differential can provide.

Again, there are a variety of special considerations in using the semantic differential. Two points are indicated in the examples: (1) The positive and negative poles should be reversed with each set to prevent respondents from merely checking down one side of the scale, and (2) it is critical that the adjectives actually be equal polarities rather than "good–terrible," and that they be in the same semantic space rather than "foolish–pleasant." This kind of scale should not be attempted without additional reading on its use.

Rank-order scales are popular and easy-to-use. This is the "beauty contest" ranking in which respondents are asked to number some items as more favorable than others. If the organization has five magazines, respondents might be asked:

```
    Please rank each of these agency publications in the
order you prefer them with '1' being the magazine you enjoy
reading most and '5' being the magazine you enjoy reading
least:
      a. Argus ____
      b. Bulletin ____
      c. Watchword ____
      d. Eagle ____
      e. Inner Voice ____
```

One problem with rankings is that there is no indication of distance between the ranks. If one respondent really enjoys the *Argus* and the *Bulletin*, reads the *Watchword* only occasionally, and never reads either the *Eagle* or *Inner Voice*, this research study will be unable to discern that pattern. It will appear as if all publications are enjoyed in relatively equal diminishing steps. The last two publications will finish in the last two places, as they should, but the *Watchword* will appear almost as favored as the *Bulletin* and the *Eagle* almost as favored as the *Watchword*. Like a beauty pageant, the most handsome contestant will be in first place and, even if the second contestant shouldn't have qualified for entry, the others will place second, third, and fourth. A better scale would be one in which the researcher can determine whether the first-place was won by a neck or by a mile.

Rank-order scales work equally well in phone, mail, and in-person interviews, provided there aren't more items to rank than half a dozen. Too many items become unmanageable for respondents to handle, particularly if they aren't very familiar with some of them. If there are more than a few items to be rated at once—perhaps content categories in one of the magazines—*rating scales* become a better scale choice.

Instead of asking respondents to compare each item against all others in a ranking system, the rating scales take each item individually. Respondents might be asked:

```
    Please rate the following items of content in the Argus
according to how well you enjoy that content. Give the item
a "10" if it's something you enjoy very much or a "1" if it's
something you don't like at all:

    a. Personalities ____      f. Quotations ____

    b. Bulletins ____          g. Classifieds ____

    c. Editorials ____         h. Agency News ____

    d. Guest Columns ____      i. Director's Notes ____

    e. Policy Changes ____     j. Team Sports ____
```

In such a rating procedure a respondent could be asked 20 or more decisions about content. The respondent doesn't have to compare each with all the others, but that is precisely what the respondent will be doing (although there are likely to be ties). Across the entire sample of survey respondents, however, the rankings probably won't be tied. If 300 respondents rate (provide a 1-to-10 rating) Team Sports, and an arithmetic average rating is derived, this content category's mean rating might be 7.64; Guest Column's mean rating might be 8.85. Not only have

Figure 10.1

Questionnaire Design Possibilities Using a Thermometer-type Scale

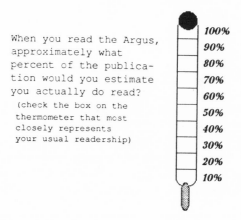

When you read the Argus, approximately what percent of the publication would you estimate you actually do read? (check the box on the thermometer that most closely represents your usual readership)

the categories been rated individually, but they are also ranked by their average score. Most important, the enjoyment distance between the two categories is known (8.85 − 7.64 = 1.21). Rating scales provide more discrete measurements than mere ranks.

Thermometer-type scales are similar to rating scales. They correctly assume everyone understands what "100 percent" means. Instead of asking for a rating on each item, respondents are asked to estimate their answers in terms of percents:

When you read the *Argus*, about what percent of the
publication would you estimate you actually do read? _____ %

Or the thermometer-type scale may take the form of a rating scale:

Now tell me about what percent of the editions of each
of these separate publications you have read in the past
year:

1. *Argus* _____ %
2. *Bulletin* _____ %
3. *Watchword* _____ %
4. *Eagle* _____ %
5. *Inner Voice* _____ %

The only care that needs to be taken with thermometer-type scales is not forcing respondents to estimate answers which in unison equal 100 percent. That would be too challenging an assignment for most of us if there are more than just a few categories to rate.

Like the rating scales, thermometer-type scales can be used in phone, mail, and in-person interviews. In fact, in their printed form they can add an attractive dimension to the questionnaire form (see Figure 10.1). And, like the rating scales, the percentages reported provide distances between the ratings: 80 percent is 30 percentage points more than 50 percent.

Another frequently used scale is called *paired comparisons*. Each item being scaled is compared with every other item and the scale score depends on how many times an item "wins" in the comparison. Using the five agency publications, respondents would be asked to circle (or select) their favorite publication in each of the following pairs:

Argus vs. *Bulletin*	*Bulletin* vs. *Eagle*
Argus vs. *Watchword*	*Bulletin* vs. *Inner Voice*
Argus vs. *Eagle*	*Watchword* vs. *Eagle*
Argus vs. *Inner Voice*	*Watchword* vs. *Inner Voice*
Bulletin vs. *Watchword*	*Eagle* vs. *Inner Voice*

Obviously such comparisons work best on paper, and just as obviously they can quickly get out-of-hand. More than a few items for paired comparisons require a long list of pair sets and will become unwieldy for efficient decision making.

The final traditional scale type is called a *cumulative scale*. Here the researcher establishes a set of statements about a concept and asks the respondent to check (or say yes to) all that apply:

```
        As you know, the company has been losing money during
   the past three fiscal years.  The firm has been able to stay
   in business by giving no raises during that time, but
   continued low revenues now require more drastic measures.
   Please indicate by checking each of the following company
   decision possibilities you think the firm should consider
   before declaring bankruptcy:

   ____  offer early retirement and a 60 percent pension to
         those who have been with the firm at least 20 years
   ____  offer early retirement and a 30 percent pension to
         minimum 20-year employees
   ____  reduce the company's current benefit package by half
         for all employees
   ____  all employees take pay reductions of 5 percent
   ____  all employees take pay reductions of 10 percent
   ____  all employees take pay reductions of 15 percent
   ____  terminate 10 percent of the work force at each pay
         level
```

The cumulative scale is arranged in ascending or descending order of probable respondent agreement. Each next statement is supposed to represent another, and equally distant, degree of attitude change from the previous. The assumption is that respondents will agree with the first two, three, or four statements, but at some point they will stop agreeing and will leave the remaining statements blank. In this scale, a "skip" (agreeing with the first three and the fifth statement) is considered an error.

The chief problem with cumulative scales is that they can be extremely difficult to construct, particularly in meeting the condition that each statement must represent an equidistant opinion change from its predecessor. Also, too frequently there are legitimate reasons for skips. In the example, an employee with few years on the job, a family to help support, and a superior performance rating may agree with the first two statements, agree to the 5 percent pay cut (but no more), and agree to the terminations being confident his or her job will be secure. Skips, then, may be errors of scale construction rather than respondent error.

PRETESTING QUESTIONNAIRES

The rough draft of the questionnaire has been compiled and edited through several discussion sessions by the public relations staff. A questionnaire focus group session has been held to ensure that the questions on the survey are properly directed to the survey's intended audience. The form has been revised through one or more attempts to make question wording more specific and to reduce the number of items to a manageable size. It is now time for the first pretest.

A pretest is a miniature field test of the questionnaire. Interviewers are trained and supervised in using the draft questionnaire. They make several calls to people who might have been in the final sample—people in the same population from which the sample was drawn—but who were not selected for the sample. There are several purposes of the pretest:

1. To find out how to close open-end questions by asking people similar to those who will be asked the final survey. The pretest answers to open-ended questions should tap enough of the range of possible responses so researchers can be confident their close-ended categories are all-inclusive and mutually exclusive. This might require calling 30 or more people in the pretest.

2. To find out if the questions on the draft are being interpreted by respondents in the manner they were intended by researchers. Even after holding a questionnaire focus group session, researchers can miss the mark by asking questions that elicit unexpected answers. The questions must be revised.

3. To find out if questions on the draft are being understood. Very often questions the researchers thought were crystal clear—questions that couldn't possibly be misunderstood by any respondent—are misunderstood by the majority. Actually, what is happening is that the researchers were wrong. Their questions weren't worded precisely enough, or the terms used didn't mean the same thing to the sample of people who received them. These questions must be reworded to improve their clarity.

4. To test instructions on the survey form. Again, instructions may seem perfectly clear until they are tried out on the audience. Then researchers find the instructions simply don't make sense in practice.

5. To determine if there are questions the respondents aren't able to answer. Either they don't have the information or they can't express it as a response to the question they were asked on the form. Questions that receive frequent ''don't know's'' are candidates for omission from the final form.

6. To determine if there are repetitive questions, or those which essentially yield duplicate answers. Again, these are candidates for deletion.

7. To be sure that every question on the form is providing necessary information. If the answers aren't germane to the research needs, these questions should be deleted. This

is another way of saying every effort should be made to limit the questions on the final questionnaire to only those that are providing valuable information.

8. To estimate the time it will take to complete the form. This information has to be provided in the final questionnaire introduction.

The pretest is the best way to ensure that the questionnaire does exactly what it is supposed to do in the most efficient manner possible. The pretest often proves that days spent getting to this questionnaire draft were not enough. Certainly the previous time is not in vain, but there is still much work to do on form correction. Depending on the number of changes indicated in the first pretest, a second pretest might be necessary. The process continues—pretest, corrections, pretest again—until the researcher is satisfied that no stumbling blocks remain on the survey form.

Actually, one pretest is probably all that will ever be done in most questionnaire testing situations, but stopping at one can be penny wise and pound foolish. It is a reasonable bet that no survey researcher has ever found a use for the answers to every single question on the final questionnaire form. While most would adhere to the principle of better safe than sorry (ask too many questions rather than too few), any unnecessary question is time and resources that should not have been spent. The best questionnaire forms are the products of enough thought and pretesting to ensure that each item on the final form will yield information that answers the research questions. That's the ideal and meeting it is a real achievement.

SUMMARY

Recognizing that answers can be no more valuable than the questions that prompt them, the chapter reminds survey researchers to consider the audience that will be answering the questionnaire. It provides suggestions to facilitate the process of developing items for the questionnaire and presents the three main portions of a questionnaire with guidelines about the introduction, the body, and the ending. Logical organization and flow of the form are reviewed along with some considerations about keeping questionnaires short. Differences between open-ended and close-ended questions are explored, and several traditional types of scales are briefly described. Pretests are recommended as a necessary final editing procedure before the questionnaire is ready to be used with sample subjects.

ADDITIONAL READING

Babbie, Earl R. *Survey Research Methods*. Belmont, CA: Wadsworth, 1973.

———. *The Practice of Social Research*. Belmont, CA: Wadsworth, 1979, pp. 395–421.

Bowers, John Waite, and John A. Courtright. *Communication Research Methods*. Glenview, IL: Scott, Foresman, 1984, pp. 91–104.

Comstock, George, and Maxwell E. McCombs. "Survey Research." In *Research Methods in Mass Communication*, eds. Guido H. Stempel III and Bruce H. Westley. Englewood Cliffs, NJ: Prentice Hall, 1981, pp. 144–66.

Fowler, Floyd J., Jr. *Survey Research Methods*. Beverly Hills, CA: Sage, 1984.

Greenberg, Bradley S. "Ethical Issues in Communication Research." In *Research Methods in Mass Communication*, eds. Guido H. Stempel III and Bruce H. Westley. Englewood Cliffs, NJ: Prentice Hall, 1981, pp. 255–77.

Lake, Celinda C., and Pat Callbeck. *Public Opinion Polling*. Covelo, CA: Island Press, 1988, pp. 19–66.

Singer, Eleanor, and M. Frankel. "Informed Consent Procedures in Telephone Interviews." *American Sociological Review* 47 (1982): 416–27.

Sobal, Jeffery. "The Content of Survey Introductions and the Provision of Informed Consent." *Public Opinion Quarterly* 48:4 (1984): 788–93.

Wimmer, Roger D., and Joseph R. Dominick. *Mass Media Research: An Introduction*. 2d ed. Belmont, CA: Wadsworth, 1987, pp. 45–86.

Yu, Julie, and Harris Cooper. "A Quantitative Review of Research Design Effects on Response Rates to Questionnaires." *Journal of Marketing Research* 20:1 (1983): 36–44.

11 Questionnaire Form Examples

To supplement the discussion in Chapter 10 on the survey questionnaire form, several completed forms are presented here with explanations of what the researchers intended these surveys to accomplish and why the forms were designed in this manner. Shortfalls and successful outcomes will be noted as attention is focused on how the forms address the primary research questions in each study.

READERSHIP STUDY (MAIL QUESTIONNAIRE)

A readership study is one of the most frequently required public relations research projects. Every organization that attempts to communicate with its publics—whether internal employees or the general public—should be interested in assessing how successfully its communication tools deliver their intended messages. Unfortunately many organizations believe the communication act itself (publishing the newsletter) is self-fulfilling. "Our employees understand the company's policies and are aware of changes that affect their jobs because we put all information in the monthly *Update* newsletter," they mistakenly assume. In fact, in most instances that is far from an accurate appraisal of the usual newsletter's communication effectiveness. Management is alerted to a problem only when a critical policy change appears in the newsletter but, weeks later, those who should have known about the change continue to perform their duties in the same manner they always have. Other telltale signs are when the company magazine is late and no once calls to ask why it didn't arrive; janitors report that the Friday morning *Weekly Managers' Message* is on the bottom of the wastebasket every Friday afternoon; or 60 families (rather than 600) show up for the company's annual picnic.

In this example, a variety of concerns prompted a readership survey of the membership of the Cumberland Presbyterian Church. Among them were the following inquiries the survey project was designed to answer:

1. The church has been publishing two major magazines for its membership: *The Cumberland Presbyterian*, a twice-monthly magazine aimed at all members, and the *Missionary Messenger*, a slick monthly magazine emphasizing the church's mission field work. The second evolved from a women's auxiliary publication that had begun some 50 years previously and was still well supported by women members of the 100,000-member church. However, the cost of printing and circulating two publications was outstripping the church's resources. Could the church incorporate the mission component into one single, combined publication and meet the same goals, with less expenditures?

2. The church believed the number of subscriptions sold for the two publications was never high enough, although the cost was quite reasonable. Recently the number of subscribers to both publications was dropping although content had not changed appreciably during the past few years. Could a combined publication reach as many subscribers? Was there a problem with the content that might explain the decrease in subscribers?

3. What did the membership think of these publications? If they were combined, which elements of both should the new publication include?

The survey research project consisted of two samples: a random sample of church members who participated in a telephone survey, and a mail survey of subscribers to the present magazines. Using two subsamples in a readership survey was more difficult but necessary under the circumstances. Fewer than one-third of the church's member families subscribed to the publications, so a random sample of 900 members would net only 300 subscribers. The likelihood of finding enough respondents familiar with the publications was low because the subscriber incidence in the population was low. Research efficiency would be increased by using two samples: a telephone survey to tap general use of the publications by a range of church members (from those unfamiliar with the publications through the frequent readers and subscribers), and a mail survey of current subscribers to tap content preferences by those most familiar with the publications. The telephone sample of 400 was expected to net about 130 subscribers; the mail survey of 800 was expected to net 400 returns (a 50 percent response rate), all from subscribers.

A systematic random sample of the computer-stored subscriber lists provided 800 mailing labels to be affixed to envelopes including the questionnaire form and a postage-paid business reply envelope. The mail survey contained no cover letter and there was no provision for followup mailings to those who didn't respond the first time. These tactics to increase response rates for mail surveys were thought unnecessary because members of the mail survey sample were expected to be among the most involved church members, hence the most willing mail survey participants. Actually, 42 percent did respond, which was less than the 50 percent response rate researchers optimistically expected, but certainly high for any mail survey. The questionnaire design problem was devising two associated forms with virtually the same questions in the same order, one of which would be delivered over the telephone, the other through the mail.

The example presented here is the mail questionnaire that has exactly the same question order as the telephone survey form, and item wording as close to the phone form as possible, although that form contained a little more instruction (''Now I'm going to ask you about . . . ''). Obviously the boxes and shaded areas were not needed on the telephone survey, but they added visual excitement and clarity to the mail survey form that was designed as a four-page booklet.

The selection of survey questions were the results of the following procedures:

1. The consultant had an hour-long meeting with the church's director and one of the magazine editors;

2. The client provided a written list of information interests;

3. Researchers discussed the problem and concluded more information (similar to what would be included in the actual survey) was needed from church members;

4. Researchers held an hour-long focus group session with six church members— selected to represent a variety of ages and church backgrounds and because they were available to participate—that was videotaped for future reference;

5. A long list of questionnaire items was compiled with each research staffer contributing as many as possible;

6. The list was discussed and edited during a research conference session;

7. An initial draft of the questionnaire form was constructed;

8. The draft was discussed with attention to deleting items, wording changes, and suggestions for reordering items;

9. A telephone pretest of the form was completed with 50 local members of the church whose names were provided by the church;

10. The questionnaire was revised during a three-hour session by researchers who had served as interviewers for the pretest;

11. Fine-tuning of the items was done prior to printing the questionnaire form.

While the process may seem unduly complicated—it is a 55-item questionnaire form—most of the steps should be employed for virtually every questionnaire. Never expect the answers to be better than the questions asked.

Design and Rationale for the Questionnaire

The form begins with a short introduction that includes the necessary elements to inform the respondent about the survey and urge participation.

The list of survey questions follows, arranged in a general-to-specific order with the earliest questions designed to allow easy answers to items about church membership. While they may seem designed merely to establish rapport with

Figure 11.1
Cumberland Presbyterian Church Publications Questionnaire

The Cumberland Presbyterian Church has asked a class at State University to do a subscriber survey to help the church improve its publications. Your name was randomly selected from subscriber rolls to provide anonymous suggestions about these publications. We hope you will help us by giving less than 10 minutes now to complete this survey form and return it in the business reply envelope provided?

Please write in the name of the state in which you reside: _____ ___ ___

1. About how many years have you belonged to the Cumberland Presbyterian Church: _____

2. Which of the following best describes the location of your own church:
    a. city __
    b. small town __
    c. country __

3. Which of the following best describes your position in the church:
    a. pastor or former pastor: __
    b. part of the church's leadership or paid staff: __
    c. serve on church committees or as a teacher: __
    d. occasionally volunteer for duties when needed: __

    (If answer to No. 3 is "d"): 4. How would you describe your church attendance:
        a. attend services twice a month or more: __
        b. attend services less than twice a month: __

THESE QUESTIONS CONCERN THE DENOMINATIONAL PUBLICATIONS:

5. Are you familiar with *The Cumberland Presbyterian*, the denomination's biweekly news publication? __ yes __ no
    (If no, skip to Question No. 28)

6. Do you read *The Cumberland Presbyterian*:
    a. hardly ever: __
    b. several times a year: __
    c. almost every issue: __

7. Do you now subscribe to *The Cumberland Presbyterian:* __ yes __ no

    (If "yes,"): 8. How many years have you subscribed:___

    (If "no,"): 9. Why don't you subscribe to this publication?

10. When you read *The Cumberland Presbyterian*, about what percent of the publication would you say you usually read: ___ %

Figure 11.1 Continued

THESE QUESTIONS CONCERN THE CONTENT OF *THE CUMBERLAND PRESBYTERIAN*.
For each type of article, mark how interested you are in it.

	Very Interested	Somewhat Interested	Not Interested
11. World News			
12. Late News			
13. Church News			
14. Seminary News			
15. Women's News			
16. Movie Reviews			
17. Prayer Calendar			
18. Soundings			
19. Bethel College News			
20. Letters to the Editor			
21. Stated Clerk's Editorial			

How much do you like each of the following in *The Cumberland Presbyterian*:

	Like It A Lot	Like It A Little	Don't Like It
22. the publication's cover			
23. the pictures			
24. quality of writing in the articles			
25. how easy it is to read the print			
26. the overall appearance			

27. Can you briefly name one article you read in *The Cumberland Presbyterian* that you found particularly enjoyable or inspiring?

NOW LET'S TURN TO THE DENOMINATION'S OTHER PUBLICATION.

28. Are you familiar with *The Missionary Messenger*,
the monthly mission publication of the church? __ yes __ no
(if no, skip to Question No. 46)

29. Would you say you read *The Missionary Messenger*:
a. hardly ever: __
b. several times a year: __
c. almost every issue: __

Figure 11.1 Continued

30. Do you now subscribe to *The Missionary Messenger*: __ yes __ no

    (If "yes,"): 31. How many years have you subscribed:__

    (If "no,"): 32. Why don't you subscribe to this publication?

33. When you read *The Missionary Messenger*, about
    what percent of the publication would you say you usually read: ___%

THESE QUESTIONS CONCERN THE CONTENT OF *THE MISSIONARY MESSENGER.*
For each type of article, mark how interested you are in it.

	Very Interested	Somewhat Interested	Not Interested
34. Articles about missionaries and mission fields			
35. Articles about world issues			
36. Monthly program material			
37. Potpourri of news and ideas			
38. Monthly Bible study section			
39. Regular columns			

How much do you like each of the following in *The Missionary Messenger*:

	Like It A Lot	Like It A Little	Don't Like It
40. the publication's cover			
41. the pictures			
42. quality of writing in the articles			
43. how easy it is to read the print			
44. the overall appearance			

45. Can you briefly name one article you read in *The Missionary Messenger* that you
found particularly enjoyable or inspiring?

46. Considering both *The Cumberland Presbyterian* and the *Missionary Messenger*,
which of the two publications do you prefer:
    a. Cumberland Presbyterian __
    b. Missionary Messenger __
    c. both equally __
    d. don't know __

Figure 11.1 Continued

47. Counting yourself, how many members of
your household read *The Cumberland Presbyterian*: __

48. Counting yourself, how many members of
your household read *The Missionary Messenger*: __

49. The denomination is considering combining the two
publications into one magazine. Do you think that is a good idea: __ yes __ no __ not sure

50. If the two are combined, would you subscribe to the new magazine: __ yes __ no __ not sure

THESE LAST FEW QUESTIONS WILL HELP THE DENOMINATION
BETTER UNDERSTAND HOW ITS MEMBERSHIP IS CHANGING.

51. Counting yourself, how many are in your household: _____

52. What year were you born: 19 __

53. Which of these categories describes your education level:
a. less than high school degree __
b. high school graduate __
c. attended college, business or technical school __
d. college graduate or more __

54. Which of these categories includes your family's annual income level last year:
a. under $10,000 __ d. $30,000 - $39,999 __
b. $10,000 - $19,999 __ e. $40,000 - $50,000 __
c. $20,000 - $29,999 __ f. over $50,000 __

55. Your sex: __ male __ female

THAT ENDS OUR SURVEY FOR THE DENOMINATION.
THANK YOU VERY MUCH FOR YOUR TIME AND EFFORT IN COMPLETING IT.

Please refold the questionnaire and mail it in the postage-paid business reply envelope enclosed to:
(return address provided here for convenience, in case envelope is misplaced)

the respondent, each of these items is part of a carefully planned set of independent variables. The researchers wanted to know if location in the United States, the number of years a respondent belonged to the church, size of the city in which the respondent's church was located, or the respondent's activity level within the church had any bearing on magazine readership or interest in magazine content. Similar types of questions would be included, of course, in a public relations research project for a company's internal publication. Management would want to know if length of employment, job responsibility level, or plant location influence the content and reading frequency of a company newsletter.

The next two sections, which comprise the bulk of the questionnaire form, assess readership of the two publications. Each section is introduced with a subheading that directs the respondent's frame of reference first to one publication, then the next. The introductory items in these sections are the same and they, too, are arranged from general to specific. A dramatic device at the beginning of each section is a screening question. If a respondent says he or she is not familiar with the publication in question, the directions instruct the respondent to skip that section entirely. That makes sense from both the researcher's interests and the respondent's capabilities. There is little point in seeking information from an individual who reports no familiarity with the topic, and further quizzing on an unfamiliar topic will only provoke the respondent. Every questionnaire form should contain screening items where needed to ensure that respondents have sufficient knowledge to continue along an avenue of inquiry.

Reading frequency and subscriber/non-subscriber items follow the screening question. These questions are critical in readership studies because content assessments made by frequent readers are likely to be more informed and different from those made by less-frequent readers. In fact, the strategy often is to find out what content draws the interest of infrequent readers so future editions can contain more articles that will lure current infrequent readers. Subscribers and non-subscribers who are familiar with the publication may have different interests that can be identified with the same strategy.

After reading frequency has been ascertained, the next sections turn to an assessment of the current content of the two magazines. Instead of assuming respondents will be able to remember and report about specific content items in the magazines, these are listed on the form with a simple, three-point scale of interest. (In the telephone survey, the interviewer would ask, "For each of the following items of magazine content, please tell me if you are very interested, somewhat interested, or not interested in that topic.") All major content elements in the magazines are included where possible. Following the content items are general appearance items—the same ones are included for both magazines. And at the end of each content section is an open-ended item asking the respondent to recall a particular article he or she enjoyed. In this survey, as in many other readership studies, these open-ended questions provided few insights because people usually can't remember such specifics. Asking for this kind of detail will probably be a mistake, as it was in this study.

After the sections on content, the questionnaire directs respondents to one of the major concerns of the study. These questions on combining the two magazines could have been placed anywhere on the form (other than in the skip portions), but they are purposely included in their most logical sequence after the two content sections. The two questions about members of the household reading the magazines (items 47 and 48) are needed to assess further the use of the magazines. If the two publications have equal numbers of subscribers, but one is read by an average of three family members and the other is read by an average of only two family members, the first magazine has a 50 percent greater reach among the church's membership.

Finally, the survey form includes the demographic items introduced by a short statement of why these answers are needed. Research ethics require honesty in questionnaire forms, and in this case the explanation given—to "help the denomination better understand how its membership is changing—was accurate. However, these items were also independent variables included to determine if church members' age, education, income, or sex had a bearing on readership of the two publications. There is no requirement to explain why the survey includes demographic questions; just introduce them with, "These are the last few items."

Anticipated Analysis of Questionnaire Results

It should be apparent from the explanation of how the Cumberland Presbyterian Church questionnaire was designed that researchers had specific analyses in mind when they constructed the form. Anticipating how the answers might be analyzed is precisely the right strategy for developing questionnaire items. Some of the analytical approaches used in the Cumberland Presbyterian Church project can be viewed in terms of data tables.

One of the client's more important information needs was determining if the two publications should be combined. It was necessary to know if women, who were expected to be more loyal to the *Missionary Messenger,* would be willing to see the publications combined. The client also might like to know if other demographic variables were related to a church member's willingness to combine the two publications. Table 11.1 offers a structure, using fictional data, that researchers would have in mind when designing the questionnaire items.

This kind of analysis is called a contingency table or cross-tabulation table. It shows respondents' answers to one questionnaire item based on their answers to another item. In Table 11.1, the percentage of respondents who were male or female, the percentage in each educational category, and the percentage in each church activity category are compared with the percent who answered yes, no, or don't know to the question about combining the two publications. While these data are contrived (few outcomes are this clear), they would be interpreted as showing: (1) Males were more likely to support combining the two magazines; (2) the more education a respondent has, the more he or she favored combining

Table 11.1

Percent Saying Publications Should Be Combined, by Selected Demographics of Church Members

	Should Be Combined	Should Not Be Combined	Don't Know or Not Sure
Sex:			
male	55%	35%	10%
female	40	25	35%
Educational level:			
less than high school degree	35%	20%	45%
high school degree	40	20	40
attended college, business or technical school	50	15	35
college graduate or more education	65	10	25
Position in church:			
pastor or former pastor	75%	10%	15%
part of leadership or paid staff	65	15	20
serve on committees or as a teacher	50	25	25
occasionally volunteer	40	35	25

the two magazines; and (3) the greater the leadership role held in the church, the more the respondent favored combining. The researchers may not have predicted these exact outcomes. That isn't important, but it is important for the researchers to have considered possible relationships among these variables before designing the questionnaire. If these relationships hadn't been considered, the questions might not have been asked.

One other data presentation from the Cumberland Presbyterian Church survey is worth considering. Table 11.2 shows a fictional analysis of outcomes respondents might have given to the *Missionary Messenger's* content.

This table requires a little more explanation. Recall the questionnaire scale used for responses to the six questions (items 34 through 39) about content in the *Missionary Messenger*. Respondents could answer they were very interested, somewhat interested, or not interested in each content item. Assuming the re-

Table 11.2
Missionary Messenger Content Preference Averages for All Respondents, Males and Females

	Interest Averages For All (n=700)	Interest Averages Males (n=325)	Interest Averages Females (n=375)
Monthly Bible study section	2.8	2.6	2.9
Monthly program material	2.6	2.3	2.0
Articles about mission- aries and mission fields	2.5	2.2	2.7
Regular columns	2.4	2.1	2.7
Potpourri of news and ideas	1.8	1.7	1.9
Articles about world issues	1.7	1.5	1.9

searchers awarded three points for a "very interested," two points for a "somewhat interested," and one point for a "not interested" response, the average responses for each item by the entire survey could be provided. The closer the average is to "3.0," the more interested respondents were in that content category. Likewise, comparisons could be made for a variety of demographic or activity levels as they are presented for the sex variable in the table. The table orders the content categories from most interested (monthly Bible section at 2.8) to least interested (articles about world issues at 1.7) for the entire survey. Table findings show which content respondents thought was the more interesting and less interesting, and the differences between average ratings for content show the extent of these preferences. For instance, there is a wide gap between Regular Columns at 2.4 and Potpourri at 1.8. Additionally, the fictional data portrayed in the table show that females always give higher ratings to the content in this publication than do males.

While it wasn't necessary for researchers to predict these outcomes in their hypotheses, it was necessary for them to consider how to structure the answer categories while designing the questionnaire. The three-point scales associated with "very interested," "somewhat interested," and "not interested" provide discrete measurements that are far more sophisticated than having asked the magazine content in another structure. For instance, had researchers merely asked: "Do you usually read . . . ," the yes—no responses would have yielded percentages for which items were read, but the data analysis would not have provided as much preference insight for the client.

RACE TRACK STUDY (TELEPHONE QUESTIONNAIRE)

Although the race track project is the central example, for survey research, used in this text, the readership study questionnaire has offered a thorough

Figure 11.2
Horse Race Track Questionnaire

Respondent Phone #: _____   I.D. #: _____

Hello, my name is _____ and I'm with John Brown Public Relations, a public issues research agency. My assignment is to speak with the oldest – youngest; male – female adult 18 or over. Am I speaking to that person in your home now? (repeat intro if necessary). This is not a sales call. We're doing a survey tonight to measure people's attitude about a new industry being proposed in this county. Your phone number was randomly selected to provide anonymous answers to a five-minute survey. We will not ask your name. Let's begin with your interest in sports:

1. Would you say you are very interested, interested, not very interested or not at all interested in sports? (circle one)

      If "not very interested" or "not at all interested," **skip to #4**
      If "interested" or "very interested," **ask:** 2. How many sports events have you
                                           actually gone to see during the past year: _____

3. Which of the following do you do on a regular basis: (check all agreed with)
    ___watch sports on TV   ___read the newspaper's sports section every day
    ___talk about sports with friends   ___make friendly bets on sports events
    ___listen to sports on radio   ___read a sports magazine regularly

4. Are you familiar with the recent proposal the state
legislature passed allowing legalized horse racing in the state? ___yes ___no ___don't know

If "yes," **ask:** 5. Do you know if the horse racing proposal allows   ___anywhere
               race tracks to be built anywhere in the state or only   ___local approval
               in cities that vote to allow race tracks?   ___don't know/not sure

6. Do you favor legalized horse racing for this state? ___yes ___no ___not sure/don't know

7. Would you vote for a horse race track in this county? ___yes ___no ___don't know

8. Why would you vote this way? (write the respondent's first answer as completely as possible)

9. How strongly would you agree or disagree with the following statement about gambling:
      "Regardless of the amount of the bet or under what circumstances a bet is made,
      I think gambling is morally wrong."
    Do you:
              a. strongly agree   d. disagree or
              b. agree   e. strongly disagree
              c. feel neutral   with that statement

Figure 11.2 Continued

These last questions will help us determine which groups of people think the same way you do on these issues:

10. How long have you lived in this county: _____

11. Which of the following best describes your religious preference:
     ___Catholic
     ___Jewish
     ___Baptist
     ___Methodist
     ___Presbyterian
     ___other Protestant denomination
     ___another religious preference
     ___no religious preference

12. Are you:
     ___Caucasian
     ___black
     ___or of another race or ethnic heritage

13. What year were you born: 19 ___

14. Which of the following categories best describes your level of education:
     ___ some high school
     ___ high school degree or GED
     ___ technical school, business school or some college
     ___ college graduate or more

15. Please stop me when I mention the category in which your family income fell last year:
     ___under $10,000
     ___$10,000 to 19,999
     ___$20,000 to $29,999
     ___$30,000 to $39,999
     ___$40,000 to $49,999
     ___$50,000 to $59,999
     ___$60,000 or over

That ends the survey. You've been very kind to talk with me tonight. Thank you. Good-bye.

16. Record respondent's sex: ___male ___female

Interviewer's signature: _____

Date survey completed: _____ Time: _____

analysis of how to design a survey form. Focusing on the differences between the two questionnaires will complete the presentation.

The race track questionnaire is structured for telephone interviews, so the emphasis is on clear layout for the interviewer rather than on graphic design to ensure mail respondents' ease in completing the form. In fact, there is less white space on this questionnaire, although its design must be neat so the interviewer doesn't get lost in a maze of jumbled typography.

This questionnaire will contain a phone number provided by the researcher from the phone directory sample. The sampling plan calls for an interview alternating between the oldest and youngest adult (18 years or older) in the household, and between a male and female. These decisions will be made in advance by the researcher who should circle the proper respondent category on the form. Interviewers will be instructed to write their names in the space provided and will be trained in handling the possible difficulties they may encounter in trying to reach the designated household respondent.

The introduction contains all the necessary facts about the survey that ethics require the respondent be told, including time the survey will take, how the respondent was selected, whether the information is anonymous, and so forth. One aspect of the introduction deserves attention: telling the respondent the survey topic is on "a new industry being proposed in this county." While the horse race track issue is being avoided for the moment, mentioning a "new industry" comes as close to the real intent of the study as is deemed practical for a questionnaire introduction on what may be a sensitive topic. Additionally, the introduction contains a statement assuring the respondent that this survey is not a sales call. In these times of computer-assisted phone solicitations and cold calls to sell aluminum siding, such a statement is advised.

The introduction leads immediately to the most general approach to the survey topic by asking the respondent about his or her interest in sports. The first three questions form a scale of sports interest. If the respondent answers "not very" or "not at all interested" to the first question, a screening item, questions 2 and 3 will be skipped. But a "very interested" or "interested" response to question 1 will prompt the next two questions. Later analysis will combine the multiple answers to question 3 with the number of sports events attended in question 2 to form the scale (discussed in the next chapter).

Next is a series of questions that move slowly into the horse race track topic. Question 4 is a general knowledge screening item which taps familiarity about the legislative measure. It also serves another purpose: to focus the respondent's attention on the issue of legalized horse racing. A yes response to item 4 prompts question 5 that seeks very specific knowledge about the legislative proposal on the track. Taken together, these two questions will form a two-tiered level of knowledge about the race track issue. The client's information needs require being able to discriminate between those segments of the public that are aware of the race track proposal at the time of this survey and those who aren't. As the referendum campaign approaches, most voters will be knowledgeable about the issue.

Two questions—again from the more general statewide item 6 to the more specific local item 7—tap current voter intentions on the race track issue. Then the study's only open-ended item allows an opportunity for individual responses. The open-ended question is intended to elicit views that can be addressed in the referendum campaign. The client will want this information in as detailed and accurate a response as the interviewer can record. The percentage of "not sure" or "don't know" answers to the open-ended item will be important, too. The last topic question on the form is item 9 that addresses how firmly respondents' attitude about gambling is held.

The questionnaire moves from topic questions to demographics and uses a vague transition about helping "determine which groups of people think the same way you do" to introduce the demographic items. In this case, some transitional device is necessary to bridge what would otherwise be a startling change for the listener between moral views on gambling and "How long have you lived in this country?"

Demographic questions are arranged from the least intrusive to the most. Asking how long the respondent has lived in the county should be the least threatening of the items. The next question, on religion, has a more extensive list of categories than the usual Protestant, Catholic, Jewish, or other. Because religion is expected to be a major factor in the referendum campaign, specificity is necessary. Arrangement of the categories, however, is based on an assumption of what will be the clearest presentation respondents can follow. For instance, a respondent who is Catholic or Jewish will not be asked the rest of the list. Baptists, Methodists, and Presbyterians will be queried first about their specific denominations before having the opportunity to say they are Protestant. In structuring the answer categories for the religion question, the assumption is that researchers have done their homework with county census data and know which religious denominations are pertinent to the client's information needs.

Interviewers may think that race, the next question, is an embarrassing question to ask. Virtually all respondents will answer the question without hesitation if it is asked as merely the next item on the form. Again, answer categories for race depend on census data that show which races are prevalent in the county, and the categories depend on the project's information goals.

Asking what year a person was born is often a more reliable approach than asking a person's age. It's difficult to fudge on years when you have to add or subtract quickly, and when the question is phrased this way it seems less intrusive.

Level of education is another item for which county census data should be used to determine categories for the questionnaire form. For instance, if the census figures show one-third of the county's adults have high school degrees, a third have some college, and a third have college degrees, asking about "some high school" is needless. Income level categories also should be built from

Table 11.3
Voter Preference for Race Track by Interest in Sports

	Vote For Race Track In County
Sports Interest Level:	
low	37%
medium	48%
high	66%

census data, but there are some other considerations as well. It is important to keep the income categories as broad as possible. Unless there's a reason to break the categories into $5,000-level spreads, keep them at $10,000, or make them $20,000 spreads if that provides sufficient detail for the research purpose at hand. Try to make the first category lower than what census figures indicate is a likely response. For instance, $10,000 or less is well below the poverty level for family income, but this category is included as a device so respondents won't have to answer in the lowest category.

The ending is brief, and the interviewer is instructed to record the respondent's sex, sign the form, and indicate the date and time it was completed.

Anticipated Analysis of Questionnaire Results

Previous chapters have described the information needs for horse race track survey. Table 11.3 offers fictional data on one of the main concerns: Whether interest in sports is associated with a decision to vote in favor of the race track.

The table shows an outcome that supports the hypothesis that the more interested in sports a person is, the more likely that person will vote for the race track.

Table 11.4 shows average ratings on the five-point scale (item 9 in the questionnaire) by a respondent's religious preference. These fictional data indicate the three Protestant denominations strongly agreed with the statement, as did those affiliated with other Protestant denominations. Non-Protestants disagreed with the statement, as did those with other religious preferences or none.

The likelihood of obtaining such clear outcomes in a survey is remote, although it does happen. The race horse track questionnaire has several more sophisticated scales that will be discussed in the following chapter on data analysis.

SUMMARY

Chapter 10 offered a theoretical overview of questionnaire design. This chapter presents specific examples of actual mail and telephone questionnaires. The

Table 11.4
Rating on Gambling as a Moral Issue by Religious Preference

	Rating on Gambling As a Moral Issue ("1" = strongly agree; "5" = strongly disagree)
Religious Preference:	
Baptist	1.3
Presbyterian	1.5
Methodist	2.2
Other Protestant	1.9
Catholic	3.7
Jewish	4.0
Other or None	4.1

rationale for items, their order of presentation on the form, and their graphic design are discussed.

After each of the questionnaires, some discussion is offered about how the items might be analyzed to draw conclusions from the research. Data analysis should be considered before a questionnaire is printed because question wording, or even whether to include a question on the form, will be influenced by how the researcher expects to analyze the data.

ADDITIONAL READING

Bailey, Kenneth D. *Methods of Social Research,* 2d ed. New York: Free Press, 1982, pp. 155–80, 207–16.

Converse, Jean M., and Stanley Presser, *Survey Questions: Handcrafting the Standardized Questionnaire.* Newbury Park, CA: Sage, 1986.

Dillman, Don. *Mail and Telephone Surveys.* New York: John Wiley, 1978.

Lavrakas, Paul J. *Telephone Survey Methods: Sampling, Selection and Supervision.* Newbury Park, CA: Sage, 1987.

Noelle-Neumann, Elizabeth. "Wanted: Rules for Wording Structured Questionnaires." *Public Opinion Quarterly* 34:2 (Summer 1970): 191–201.

12 Data Analysis

The previous sections on survey research correctly indicate that early steps in any research project must be correlated with later steps. For instance, even as the researcher considers what items should be on the questionnaire form, decisions are being made based on the previous stages of stating hypotheses and the anticipated stages of data analysis. The questionnaire design chapter appropriately mentioned how items on the form would be used to create comparison scales when the data had been gathered. At this stage of the scientific method, the data-gathering or survey field work has been completed and the questionnaire forms are in a stack, ready to be put into the computer.

CONSULTING A PROFESSIONAL

The discussion of formal research strategies began by considering how much hands-on work a public relations professional might actually be expected to do and how much would be contracted out to a consultant or commercial research firm. The answer was that while most organizations' public relations departments do little more than oversee a formal research project, the public relations director is still responsible for the project's successful completion. Should something go wrong during the process—or should the information prove inaccurate—the public relations director's job may be on the line, not the hired consultant's. So a professional public relations practitioner must possess a working knowledge of all the formal research procedures to ensure a project's success. In the 1990s, more organizations are expecting their public relations professionals to have these skills.

But most public relations practitioners cannot be expected to possess the level of knowledge of formal research necessary to personally direct a project from initiation to completed report. The vice-president of public relations may take an active, working role in producing the organization's annual report and may, in fact, do most of the writing and editing. But the vice-president will not be expected to ink the color presses or even know how to perform that task. Similarly, at some point in the formal research project, the skilled expertise of a consultant or commercial firm may be required. As this text's early discussion of formal research suggested, the hired professionals should be brought in at the beginning of the project rather than be expected to tie together loose ends after the research is underway. The entire success of a project may be in jeopardy by not relying on expert advice until a stumbling block is hit.

Data analysis is probably the stage of formal research with which public relations professionals need outside expertise. Some of the skills required are routine chores that can easily be performed by untrained clerical staff personnel hired as temporaries. But some skills require graduate-level college training in statistics and computer science. These are the skill areas for which a consultant may be needed, although the public relations professional must possess enough knowledge to communicate with such experts. This chapter provides an overview of the routine chores and some concepts about the statistical analysis.

CREATING A CODEBOOK

A codebook is the set of guidelines used to convert questionnaire form answers into numbers that can be read by a computer. Making this translation from close-ended or even open-ended items consisting of paragraphs in the respondent's own words is not a difficult procedure. However, there are some points to remember and some suggestions for making the conversion easier.

Figure 12.1 is a codebook for the horse race track survey form. There were 16 items on the questionnaire; the codebook contains these 16 plus a first item, the identification number at the top of the questionnaire (a three-digit number from 001 to 700, if 700 questionnaire forms were completed).

Before continuing, consider Figures 12.2 and 12.3. The figures approximate coding sheets—forms coders will use to actually write the codes into the boxes on the coding sheets as instructed by the codebook. Hand processing with a coding sheet is becoming outmoded because of the advances in computer character recognition and laser scanning. Although it is unlikely that a research project in the 1990s will require hand coding, understanding the process is part of preparing the data for analysis. Coding sheets actually have 80 columns across (80 boxes), although only 30 boxes are shown in the figures. There are actually 20 vertical lines of boxes, although only five lines are shown in the figures.

For the horse race survey, according to the left-hand margin column of the Figure 12.1 codebook, only 26 of the columns (the boxes on the coding sheets in Figures 12.2 and 12.3) will be used. The process begins by picking up the first completed questionnaire form and looking at the upper right-hand identification number for this form: 001. Each questionnaire, regardless of whether it

Figure 12.1
Horse Race Track Survey Codebook

COL-UMN	ITEM #	VAR-IABLE	QUESTION	CODES
1-2-3	I.D.	ID	Questionnaire #	(code 3-digit number top right corner)
4	1.	V1	Interested in sports?	(1) very interested (2) interested (3) not very interested (4) not at all interested (0) blank
5	2.	V2	Number sports events attended	(code actual number up to "8;" code "9" if over 8 events; "0" if blank)
6 7 8 9 10 11	3.	V3 V4 V5 V6 V7 V8	Watch TV sports Talk sports Sports on radio Newspaper sports Friendly bets Sports magazine	Use this code for series: (1) checked (2) not checked (0) whole series blank
12	4.	V9	Familiar with legislative proposal	(1) yes (2) no (3) don't know (0) blank
13	5.	V10	Specific knowledge question on track	(1) anywhere (2) local approval (3) don't know/not sure (0) blank
14	6.	V11	Favor racing in state	(1) yes (2) no (3) don't know/not sure (0) blank
15	7.	V12	Vote for race track in this county	(1) yes (2) no (3) don't know (0) blank
16	8.	V13	Why would you vote this way	(1) favor to raise revenues (2) favor to keep dollars in state; neighboring states have tracks (3) favor, brings jobs/tourists (4) favor, likes racing; wants to attend (5) favor, other reason given (6) opposed moral/religious grounds (7) opposed, fear crime potential (8) opposed, other reason given (9) don't know/not sure (0) if blank

Figure 12.1 Continued

COL-UMN	ITEM #	VAR-IABLE	QUESTION	CODES
17	9.	V14	Gambling morally wrong	(1) strongly agree (2) agree (3) feel neutral (4) disagree (5) strongly disagree (0) blank
18-19	10.	V15	How long lived in this county	(code actual two-digit number; "01" for one year or less, "02," "14," etc.; "00" for blank)
20	11.	V16	Religion	(1) Catholic (2) Jewish (3) Baptist (4) Methodist (5) Presbyterian (6) other Protestant denomination (7) another religious preference (9) no religious preference (0) blank
21	12.	V17	Race	(1) Caucasian (2) black (3) other race (0) blank
22-23	13.	V18	Year born	(code actual two-digit year; use "99" for years 1900 and below; use "00" for blank)
24	14.	V19	Educational level	(1) some high school (2) high school degree or GED (3) technical, business, some college (4) college grad or more (0) blank
25	15.	V20	Income level	(1) under $10,000 (2) $10,000-$19,999 (3) $20,000-$29,999 (4) $30,000-$39,999 (5) $40,000-$49,999 (6) $50,000-$59,999 (7) $60,000 or over (0) blank
26	16.	V21	Sex	(1) male (2) female (0) blank

Figure 12.2
Coding Sheet, Blank Except for First I.D. Number

columns ⟹

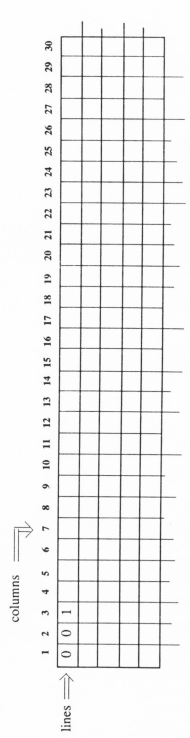

lines ⟹	1	2	3	4	5	6	7	8	9	10	11	12	13	14	15	16	17	18	19	20	21	22	23	24	25	26	27	28	29	30
	0	0	1																											

Figure 12.3
First Three Questionnaires Completed on Coding Sheet

1	2	3	4	5	6	7	8	9	10	11	12	13	14	15	16	17	18	19	20	21	22	23	24	25	26	27	28	29	30
0	0	1	1	6	1	1	2	1	1	1	1	2	1	1	3	4	2	0	4	1	3	8	3	4	1				
0	0	2	3	0	0	0	0	0	0	0	2	0	2	2	5	2	0	8	6	1	6	0	2	5	2				
0	0	3	2	2	1	1	1	2	2	2	1	3	3	1	1	3	1	7	3	2	5	5	4	3	2				

204

was completed in this order, gets a consecutive ID number. If there is a problem on the coding sheet or with the later computer analysis, it will be possible to locate the questionnaire form that contains the error by looking up the three-digit ID number to correct the translation error. Using the codebook as a guide, some fictional data will be translated to the code sheet. The first is the ID number, 001, written into the first three columns (boxes) on the first line of the code sheet (Figure 12.2). That line will contain all the digits depicting answers to the questionnaire numbered 001, shown in the first line across Figure 12.3. After the ID number, the codebook instructs that column 4 is the response to item 1 on the survey form, and that this is variable number 1 (written V1 on the codebook). The question was: "Would you say you are very interested, interested, not very interested, or not all interested in sports?" The interviewer will have circled one of those responses, and they are listed as codes for the item in the codebook. Because respondent 001 said very interested, a "1" is placed on column 4 of this line.

Column 5, according to the codebook, will contain the answer to the second item on the questionnaire, "How many sports events have you actually gone to see during the past year?" Respondent 001 said he attended six, so this number is actually placed in that column box on the coding sheet, according to the instructions on the codebook. The best way to handle the answers to item 3 on the questionnaire is to make them individual variables: A respondent could answer each one yes, in which case there would be a check on the form, or no, in which case that space would be empty. However, it is also possible that none of these questions was even asked. If the respondent was "not very interested" or "not at all interested," items 2 and 3 were not asked. The researcher has decided to make a distinction between these two possibilities by coding a yes in the space as "1," a no as "2," and by coding a "0" if these questions weren't asked because of the skip. The answers to these six questions constitute six variables on the codebook, and the correct number for each must be placed in the designated column on the coding sheet (columns 3 through 8).

Questionnaire items 4 through 7 are self-explanatory, but item 8 on the questionnaire is an open-ended question which asked respondents, "Why would you vote this way?" The answers to open-ended questions must also be converted to digits, and there are potential problems associated with the decision on how many categories to include. For instance, there are easily more than 20 possible responses to the question ranging from "gambling is the devil's handmaiden" to "the more tax revenues we have, the better my kids' education." With some diversity, the researcher must decide which comments pertain to the client's information needs, which are repeated frequently enough to be categorized, and which are closely enough related to be combined as one category. Using this question as an example, some considerations are:

1. What information does the client need to plan the referendum campaign? Obviously, the campaign will include such issues as economics, tourism, jobs, taxes, fear about

crime, and people's moral and religious feelings about gambling. If preliminary research has shown that taxes and education were critical concerns in referendum elections in other states, those items should be separate categories so the client will know what percent of the voting public is likely to be considering these issues. Anything that surprises the researcher on a read-through of 20 or 30 completed questionnaires is a candidate for one of the open-ended question categories, assuming there are enough similar answers.

2. Unless there are enough answers of a similar nature, there is no justification for creating a category. In the horse race survey, tax dollars for education was discussed as a reason people might give for supporting the track. However, the reason isn't among the open-ended question's categories on the codebook. The probable explanation for not including either education or taxes as separate categories is that too few respondents mentioned these aspects among reasons for their voting decision. In fact, we may assume too few respondents mentioned either of these two topics because there isn't even a combined answer category called "taxes or education." Open-ended question coding categories are developed by reading perhaps ten percent of the respondents' answers from randomly selected questionnaires. Answers that aren't repeated among this smaller sample probably won't be found with any frequency in the sample as a whole. Since the purpose of surveys usually is to determine the opinion of groups of people—not individuals—every category should contain a dozen or more similar responses. One dozen isn't a rule-of-thumb, but little meaningful information can be gained from an answer given by five people in a 700-person sample . . . other than only five people answered that way.

3. It often happens—as may have occurred in the horse race track survey—that categories with too few answers will be combined (or collapsed) into other similar categories to increase the numbers of category respondents. Code 1 for the open-ended question is any comment related to revenues other than comments covered by code 2 (dealing with keeping the dollars inside the state rather than losing revenues to nearby states) and code 3 (in which a respondent mentioned jobs or tourists). Apparently three of the four reasons for favoring the track were money-related, but there was sufficient discrimination among the three to require separation.

Discriminating between open-ended response categories is probably the single most difficult decision a coder has to make. The researcher must define the categories carefully enough to ensure reliability in coder decisions. For instance, in which category should this comment be put: "I think this county needs the income and the new jobs a race track would bring." To discriminate between categories 1 and 3, coders must be told to put any response with the words "jobs" or "tourism" into category 3 instead of 1.

The more obvious example of combining responses into a single category is that of moral/religious reasons for opposing the track. Apparently respondents used the terms interchangeably. Researchers decided it would be impossible for coders to discriminate between the two categories, so they combined these two responses into a single category.

The rest of the codebook is straightforward, with the exception of some possible confusion among coders on the remaining two-digit responses. Item 10 in the questionnaire asks how long the respondent has lived in the county, and it requires remembering to put a zero before the second digit for years one through nine. Item 13 on the questionnaire form is a two-digit code for year born if the respondent was born after 1900. Those who were born before that time will be coded "99" on the coding sheet.

The codebook instructs coders to use a zero or double zero for every answer left blank on the form. The computer will be programmed to recognize a zero as missing data, not to be included in the analysis.

Do the code numbers ("1" for yes, "2" for no) have any real meaning? In most cases, they don't; they are only digits selected for convenience. The data are nominal, the lowest form of data sophistication. In fact, it would be just as meaningful to code a yes answer "4" and a no answer "9," as long as the number 4 is later labeled as standing for yes and the 9 for no. However, some of the code numbers do have real meaning. For instance, in item 2 on the questionnaire, a response of attending one sports event is coded "1"; two events gets a "2." Here a "2" represents twice the attendance as a "1." These data are interval data, the third most sophisticated level of measurement. Likewise, years lived in the country and year of birth are interval data. Item 14, educational level, is coded in ordinal data. A "1" response indicates some high school, a "2" indicates a high school diploma, and so forth, with each higher number representing more education. But the number codes for education are only ranks because a "1" might be a person with only six years of schooling or it might be a person with 11 years of schooling.

USING THE COMPUTER

With the recent advances in technology, computer analysis of survey results is open to virtually everyone. Extremely sophisticated statistical programs are available for personal computers and office machines purchased primarily for word processing. Computer hardware is as commonplace in the 1990s as typewriters were in the 1970s, and today's $200 software program can duplicate the capabilities of a $2 million mainframe computer of only 20 years ago. The research capabilities—and responsibilities—of today's public relations practitioner are awesome. While it would be impossible to itemize the dozens of excellent statistical software packages, one program has been the mainstay of social science research for more than 20 years: SPSS^x Batch System. Statistical Package for the Social Sciences (SPSS^x*— "x" stands for a recent mainframe computer version) provides the entire range of capabilities a public relations researcher might need, and it will be described here in a brief overview, just to present an idea of how computer analysis is done.

The codebook again serves as a guide to computer programming for translating the analysis instructions into "commands" the machine can read. In this case,

*SPSS^x is a trademark of SPSS Inc. of Chicago, IL, for its proprietary computer software

Figure 12.4

SPSS[x] Command File for Horse Race Survey

```
FILE HANDLE RACEDATA / (more instructions depend on computer)
DATA LIST FILE = RACEDATA / ID 1-3 V1 4 V2 5 V3 6 V4 7 V5 8
    V6 9 V7 10 V8 11 V9 12 V10 13 V11 14 V12 15 V13 16 V14 17
    V15 18-19 V16 20 V17 21 V18 22-23 V19 24 V20 25 V21 26
MISSING VALUES V1 TO V21 (0) / V18 (99)
VARIABLE LABELS V1 'interested in sports'
    V2 'how many events' V3 'watch tv sports'
    V4 'talk sports with friends' V5 'listen radio sports'
    V6 'read newspaper sports' V7 'make friendly bets'
    V8 'read sports magazine' V9 'know legislative measure'
    V10 'know proposal detail' V11 'favor racing in state'
    V12 'favor racing in county' V13 'why vote this way'
    V14 'gambling morally wrong' V15 'years in county'
    V16 'religious preference' V17 'race' V18 'year of birth'
    V19 'educational level' V20 'income level' V21 'sex'
VALUE LABELS V1 1 'very interested' 2 'interested'
    3 'not very interested' 4 'no interest at all' / V3 to V8
    1 'yes' 2 'no' /
    V9, V11, V12 1 'yes' 2 'no' 3 'don't know' /
    V13 1 'pro-revenues' 2 'pro-neighbor states'
    3 'pro-jobs or tourists' 4 'pro-likes racing'
    5 'pro-other reason' 6 'con-moral or religious'
    7 'con-crime fears' 8 'con-other reason' 9 'don't know /
    V14 1 'strongly agree' 2 'agree' 3 'neutral' 4 'disagree'
    5 'strongly disagree' / V16 1 'Catholic' 2 'Jewish'
    3 'Baptist' 4 'Methodist' 5 'Presbyterian'
    6 'other Protestant' 7 'other religion' 8 'no religion' /
    V17 1 'Caucasian' 2 'black' 3 'other race' /
    V19 1 'some h.s.' 2 'h.s. degree or GED'
    3 'tech-busi-some college' 4 'college grad-plus' /
    V20 1 'under $10,000' 2 '$10-$19,999' 3 '$20-$29,999'
    4 '$30-$39,999' 5 '$40-$49,999 6 '$50,$59,999'
    7 '$60,000 or over' / V21 1 'male' 2 'female'
COMPUTE AGE = (90 - V18)
IF (V15 LT 5) RESIDENT = 1
IF (V15 GT 4 AND V15 LT 11) RESIDENT = 2
IF (V15 GT 10 AND V15 LT 20) RESIDENT = 3
IF (V15 GT 19) RESIDENT = 4
VALUE LABLES RESIDENT 1 'under 5 years' 2 'five to 9 years'
    3 '10 to 19 years' 4 '20 years or more'
FREQUENCIES VARIABLES = V1, V3 TO V14, V16, V17, V19 TO V21,
    RESIDENT
FREQUENCIES VARIABLES = V2, V15, AGE / STATISTICS ALL
FINISH
```

however, the SPSS[x] program requires learning only a few special computer-sensitive conventions. These instructions trigger the program and it, in turn, triggers the computer. Figure 12.4 is an SPSS[x] file, or set of commands and labels, for the horse race track survey. It was constructed using the codebook and an SPSS[x] manual.

The FILE HANDLE or first line of the file is called a command, meaning that SPSS[x] will recognize the words FILE HANDLE (beginning in column one of the line) as an order to begin and name this file. All command lines must begin in the first column; all of the continuing lines must be indented at least one column (they may start in column two or three, but not in column one).

The FILE HANDLE line contains the name of the file in which the data are located. The assumption is that a file with 700 lines of numbers, each representing a completed questionnaire, has already been created. That file was named RACEDATA. Researchers are now creating a command file to instruct the computer what the string of numbers means. The remaining portion of the FILE HANDLE line has specific machine start-up information required by the individual computer center being used.

The second line, DATA LIST FILE, is also a command line (it begins in the first column) that reminds the computer it is being told how to interpret a data file called RACEDATA. DATA LIST FILE then begins giving interpretative information by listing the variables in the data set and columns on which each is found. The columns and variables are listed in the codebook, so the process is merely a matter of telling the computer where to look: A variable called ID is located in columns 1 through 3 of the data set (remember 001 for the first questionnaire form coded); a variable called V_1 (variable one) is located in column 4; V_2 is in column 5; and so forth through the entire list of variables. It is critical to remember that some variables will have two or more columns such as V_{15} in column 18 and 19, and V_{18} in columns 22 and 23. The DATA LIST FILE command continues to a second line (beginning with V_6) and third line (beginning with V_{15}. These aren't command lines, so they must be indented at least one column.

MISSING VALUES is the next command line used to tell the computer that some of the respondents didn't answer the questionnaire item, hence that data should not be included in the analysis (although it should be noted as missing). Here it is possible to use a string convention to say that in the entire list of variables, from V_1 through V_{21}, a zero stands for a missing value. But the year-of-birth variable, V_{18}, was coded 99 for birth years 1900 and before. If there are values in this survey, for simplicity they will be declared missing.

The next command line is VARIABLE LABELS. Here, the researcher is allowed to add labels to the V_1, V_2, etc., codes. One of the major advantages of SPSS^x is that it maximizes the use of English language labels, making it easier to read the computer printout. If labels aren't used, researchers will have to remember what V_8 is—which questionnaire item it denotes. VARIABLE LABELS allows a label—up to 40 characters, if necessary—to appear every time a variable is printed in the data analysis output. The command continues through several lines, first with the variable name, then with the label in single quote marks: V_1 'interested in sports,' etc.

VALUE LABELS allows the same labeling technique for the categories of variable answers. The first variable denotes the first item on the questionnaire about a person's interest in sports. Possible answers and the code values shown on the codebook are: (1) very interested, (2) interested, (3) not very interested, and (4) not at all interested. The program allows a label up to 20 characters for each of the values in the format shown: V_1 1 'very interested,' 2 'interested,' etc. To keep the fourth value label within the 20-character limit, it has been changed to 4 'no interest at all.' Labeling of one variable is separated from the next with a slash to let the computer know another variable is being labeled. The same procedure is used for most of the other variables in the list, although one string of variables (V_9, V_{11}, and V_{12}), has the same value labels, so those values can be included as a set for all three variables. Not all variables need be labeled. In fact, V_2 (how many sports events were attended), V_{15} (years in the country), and V_{18} (year born), aren't included in the value label list. That is because their values are self-explanatory. A respondent who has attended three sporting events will already be identified with a value of "3" for this variable.

COMPUTE is a special command line being used in this study to convert the year a person was born to that person's actual age. The command tells the computer to create a new variable called AGE by subtracting the value in V_{18}—the year the person was born—from a value of 90, and to do that for every respondent in the study. If the current value in V_{18} (a two-digit number) is 53, indicating the person was born in 1953, this value will be subtracted from 90 (the survey year 1990). AGE for this respondent will be 90 minus 53 equals 37 years old. AGE should be a range from 18 (the youngest qualified respondents) to 89 because years of birth for 1900 and before were coded "99" and a value of "99" was declared a missing value.

Finally, the program includes four IF command lines. Their purpose is to create a new variable labeled RESIDENT, depending on the value of V_{15}, the number of years a person has resided in the county. For data analysis ease, length of residence in the county is being divided into four segments. Where V_{15} is less than (LT) five years, the new RESIDENT variable equals "1"; where V_{15} is greater than (GT) four years but less than 11, RESIDENT equals "2," etc. Then the researcher declares values for length of residence as: "1," under 5 years: "2," 5 to 9 years; "3," 10 to 19 years; and "4," 20 years or more.

The last command lines, before telling the computer to FINISH, are FRE-QUENCIES commands. FREQUENCIES instructs the computer to do an analysis of the variables listed. The first FREQUENCIES command asks for a listing of all variables that contain nominal data. The second FREQUENCIES command instructs the computer to do a listing of all variables containing interval data (sports events attended, years in the county and the newly created AGE variable, converted from year of birth).

SOME STATISTICAL PROCEDURES

Before looking at a statistical computer printout, it is necessary to consider a concept called *significance level*. Significance—sometimes called *confidence level* or *probability*—is the researcher's tool to determine if differences found in the sample can be generalized to the population under study. Significance is the probability that a difference found in the sample may have occurred by chance. It may not be a real difference that would be found if everyone in the population had been asked the question. Instead it may be an artifact of this sample of respondents who happened to be selected. Had another sample been selected, the difference would not be present. Obviously, this concept requires more explanation.

Consider a CEO who is contemplating an annual employee pay raise of five percent. There were no raises last year because the company was losing money. This year the company made a small profit, but not enough to provide pay raises of ten percent. The union voted last year to accept the no-pay-raise without protest, but it warned management that a second year of unsatisfactory raises might result in a strike. The CEO wants to know if five percent raises this year will avert a strike. The public relations vice-president is asked to provide the answer and to be ready to stand behind the recommendation given.

A sample of 200 employees is surveyed and asked, among other things, if a five percent pay raise will be acceptable considering there were company profits this fiscal year, but they were slim. Fifty-seven percent of the employees sampled say yes (43 percent say no). The margin of error for a sample of 200 is about ±7 percent. The significance level for this finding (calculated by the statistical program in the computer) is 0.12 which means that 12 times out of a hundred such samples, a difference of 57 percent vs. 43 percent might be found merely by chance. Is the difference a chance finding this time (one of the 12 times out of 100 that it could be), or is this one of 88 times out of 100 samples in which the same percentage split will occur when all employees are asked the question? A 0.12 significance level offers reasonable confidence, but not enough on which to stake your job. The public relations vice-president can either report the vote is too close to call, or do another survey. In this instance, the best decision is another survey. If another study is done with another sample of 200 and the yes vote is 60 percent with a significance level of 0.03 (a percentage split of 60 percent vs. 40 percent could happen only three times out of hundred such samples), the vice-president may decide to report to the CEO that employees will accept the pay raise without a strike.

However, the best approach would have been to use a larger sample in the first place. If a sample of 600 had been asked and 57 percent said yes, the margin of error would have been about ±4 percent and the significance level might have been as low as 0.01 meaning a percentage split as large as 57 percent vs. 43 percent could happen by chance only once in 100 samples. Such a significance level would be adequate to tell the CEO all is well.

Significance level is associated with margin of error—the larger the sample, the more reliable the findings. But the two are not the same principle. Margin of error provides a range of assumed accuracy based solely on sample size. Significance level is a statistical formula that includes sample size, but tells researchers how confident they should be that the differences found in any single research study were either found by chance or were a real difference that will be found in the population.

The levels of significance associated with social science research are the 0.05 level, the 0.01 level, and the 0.001. They mean, respectively, that the outcomes

Table 12.1
Frequency Table for V₁; Interest in Sports

V1   INTEREST IN SPORTS

CATEGORY LABEL	CODE	ABSOLUTE FREQ.	RELATIVE FREQ	VALID FREQ.	CUM FREQ.
VERY INTERESTED	1.	228	32.6	32.6	32.6
INTERESTED	2.	275	39.3	39.3	71.9
NOT VERY INTERESTED	3.	119	17.0	17.0	88.9
NO INTEREST AT ALL	4.	78	11.1	11.1	100.0
	TOTAL	700	100.0	100.0	100.0

VALID CASES 700   MISSING CASES   0

found in this study could happen by chance five times out of 100 samples, once out of 100 samples, or once out of 1,000 samples. Because no research project involves doing 100 samples, researchers rely on the significance level statistic for their estimate of the validity of outcomes found in one sample. The "higher" the significance level (the least probability that these outcomes might be found by chance; once out of 1,000 is much less chance than five times out of 100), the more confidence researchers have in their sample findings. Margin of error always has the plus-or-minus (± 3.5 percent); significance level is reported a a two- or three-digit decimal (0.05, 0.001). In social science, other than predicting some election outcomes, a 0.05 significance level is considered a real difference.

Significance levels are used in all research projects. For instance, a grade-school principal wants to know if a new reading text is a more effective teaching tool than the one now being used. The principal has first-grade teachers use each text in different classes for six months and tests the students' reading level at the end of that time. Those classes using the old textbook score an average of 82 on the test; those using the new book score 86. There is a difference of four points, but is it a statistically significant difference? Perhaps the difference is a chance finding, an outcome of these teachers and these students. The significance level can be calculated to determine if the new reader should be adopted.

With significance level in mind, several statistical analyses will be presented in brief overview. All of the data are fictional and the tables are approximations of actual SPSS[x] computer printouts.

Frequencies

A frequency table is merely a tabulation of the percentages of respondents who have given answers to each of the values in the variables asked. Table 12.1 is a frequency table for V₁ 'interested in sports' in the horse race track survey.

The table provides the variable label and the value labels that have been programmed into the computer. It shows, at the bottom, the number of valid

Table 12.2
Frequency Table with Statistics for V₂; Events Attended

```
V2   HOW MANY EVENTS
```

CATEGORY LABEL	CODE	ABSOLUTE FREQ.	RELATIVE FREQ	VALID FREQ.	CUM FREQ.
	1.	82	11.7	16.5	16.5
	2.	98	14.0	19.7	36.2
	3.	65	9.3	13.1	49.3
	4.	44	6.2	8.9	58.2
	5.	58	8.3	11.7	69.9
	6.	32	4.6	6.4	76.3
	7.	26	3.7	5.2	81.5
	8.	16	2.3	3.2	84.7
	9.	76	10.9	15.3	100.0
	0.	203	29.0	MISSING	MISSING
	TOTAL	700	100.0	100.0	100.0

```
VALID CASES 497    MISSING CASES 203

MEAN    3.159    STD DEV  1.606    MEDIAN   3.007    MODE    2.000
RANGE   8.000    MINIMUM  1.000    MAXIMUM  9.000
```

cases—those who actually answered the question in one of the value categories—
and the number of missing cases. Everyone in the survey answered V_1 in one
of the four categories. The first column titled "code" is the value number coded
for each category: "very interested" was coded "1." The second column,
absolute frequency, is the number of respondents who gave each coded answer:
228 respondents said they were "very interested." Relative frequency is the
percent of all survey respondents represented by the number in each category:
228 respondents is 32.6 percent of 700 completed questionnaires.

Valid frequency is the percent 228 represents of all those answering the question. Because everyone answered this question—there are no missing cases—
valid frequency is the same as relative frequency. However, most variables do
have missing cases, so valid frequency is the column usually referred to in a
frequency table. It shows that about one-third of the survey were very interested
in sports, about 40 percent were interested, 17 percent were not very interested,
and 11 percent said they were not at all interested in sports. The cumulative
(CUM) frequency adds the valid frequency percentages: 32.6 percent plus the
next valid frequency of 39.3 percent equals 71.9 percent; 71.9 percent plus 17
percent equals 88.9 percent; 88.9 percent plus 11.1 percent equals 100 percent.
The cumulative frequency shows more quickly that about 70 percent of the
survey generally was interested in sports (those "very interested" and those
"interested" combined).

One other frequency table (Table 12.2) shows an additional advantage of frequencies in providing information. It indicates how an interval-measure variable (in which the value in a meaningful number rather than a label) can be viewed with summary statistics.

Again, the frequency table provides the variable label, "how many events," and the number of valid and missing cases. Here, however, there are 203 missing cases, which should be expected because those who answered they were not very interested or not at all interested in sports were not asked the question. We know from the V_1 frequency table that 28.1 percent of the respondents weren't asked the question, so they are missing cases in V_2. And, apparently, a few other respondents couldn't provide the number of sports events they attended, so their answers would have been coded zero and they become missing cases in V_2. Having missing cases for V_2 demonstrates the valid frequency column's importance. For example, it would be a mistake to say 11.7 percent of the sample had been to one sports event during the past year. Actually, nearly a third weren't asked the question, so the proper assessment is to say 16.5 percent of those who answered the question attended one sports event. The cumulative frequency column also deletes missing values. It shows that just as half the respondents who answered this question has attended three or fewer sports events, slightly more that three-quarters had attended fewer than seven sports events.

But because this variable's measurement level is an interval, the numbers can be averaged to yield measures of central tendency and dispersion. The mean (arithmetic average) of sports events attended, by those asked the question, was 3.2 events; the standard deviation was 1.6. Standard deviation indicates spread around the mean. For instance, in the example of the new first-grade reader, the mean score on the reading test for classes using the old reader was 82 and the mean score with the new text was 86. However, perhaps with the old book student test scores might have ranged fairly evenly from a high of 90 to a low of 75; with the new book the scores might have ranged fairly evenly from a high of 94 to a low of 43. The standard deviation (range of scores around the mean) for the old book might have been about 4 points; the standard deviation for the new book might have been 18 points. Knowing just the mean and the standard deviation would tell us that the old book is the superior reader. The best readers scored almost as high using the old book as those using the new, but the worst readers scored much higher with the old book. We could conclude that this new book will leave a lot of first-graders at an unacceptably low reading level, and justifiably reject the new text on that basis.

The higher the standard deviation (in relation to the mean), the more variability there is in scores. Median is the score at which half the respondents are below and half are above. The cumulative frequency often allows a quick estimate of the median because it usually shows the halfway point: 49.3 percent of the respondents had attended one, two or three sports events; the median actually is 3.007. Mode is the value most respondents answered. Since most respondents (98 of them) said they attended two sports events, the mode is "2." Zero, with its 203 respondents, would have been the mode, but zero has been declared a

Figure 12.5
Crosstabulation of Sex and Interest in Sports

```
*   *   *   *   *   *   *   *   *   *   *   *   *   *   *   *   *   *   *   *   *   *
    V21     SEX                         BY    V1    INTEREST IN SPORTS
*   *   *   *   *   *   *   *   *   *   *   *   *   *   *   *   *   *   *   *   *   *

                    | V1
           COUNT  |                        |  NOT    | NO IN   |
           ROW %  | VERY    | INTER    |  VERY   | TEREST  |
           COL %  | INTER   | ESTED    |  INTER  | AT      |
           TOT %  | ESTED 1 |       2. | ESTED 3 | ALL  4. |
    V21    ---------+---------+----------+---------+---------+
              1.  |   168   |   133    |    38   |    22   |  361
    MALE          |  46.5   |  36.9    |  10.5   |   6.1   | 51.6
                  |  73.7   |  48.4    |  31.9   |  28.2   |
                  |  24.0   |  19.0    |   5.4   |   3.1   |
           ---------+---------+----------+---------+---------+
              2.  |    60   |   142    |    81   |    56   |  339
    FEMALE        |  17.7   |  41.9    |  23.9   |  16.5   | 48.4
                  |  26.3   |  51.6    |  68.1   |  71.8   |
                  |   8.6   |  20.3    |  11.6   |   8.0   |
                  ---------+----------+---------+---------+

           COLUMN    228       275        119        78        700
           TOTAL    32.6      39.3       17.0      11.1      100.0
```

CHI SQUARE = 12.835   3 DEGREES OF FREEDOM   SIGNFICIANCE = .012
NUMBER OF MISSING OBSERVATIONS =   0

missing value for this variable. The last row of numbers is the range, the minimum and the maximum. "Range" is derived by subtracting the minimum value from the maximum value.

Frequencies is normally the first computer run done on a data set. Researchers learn a lot about the general scope of answers from the first read-through of the frequencies data. In fact, frequencies provides enough data description to usually answer most of the research questions without going further into the data set. In the horse race track survey, the researcher will know what percent of people are interested in sports, attend events, favor the track, think gambling is morally wrong, have lived in the country ten years or less, are Methodist, or make less than $30,000 a year. What won't be known is how these variables interact: Are the poorest residents more interested in sports and more likely to favor the race track? Frequencies hint at the interacting relationships but can't provide definitive answers. More sophisticated statistics are needed.

CROSSTABS, or contingency tables, are probably the next most heavily relied upon statistical tool. Figure 12.5 shows a contingency table printout for two variables in the horse race study. The objective is to determine if there is a difference between men's and women's interest in sports. A lot of information is presented in a CROSSTABS table, and that often makes it difficult to interpret.

However, it is easier to read if viewed in its constituent portions. The table is labeled at the top to indicate that V_{21}, 'sex,' is being compared with V_1, 'interest in sports.' Variable 1 is the column variable, with values printed and labeled at the top of each of the four columns; V_{21} is the row variable with its values, "1" for male and "2" for female, printed at the left of each of the two rows.

The next label is the reminder in the upper-left corner of the boxes that the four numbers inside the boxes refer, respectively, to count, row percentage, column percentage, and total percentage. Looking at the first enclosed box— that for males who said they are very interested in sports—the top number of 168 means that many respondents were males and said they were very interested in sports. This count is the actual number of respondents who fit the two criteria of being male and very interested. The second number in the box, 46.5 percent, is the row percentage. Reading across it indicates that 46.5 percent of the males were very interested in sports. The third number is the column percentage of 73.7 percent. It is read down the column to determine that 73.7 percent of those who were very interested in sports are males.

The last number inside each box is the percentage that the respondents in the box constitute of all respondents. All respondents are given at the lower right-hand corner of the table, outside the box. The fourth number in box one indicates that 168 respondents who are very interested males constitute 24 percent of the entire number of respondents who answered this question.

Row totals are given at the right, outside the boxes. The top figure shows there were 361 males or 51.6 percent of the total respondents, and 339 females or 48.4 percent of the respondents. Column totals are outside the boxes at the bottom of each. There were 228 people who were very interested in sports (32.6 percent of the total people); 275 or 39.3 who were interested in sports; 119 or 17.0 percent not very interested; and 78 or 11.1 percent not at all interested in sports.

At the bottom of the CROSSTABS table is a row of statistical outcomes for the observations reported in the boxes of the table. Two of these are pertinent to the discussion: number of missing observations (in this case, none), and significance. Significance is the probability of significance level that indicates here that differences as great as the ones reported in the table could be expected to be found by chance only 0.012 times out of 100 such samples. Differences this great would occur by chance less than two times out of 100, so the differences found here can be assumed real differences worthy of reporting to the client.

What are these differences? The row percentages show that males are much more likely than females to be interested in sports: There is a steady drop in the percentage of males as interest moves from very interested to no interest. Nearly 85 percent of the males are either very interested or interested in sports. The row percentages show females are less interested in sports than males, but the pattern is not exactly opposite. Instead, a majority of females are interested in sports too, but they're split about 60 percent interested and 40 percent not interested. Looking at the column percentage in the boxes (the third number), it is evident that males are nearly three times as likely to be very interested in sports as females. However, both sexes are equally likely to be "interested" in sports. Three times as many females as males are not interested in sports.

These findings aren't particularly surprising, except that researchers may not have anticipated that the percentage of females "interested" in sports is equal to the number of males giving this particular response. But the CROSSTABS does support the common assumption that males are more interested in sports than females. Based on the CROSSTABS outcome, the client might be told to include some female interest messages in a campaign emphasizing that horse racing is a sport. "Thoroughbred racing is the sport of kings . . . and queens," should be a more effective campaign theme than ignoring the female interest potential.

The CROSSTABS procedure requires care in interpretation, but it does offer a lot of information about the interrelationship of two or more variables in the study. It is the statistic of choice for most comparisons between demographic variables and opinion measures. Using it allows data analysts to determine if some kinds of people possess different views than others. For instance, the income, race, and religion variables may be critical in isolating which groups of people favor the track. Knowing the views of particular types of people will help the client aim specific messages at target audiences during the campaign.

But a limitation of the CROSSTABS (chi-square) statistic is that it is used on nominal data: categories rather than ordinal or interval data. Another analytic procedure is appropriate for these more sophisticated levels of measurement.

BREAKDOWN is the procedure for the analysis of variance statistics used with interval data. The objective is to determine if there are differences in means among three or more groups. Figure 12.6 presents a BREAKDOWN table for age based on the response to V_{12}, "Would you vote for a horse race track in this county?"

As with the CROSSTABS table, BREAKDOWN is clearly titled to show that age, the criterion variable, is being "broken down" by answers to the voting question. The researcher is interested in knowing the average age of the respondents who said yes, no, or don't know to the voting question. Additionally, there are significant differences in the mean age of those who gave each of these answers to the voting question. Variable 12 is a nominal variable with three categories ("1" for yes; "2" for no; and "3" for don't know). Age is an interval variable in which the values stand for numbers of years a respondent has lived.

Using the three values in V_{12}, BREAKDOWN shows the average age of the people who gave each of the three value answers. It shows that the entire population's mean age (in this case the 676 people who answered the voting question and gave their year of birth; 24 didn't answer one or more of the two questions) was 43.8 years old. The entire population's age standard deviation was 12.6 years, suggesting that about two-thirds of the sample were between age 31 and 55. But the average age of the respondents who said they would vote for a horse race track in the county was 35.2 years old. This is in distinct

Figure 12.6
Breakdown of Age by "Favor Racing in County"

```
------------------------------------------------------------
    D E S C R I P T I O N    O F    S U B P O P U L A T I O N S
------------------------------------------------------------

    CRITERION VARIABLE    AGE
    BROKEN DOWN BY        V12   'favor racing in county'
------------------------------------------------------------

    VARIABLE       VALUE LABEL      MEAN      STD DEV   CASES

FOR ENTIRE POPULATION                43.822    12.597    676

       V12         1 yes            35.157     9.323    328
       V12         2 no             46.491    14.875    189
       V12         3 don't know     48.824    15.246    159

        TOTAL CASES =    676
      MISSING CASES =     24 OR   3.4 PCT.
              SIG. =     .034
```

contrast with those who said no (average age 46.5) and those who said they didn't know (48.8 years old). We know these differences in age are real differences because the significance level (SIG.) is 0.034, or only about three times out of 100 samples could differences in age this great be found by chance.

The researcher should report this finding to the client noting that those opposed to the horse race track and those who haven't yet made up their minds are older. Campaign messages to persuade voters whose average age is in their late 40s should avoid recent rock-'n-roll background music and other possible appeals to a younger audience. Instead, upbeat music from the late 1950s or 1960s might be more likely to grab this audience's attention. Also, there is likely to be a difference in the periodicals these older target audience members read and the radio stations they listen to. Such media purchasing suggestions also should be reported to the client.

CONCLUSION

The data analysis procedures described are only a few of the possible methods used to determine outcomes of a formal research survey. The presentation indicates data analysis is, in some respects, not as difficult as the beginning researcher might have imagined. Even with the brief overview presented, it is certainly possible to understand the process and grasp implications that might be applied to other hypotheses in the horse race track study—or in a wide variety of more usual public relations research projects. On the other hand, the presentation suggests many of these data analysis procedures are complicated. An underlying theme has been that there are dozens of more sophisticated procedures beyond the scope of a beginning research methods text and beyond the capabilities of a public relations professional who is directing his or her first formal survey project.

Many organizations need information that can be obtained only through survey research. It is the public relations practitioner's responsibility to ensure that an organization has the information it needs. The public relations professional has a further duty to encourage management to support survey research projects when that is the appropriate strategy for meeting information needs. Practitioners who are less than comfortable with the procedures should rely on hired assistance including commercial consulting firms and faculty research expertise at nearby universities. There is no requirement to jump into a survey research project without a reliable life preserver.

SUMMARY

When the survey is complete and the questionnaire forms are stacked on the public relations researcher's desk, it is time for serious data analysis. Many practitioners call upon statisticians and commercial consulting firms at this point (outside experts should have been called in at the beginning if it could be anticipated their help would be needed at the data analysis stage). But with the recent advances in statistical programs available for personal computers, practitioners can attempt even sophisticated data analysis themselves. This chapter provides the steps of: (1) creating a codebook; (2) using coding sheets to transform the answers into numbers a computer can analyze; (3) accessing SPSS^x; and (4) selecting the proper program analysis commands. The concept of statistical significance is also presented.

While the data analysis procedures shown are only a few of the possible ones, most practical public relations projects require no more than this level of sophistication. Still, the public relations professional is responsible for providing reliable answers to clients or management. The assistance of data analysis experts should be sought when it is needed.

ADDITIONAL READING

Babbie, Earl R. *The Practice of Social Research*. Belmont, CA: Wadsworth, 1979, pp. 357–75.

Bowers, John Waite, and John A. Courtright. *Communication Research Methods*. Glenview, IL: Scott, Foresman, 1984, pp. 174–90.

Danielson, Wayne A. "Data Processing." In *Research Methods in Mass Communication*, ed. Guido H. Stempel III and Bruce H. Westley. Englewood Cliffs, NJ: Prentice Hall, 1981, pp. 105–18.

Kerlinger, Fred Nichols. *Behavioral Research: A Conceptual Approach*, 2d ed. New York: Holt, Rinehart and Winston, 1979.

Norusis, Marija J. *SPSS^x Introductory Statistics Guide*. New York: McGraw-Hill, 1983.

SPSS, Inc. *SPSS^x User's Guide*. New York: McGraw-Hill, 1983.

Wimmer, Roger D., and Joseph R. Dominick. *Mass Media Research: An Introduction*, 2d ed. Belmont, CA: Wadsworth, 1987, pp. 409–25.

13   Reporting Survey Results

Although the examples used in the text to explain survey research have been one-shot studies designed to answer specific information needs, usually on deadline, such studies are far from the ideal. In fact, public relations practitioners should consider survey research part of their arsenal of tools to remain abreast of current attitudes and to tap changes in attitudes.

TAPPING TRENDS

Survey research is a powerful tool for maintaining constant surveillance of the environment. It can be used to answer specific public relations questions in emergencies, but it is a far better resource for tapping trends over time. For instance, the Cumberland Presbyterian Church readership study served a specific need at a special time, but the church would probably have served its members better, improved its two magazines, and saved money during a 30-year period had it instituted readership studies of its publications on a continuing basis, say every five years, from 1960 through 1990. Comparisons of reader interest in content would have suggested deleting some regular magazine columns and developing others. Additionally, the changing interests of readers would have been identified and the church would have been more aware of the changing demographics of its members.

If an organization hopes to remain a viable institution—a leader in its field and an innovator in products or services—it will have a formal research program to tap the trends that foreshadow social or industry changes destined to influence company policy. Public relations professionals should be sensitive to the changes, identified in on-going survey projects, and include these trends in their reports to management. For instance, it is sensible to include items on questionnaires that ask employees about job satisfaction today compared with five years ago, or to ask if today's newsletter is more or less informative than it was three years ago.

REPORTING TO MANAGEMENT

When the data from a survey have been analyzed, it is time to write a report to the client or to management. Public relations practitioners often worry that reporting the results of formal research is beyond their writing expertise. Actually, the public relations writer is probably the best trained professional to put together such a report. He or she has several distinct advantages over even a commercial research firm:

1. Public relations training emphasizes the specific writing skills of taking someone else's information, sometimes very technical, and writing about it in a manner that can be understood by a general audience.

2. The public relations professional works directly with management, or the client, and is familiar with the background information needs that initiated the research project.

3. By overseeing the project, the public relations professional has knowledge about how the study was done, why the questionnaire items were chosen, and what the outcomes were as they relate to the client's specific concerns.

4. No one is in a better position—after doing the informal literature review—to relate the outcomes of this study to similar situations in the past.

5. No one is in a better position than the public relations professional to make recommendations about how to achieve results, based on the survey's findings.

Some considerations about reporting survey results to management or the client are discussed in the following sections.

Management Is Accustomed to Research Reports

Remember that organization presidents and division heads read a lot of technical reports as part of their daily routine. People at this level of leadership prepare budgets, read research and development reports, sales projections, marketing studies, etc. They are familiar with the technical jargon associated with research. In fact, the public relations vice-president may worry that a survey research report is too technical, but will probably find no one at the monthly board meeting asks what margin of error is because they understand this concept; not including it would raise questions. Business reports are loaded with figures, tables, and the jargon of statistical probability. Management is likely to be pleasantly surprised when the public relations department offers solid documentation of attitudes and opinions, couched in the same business terms used by professionals in marketing, sales, or quality control.

Simplicity of Style

The public relations professional's writing skills should be able to improve the usual business report's readability. Knowing the jargon is no excuse for parading it in a manner that interferes with clarity. Keep the survey report as simple as possible.

Highlights

Begin the report with a summary of highlights: major findings from the survey that contain the answers to key questions the client asked. Highlights may include findings that go beyond the specific information needs sought through the project; certainly any major, unexpected findings should be included in this first section of the report. The highlights section may be one or two pages long. Each finding included should be no more than one paragraph in length, and there should be a reference at the end of each finding to the page in the report where this outcome is fully explained. If possible, the highlight findings should be arranged in descending order of importance—an inverted pyramid presentation—to focus attention on the most critical outcomes of the study. Highlights, then, are the study's major results, presented in brief at the beginning of the report so they stand out even on a hurried read-through.

Methodology

Following the highlights, the first full text section of the report should contain complete details on how, when, and why the study was done, as well as certain key elements of the research method. A methodology section usually begins with the concerns that initiated the study—a brief overview of why the research project was done.

Other elements that belong in the report are those suggested by the American Association for Public Opinion Research (AAPOR), a national organization of opinion research firms and consultants. The following are considered the minimum standards of professional practice for reporting survey results:

1. Who sponsored the survey and who conducted the poll? While the client or company management may be familiar with these facts, they should still be included in the methodology of the report in case others who don't know receive the report.

2. When was the survey done? Be specific about exactly when the field work—the interviews—was carried out. If there were "news" events or policy changes that occurred before the field work, during the field work, or between field work and the time the report was written, this information should be included because it might influence how the report's findings should be interpreted.

3. What group or groups of people were polled? The population sampled should be clearly stated in the report. Did the study involve all company employees or only

hourly paid workers? Was the survey population defined as registered voters or every-one 18 and older?

4. Was a probability sample used? If the study was not based on a random sample of the population, the findings can't be generalized to the population. Be specific about how the sampling was done. Often there are limitations that affect the results. For instance, if interviewers were told to alternate between male and female respondents, the sample will reflect a 50—50 percent split in sex when that might not be the case in the population under study.

5. How were respondents contacted: mail, phone, or in-person? Fully explain the inter-viewing procedure because it frequently does affect survey results.

6. How many people were surveyed? What is the exact size of the sample? Additionally, it is necessary to indicate the response rate because a large percentage of refusals makes the final sample a potentially biased segment of the initial sample.

7. What is the margin of error? Give the figure and explain what margin of error means.

8. How many in the survey responded to each question? It isn't necessary to provide an exact count of responses to every item because several people are likely to be missing values for each question. But it is necessary to note items for which a substantial portion of the respondents did not answer, perhaps because they weren't asked. Screen-ing questions in a survey can decrease later responses significantly. A survey of 700 may have postscreening questions to which only 400 responses were made. These details must be specified in the report.

9. Is the exact wording of key questions given? The wording of questions is one of the primary error-producing aspects of a survey. Unexpected and unexplainable outcomes of a study are often attributable to peculiarly worded questions rather than true attitude measurement. Those reading a research report deserve to know the exact wording of the survey's key questions.

The methodology section could be five- to ten-pages long. Many readers may only skim through this section, but the minimum information reporting standards still must be met. Readers who have little knowledge about this study or about survey research generally, will go through the methodology section carefully.

Optional Review Section

The report may contain a slightly longer section on why the study was done. Although some explanation of "why" will introduce the methodology section, more details of purpose may be required; how many depends on the complexity of the problem. This section should contain a list of the hypotheses or research questions with some explanation of why these questions were selected to guide the study. The review section is the proper place for any review of the literature that will be included in the report. Findings of past studies, which may have prompted the current study's questions, belong in the review section, as do summaries of similar situations the public relations director may have uncovered in the informal information-gathering process. Because outcomes of similar studies usually have relevance to this survey, an overview of previous findings should precede the present study's findings so comparisons can be made in the body of the report.

Body of the Report

This section should provide a detailed analysis of the survey's findings and how they were derived. The body of the report is a step-by-step rendering of the processes that led to development of the survey scales, the order of questions, the decision about which demographic items to include, and any other procedural matters that may influence the findings.

Findings, however, are the mainstay of the body of the report. It may be necessary to divide the body into subsections, perhaps using the hypotheses as headings to direct the reader from one set of findings to the next. Whereas the highlights section gave an overview, this section should detail the findings, including the significance level of the major differences found. Tables should be included in the body of the report. The following rules govern when and how to use tables effectively:

1. A table is designed to provide a quick graphic overview of the finding being discussed. If it is more efficient to merely state the finding in the text of the report, do that instead of using a table. But if the finding involves several figures that can be summarized in a table, the table is preferred. Even if a finding is presented in a table, it should be included in the text of the report with further explanations of its importance.

2. Tables should be titled with as many words as are necessary to tell the reader exactly what the table's contents are. Vague titles won't quickly orient the reader to the table.

3. Label the contents of the table as completely as possible so there is no question about which variables are being displayed or what the values in those variable were. Use full column headings where possible so the reader doesn't have to interpret abbreviations or decide if the numbers are percentages, averages, or some other statistic.

4. Don't crowd a table with too much information. Crowding confounds the reader and makes the table look like a jumble of numbers. It defeats the quick graphic read a table is supposed to provide. Leave white space and round off the numbers to the nearest whole number or to one decimal place, if that is possible (usually it is).

5. Use explanatory footnotes in the tables, if that helps promote quick reader understanding. But don't get carried away with footnotes. Too many required explanations suggest the table presentation is too complicated. Remove the least important information in the table or reconstruct it in a way that avoids footnotes entirely.

Although each of the findings will be accompanied by explanations and recommendations, the body should conclude with a summary of major recommendations from the study. If there are enough outcomes from which recommendations can be made, a separate recommendation summary section should be added after the body of the report.

Appendixes

Additional elements after the report's body should be kept to a minimum, but it is proper to include the questionnaire form as an appendix. Other elements appropriate to an appendix might be a margin-of-error table or detailed footnotes, but only if these are essential in explaining some aspect of the report at a level that would interfere with easy reading of the text.

NEWS RELEASES

Should the media be informed about public relations research results? It depends on the study's purpose, but frequently the answer is yes. A survey's results often are worthy of public attention. Whether the client or the boss agrees usually depends on survey outcomes. Sometimes findings are part of an organization's competitive assets. Divulging them would decrease the competitive edge gained by underwriting the survey in the first place. Sometimes the results are of interest only to internal audiences or management. Sometimes the results are simply embarrassing to the organization. In these instances, the survey findings will not become part of a news release any more than the organization would wish to divulge union problems or a discrimination settlement.

The public relations professional can face an ethical dilemma when some of the survey findings are positive and some are negative. Naturally the firm would like to promote the positive and stifle the negative. In these instances the best public relations advice to clients or to management is to release either the entire report or none of it. The news media have become more adept at interpreting survey research reports. Journalists are likely to uncover any attempt to withhold portions of a report; this will generate more negative publicity than any damage an unfavorable report is likely to. And the media will probably not publish a survey-based news release unless it is accompanied by the full report. Major newspapers and magazines have established policies governing their publication of survey research reports. These rules usually include receiving the full report in sufficient time to analyze it before publication.

However, some clients hope the findings of research reports—such as the horse race track survey—will serve as the basis of a positive news release to the media. If there is enough favorable public attitude toward the race track, the client will be anxious to have the researcher supply the media with a news release and the entire survey report. Such a news article will be of interest to the public and will serve the client's purposes. The news release may be used as the kick-off piece for the referendum campaign.

Here, in a slightly altered form, is the horse race track story that appeared in a local newspaper. It was the result of a 1985 survey done in a manner approximating the one discussed in this text, with a similar questionnaire. The researcher provided the newspaper with a story similar to this one as a public information release.

A horse race track in Eastgate would have won by a couple of lengths if the issue had been put to a vote here in March. That is the conclusion of a telephone survey taken in the country by John Brown Public Relations, Inc., for the group of local promoters sponsoring the track referendum. When asked, "Would you vote for a horse race rack in the Eastgate area," 60 percent of the survey said they would, 30 percent said they would not, and 10 percent were undecided.

The 60 percent favorable figure is beyond the margin of error rate of about 5 percent for this survey. With more than 55 percent saying they would vote for a race track, had the issue been on a ballot during March, it would have passed.

Many survey respondents said if the majority of Eastgaters want a pari-mutuel track, it should be built. Typical was a high-income male respondent who said, "People should have a choice; gambling should not be legislated against."

Other survey findings were:

- A horse race track for Eastgate is not a racially split issue. Both blacks and whites said they would vote for a local track in nearly equal proportions of more than three out of five.
- Men would have carried the issue with 73 percent favoring the track versus 57 percent of women favoring it.
- Seventy-three percent of the better educated residents—those with college degrees or post-college years—said they would vote for the measure versus only 54 percent of those with less education.
- Residents of the area who had been in town less than 10 years favored the track more than those who had lived here longer. Some 72 percent of the newer residents said they would vote for the track versus about 62 percent of residents who have been here more than 10 years.
- Survey respondents under age 55 favored the race track at slightly above 66 percent while only about half of those over age 55 said they would vote for it.
- Of those who said they generally vote Republican, 67 percent favored the track versus 60 percent of those who said they generally vote Democratic.
- Moral or religious grounds were the chief reason given for opposing the race track.

The survey involved a sample of 403 persons chosen by randomly selecting residential numbers from the Eastgate and adjoining cities telephone directory, then replacing the last two digits with random numbers—a frequently used method of local survey sampling. Although the survey sample is relative small, it is representative of the Eastgate area population.

Moral Arguments Spark Opponents

A recent arrival to Eastgate said, "I don't approve of gambling in any form or fashion." Another respondent, a white male in the middle-income range, said: "It brings on more corruption and crime. The increase in revenues isn't enough to justify the increase in the police force."

Other comments against gambling were: "People would spend their wages at the track and not support their families"; "There are already too many bets going on in Eastgate"; and "It would bring a lot of bad, drunken people into town."

Increasing the state's income was by far the chief reason for supporting the track. Two of five persons who said they would have voted for the race track said it would keep dollars in the state, bring jobs and tourists, or raise state income.

Favoring the track for Eastgate apparently is closely tied to a person's general interest in sports: The more interest, the more likely the survey respondent was to favor a track.

Survey Done at Legislation Start

Interviewing for the survey was done when the race track proposal had just completed its final stages of consideration in the legislature.

Although the race track was not receiving as much media attention during the survey as it is now, slightly more than half the respondents said "yes" when asked, "Are you familiar with the proposal being offered in the state to allow legalized horse racing?" Only 37 percent were able to say for sure that the bill called for local approval before a new track could be built in a county.

Those favoring having a track in Eastgate said they view the issue as an economic rather than moral consideration. One middle-aged male with some graduate work said, "A horse track will bring in more revenues and a better cash flow to Eastgate, utilizing its hotels and restaurants."

A lifelong Eastgate woman said, "It would bring in tax revenues we wouldn't have to pay out of our own pockets." Tax considerations were instrumental in many respondents' views.

Although favoring the track did vary with family income levels, there was no consistent pattern of how income might affect a voter's view about the track.

Sports Interest also Measured

A "sports interest scale" was established by responses to six survey questions about "which of the following do you do on a regular basis": watch sports on television, listen to sports on radio, read a sports magazine, read the newspaper's sports section every day, talk about sports with friends, or make friendly bets on sports events. The average number of yeses to this series of questions was 2.3, with 27 percent of the survey saying no to all questions.

Survey respondents were also asked, "How many sports events have you actually gone to see in the last year?" The average number was 3.5, although 35 had attended no events in the last year.

Other considerations overshadowed non-interest in sports among some respondents. A young high school graduate who scored zero on all sports-interest questions said he would vote in favor of the track because it would "keep the money on this side of the river instead of everyone going to the other state for horse racing."

However, another male scoring the highest possible mark on all sports-interest questions said he wouldn't want a race track "because I don't like gambling around the area in which I live."

In viewing the results, caution must be taken that the favorable community "vote" by a sample of respondents in March does not imply an actual vote on the issue at some future time would result in the measure passing.

Table 13.1 was prepared with the news release on the horse race track survey.

Table 13.1
Percentage of Respondents Saying They Would "Vote for a Horse Race Track in the Eastgate Area" during March, 1985 Survey

	Percentage Voting "Yes"
AGE:	
25 to 34 years	67%
35 to 54 years	65
Over age 54	56
LENGTH OF RESIDENCE:	
under 10 years in area	73%
10 years or more in area	62
INCOME:	
under $15,000 annually	72%
$15,000 - $24,999	56
$25,000 - $39,999	6
$40,000 and over	74
EDUCATIONAL LEVEL:	
finished grades 1 - 12	56%
some college	63
college degree or more	77
RACE:	
black	69%
white	63
SEX:	
male	73%
female	57

SUMMARY

Methods for reporting survey results to management and clients are discussed in the chapter. Particularly important are those findings that can be documented over time: trend comparisons that show how opinions develop and change. Such comparisons can be made only if organizations adopt formal research as a continuing strategy for information gathering.

Actually writing the report is part of the arsenal of tool skills public relations professionals possess. In most instances, once the data analysis is complete, the public relations practitioner is the individual most capable of writing the report. The practitioner should be aware that organization management or a client are likely to possess extensive background in reading research reports. Still, a report should be written in a manner that offers the reader a quick, easy grasp of the findings and their implications. Sections of the report are discussed along with AAPOR guidelines for minimal disclosure of research methods. Often public relations practitioners will provide research findings to the mass media through news releases. A news story on the horse race track survey, similar to one that actually appeared in a local newspaper, is presented.

ADDITIONAL READING

Beauchamp, Tom L., et al., eds. *Ethical Issues in Social Science Research*. Baltimore: John Hopkins University Press, 1982.

Lake, Celinda C., and Pat Callbeck. *Public Opinion Polling*. Covelo, CA: Island Press, 1988, pp. 103–21.

Nager, Norman R., and T. Harrell Allen. *Public Relations: Management by Objectives*. New York: Longman, 1984.

Rivers, William L., and Susan L. Harrington. *Finding Facts: Research Writing Across the Curriculum*, 2d ed. Englewood Cliffs, NJ: Prentice Hall, 1988.

Rubin, Rebecca B., Alan M. Rubin, and Linda J. Piele. *Communications Research: Strategies and Sources*. Belmont, CA: Wadsworth, 1986, pp. 43–49.

14 Experiments

The formal research method most closely associated with survey research is experiments, but this decision-making strategy is infrequently used in public relations practice. Infrequent use of experiments is unfortunate because experiments can be the most effective way to derive important answers related to an organization's internal operations. There are possibly three reasons experiments aren't relied upon more in public relations:

1. Practitioners are less familiar with experimental procedures; hence they are less likely to consider using an experimental design. Survey research, a common textbook method of measuring public opinion, now is a time-honored procedure that gets a lot of media attention and considerable space in public relations journals. Examples based on survey research abound in public relations case problems, PRSA Silver Anvil awards competitions, and even local public relations campaigns. Surveys are the "in" methodology, so they come to mind more frequently.

2. Experiments are associated with academic research rather than practical applications. Exceptions are experiments that measure the effectiveness of television commercials or advertising campaign messages. But these practical applications often seem foreign to public relations needs. Practitioners don't see the transition from an experimental "laboratory" setting to the organizational workplace as the simple and practical progression it actually is.

3. Experimental research can be a public relations nightmare if it isn't done properly. There is always a danger in working closely with human subjects. The potential for embarrassing or compromising the organization multiplies when subjects are employees.

While these reservations keep experiments from being as popular in public relations research as surveys, there are hundreds of instances in which experiments should be the research methodology of choice.

RANGE OF APPLICATIONS

Experiments should be used to test the effectiveness of communication messages. Public relations messages may range from the contents of a newsletter or magazine—as well as its graphic design—to slogans for a public relations campaign. An effective monthly newsletter may become stale over time without the editorial staff members noticing that their subtle changes in content and graphics have lessened reader interest. An experiment is the appropriate method to learn quickly if the intended audience believes this month's newsletter is as interesting as the one published this time last year.

Consider a public relations campaign designed to promote safety in a factory during the summer months. The intended slogan or theme for the campaign, thought appropriate because it is tied to a company-sponsored employees' baseball league, is "Strike Out for Safety." An experiment might remind the public relations director that "strike" is not the kind of word the company likes to promote. Or an experiment might signal the public relations director that workers exposed to the "Strike Out for Safety" slogan fail to see its relation to safety. Instead of trashing a ton of posters, the safety slogan can be changed before it becomes an embarrassing campaign theme.

Experiments should be used to pretest organizational innovations. Improvements in products, technology, and even plant facilities can be tested on a segment of the organization's workers before their acceptance is mandated for all workers. The experimental testing can identify any unanticipated problems with acceptance and it can result in a smoother acceptance of the innovations. For instance, newspapers found in the 1970s that computers could reduce costs, increase speed, and improve accuracy. Many editorial departments merely removed the typewriters from reporters' desks and replaced them with video display terminals. The result was chaos as the older reporters rebelled against the machines and resented management's interference in their daily work environment. Instead of reaping the expected benefits from new technology, many newspaper managers found they had created an internal public relations problem that interfered with workers' routines and productivity. Newspapers that adopted computers later learned from the innovators' mistakes and planned careful experiments to introduce the machines to segments of their newsroom personnel in a less threatening manner. At these newspapers, journalists viewed receiving a desktop computer as a reward instead of a punishment. The result was a smooth adoption which led to management's expected benefits in cost, speed, and accuracy.

Experiments are the correct research strategy in planning organizational policy changes. Too often a company's or agency's directors mandate policy changes without regard to potential resentment or misunderstanding. The more dramatic the planned policy change, the more crucial it is to use an experiment to determine how best to implement the change. A wise management team will rely on the public relations director for advice on the correct method to affect change. These are the situations in which public relations practitioners can earn their bonuses or risk termination. A situation involving policy change management will be used to describe the steps in doing a public relations experiment.

SURVEYS VERSUS EXPERIMENTS

Surveys are designed to gather data in real-world settings and to look at comparisons in the data that support (or fail to support) expectations (hypotheses). Because they take place in the "real world," surveys have a built-in element of validity. We can assume if a survey shows 60 percent of the electorate intends to vote for a candidate in next week's runoff, barring an unexpected event in the interim, that candidate will win the election.

An example more appropriate to public relations is a survey to determine local residents' attitude toward their utility company. But because surveys occur in the real world, there is usually a confluence of influences that mitigate against finding effects. The utility company survey may show that residents don't know much about the utility company and certainly can't answer specific questions about rates, products, or progress the company has made in the past five years. The survey may only show that residents' attitude toward the company is undefined. That, of course, is a research outcome worth knowing, but it is of little help to the utility firm's immediate planning. A survey often produces few significant findings because the public doesn't have enough information to possess a measurable attitude. There are too many distractions in the "real world"—work, school, family, television, shopping, etc.—that decrease knowledge possession.

The variety of everyday life occurrences create other problems for survey research. It is often difficult to determine which independent variables are responsible for the significant findings that might be found. For instance, the horse race track survey included several demographic and attitude measures assumed to influence a respondent's preference for or against the race track. Which of these independent variables is most influential to the decision? Perhaps more important, is there an intervening variable–a reason not measured because it was not included in the survey—that actually explains a respondent's decision for or against the race track?

There are two distinct drawbacks in survey research that experiments are designed to overcome:

1. The "laboratory" setting of an experiment allows researchers to inject a heavy dose of the experimental variable so every subject in the study will be exposed to it and will have knowledge about it. Researchers are likely to find more significant outcomes after an experiment because every subject is exposed to the experimental variables: There will be fewer "don't knows" after the experiment. Infusing the subject with the experimental variable certainly has its associated problems, but it does overcome the lack-of-knowledge disadvantage of surveys.

2. Because the experimental setting is similar to being in a laboratory, external influences that might be intervening variables can be controlled.

PURPOSE AND EXAMPLE

The classic purpose of an experiment is to test hypotheses under controlled conditions. This means the objective is to test a very specific research problem in a manner that provides great confidence in the outcomes reached. When an experiment is completed, researchers should be highly satisfied that their recommendations are correct. Such assurances can be obtained only in controlled situations that allow the experimenter to say "A," the experimental or independent variable, resulted in "B," the dependent variable or outcome. The assumption, then, is that the independent variable caused the outcome.

A public relations situation we will use as an example for experiments is one of the recent corporate management trends: quality circles. Briefly, as described by Thomas J. Peters and Robert H. Waterman, Jr., in *In Search of Excellence,* U.S. corporations adapted the concept of quality circles from management successes in Japan. In the United States, companies have traditionally expected employees to be concerned about product quality because supervisors directed them to be concerned. The management style is vertical and authoritarian. Japanese businesses, however, expect more involvement from employees and allow them more participation in the decision-making process. The Japanese management style is horizontal and more democratic.

Quality circles promote the formation of employee groups aimed at discussion and innovation. Instead of a department's workers being led by their supervisors, employees are in groups composed of an amalgamation of workers and managers from a variety of departments across the organization. The groups are loosely structured and less threatening because members aren't placed in departments according to the corporation's organizational chart. Continuing themes of the quality circle are how to improve the product, production procedures, and workers' satisfaction. The idea is that a better product will be more competitive in world markets, and a better product can only be achieved if quality is every worker's goal.

In 1988, Eastman Kodak Corp. received favorable publicity by instituting quality circles in its copier division. During a year's experimentation, Kodak copier plant managers changed their policy from rewarding production of more machines to rewarding production of better machines. Quality circles were part of Kodak's strategy. In less than one year, the division was able to cut a staff of 700 quality inspectors to about half that number and to post huge gains in copier sales and in profits for two quarters during which American business generally showed little gain. Quality circles got credit for much of the success.

To help you understand public relations experiments, imagine that you are now vice-president of public relations for Precision Industries, a 10,000-employee corporation whose CEO is considering instituting quality circles throughout the work force. The CEO wants you to determine if they will work at Precision. Additionally, the CEO has been approached by a firm called Quality Circle Managers that has offered to organize and operate a quality circle system throughout Precision Industries at a price of $1 million per year. Although QCM's $100-per-employee price seems high, it may be necessary to spend that amount for guaranteed results. Come back in two days with a plan the board can approve.

A less professional public relations vice-president might be shaken by this assignment, but you are on top of this situation. You are familiar with quality circles because you regularly read general business periodicals, newspapers, and public relations trade publications. You know that companies have had success with quality circles; in fact, you've never read about an instance where they didn't work. You have some general impressions about how to organize them, and you can get some pointers by phone this afternoon from colleagues across the country who may have some direct experience with them, or can suggest another public relations contact who has. You aren't even visibly upset about the last-minute notice because, as the professional you are, you knew about QCM's sales pitch to your CEO last week. But a busy couple of days will be required to prepare for the board meeting. You instruct your staff to (1) gather information about QCM, including its proposal to your CEO, its past performance record, and a lengthy interview with a major firm that recently purchased QCM's services; (2) do a library search on quality circles; (3) do a data file search on quality circles; (4) try to locate any published examples of problems associated with quality circles; and (5) prepare a written report overviewing quality circles and a written report on QCM's services, especially those comments from the interview. While the staff is preparing this information package, you will contact your public relations associates and get detailed accounts of their experiences with quality circles.

We will assume all goes well with this preliminary research: No major problems are unearthed in regard to either QCM or quality circles generally. Your report to the board will be ready on time. Your only concern is to plan the best formal research methods to complete your CEO's information needs.

EXPERIMENTAL DESIGN

Hypotheses

The research method is an experiment to answer the following two hypotheses:

1. Quality circles at Precision Industries will result in improved production quality levels and increased employee satisfaction with the company. Improved production quality levels and employee satisfaction levels will result from quality circles organized by QCM and by those organized by Precision's public relations department.

2. There will be no significant difference in production quality levels and employee satisfaction levels between quality circles organized by QCM and those organized by Precision.

The operational definition of the dependent variable "production quality levels" is the same as the one being used now to determine product quality at

Precision Industries: the number of unacceptable units per 100 units produced as determined by the quality control department staff currently assessing standards of product quality. "Employee satisfaction" will be measured by a questionnaire designed to assess employee attitude toward Precision Industries.

Although employee satisfaction with Precision Industries may not be a critical outcome for the present experiment, most public relations programs don't have the advantage of an easily demonstrable dependent variable such as measuring a plant's unacceptable units per 100 units produced. That is one of the chief disadvantages of public relations research. In sales or marketing, it is relatively simple to determine the success of different programs by counting increased product sales. Public relations program outcomes frequently are more ephemeral because their goals relate to attitude changes. Attitudes and opinions are more difficult to measure than dollars or volume increases in product sales. Additionally, when it is possible to measure a change in attitude there is still some question abut the direct, monetary benefits attitude changes have for the organization. Yet the assumption is that if employees' attitudes toward the company improve, there will be an increase in the quality (and perhaps the quantity) of their work. This assumption should be included as an additional check on instituting quality circles in the present example. If nothing else, this additional dependent measure demonstrates how to assess the more ephemeral public relations dimension of attitude change.

General Design

You propose the following experiment:

1. QCM will be paid to do a microcosm quality circle in one production unit during a one-month experiment.
2. Precision's public relations department will organize a similar microcosm quality circle in another production unit for a one-month experiment.
3. Two other production units, similar to the two experimental groups, will be used as control groups. No quality circles will be organized in these units.

The experiment will be designed to maximize control of variables, which is what experiments are particularly adept at doing. The design for this experiment is shown in Figure 14.1. It serves as the discussion point for the remainder of the quality circle experimental example.

When the experiment is finished, you want to be able to tell your CEO that it was the quality circles—rather than some other variable—that resulted in improved attitude and higher production quality levels.

Group Selection

As in survey research, sample selection is equally important in an experiment. But the objectives of an experiment are different from those of a survey. The

Figure 14.1
Quality Circle Experimental Design

	Control Group #1	Control Group #2	Experimental #1 - QCM	Experimental #2 - PR
RANDOMIZE	yes	yes	yes	yes
PRE-TEST	yes			
EXPERIMENT			yes	yes
POST-TEST		yes	yes	yes

survey attempts to generalize from a sample to its defined population, so the sample must be representative of the population. An experiment controls variables, so the samples—or experimental groups—must be selected in a manner that maximizes control of independent variables. This group selection process is called *randomization* and it is done to neutralize potential intervening variables in an experiment.

Let's assume an experiment will take place on two employee groups in the accounting department to determine which of two new computer systems should be purchased for the entire accounting department. One computer is very powerful but less user-friendly; the other is very user-friendly but has limited capacity. Accounting department employees are offered an extra day of vacation if they volunteer for the four-hour experiment and 60 volunteers assemble for the test. They may enter either Room A (powerful computer room) or Room B (friendly computer room). After the four-hour test, it is found that employees simply couldn't cope with the powerful computer instructions. The friendly computer group accomplished its tasks easily.

But before reporting to management that the friendly computer be purchased for the entire department, a questionnaire at the end of the experiment reveals the two groups of employees were not equal. Those who selected the powerful computer room were allowed to go in with their friends—the people they had been talking with in the hall before the experiment. These employees usually had lunch together, were friends away from the plant, had family outings together, etc. The same was true for those who had been talking together in the hallway and chose the friendly computer room. The post-test (after-the-experiment) questionnaire revealed not only that each group was homogeneous but that those in the powerful computer room had completed an average educational level of 12th grade. Those in the friendly computer room had completed an average of two years of college or technical school. The experiment was ruined by an intervening variable, education, which in this case prevented the powerful computer from having a fair test of its potential. Similar intervening variables in an experiment can be the group's sex, occupational level, income, race, length of time with the company, etc.

The best way to neutralize all of these possible intervening variables that might ruin the experiment is to randomize group members. Instead of allowing experimental participants to select which group they will join, the experimenter makes this decision by randomly assigning subjects to groups. Each of the 60 volunteers should have been given a numbered card in the hallway. Those with even (or odd) numbered cards would be assigned to one of the rooms; the others would be assigned to the other experimental room in a random manner. If participants in an experiment are assigned randomly among the control and experimental groups, the assumption is that attribute variables such as sex, age, education, etc., will be neutralized because they will be spread evenly across all groups.

There is another potential bias in group selection for the quality circle example. *Volunteers* for an experiment are often dissimilar to non-volunteers. Having volunteered for the experiment might not be crucial for the accounting computers, particularly if most of the accounting employees were willing to participate. But with quality circles, a volunteer is likely to possess a personality trait different from those in the plant who might want to avoid participation. Volunteers for experiments generally are more curious, more outgoing, more willing to interact with other people, more innovative, etc. Such individuals should thrive in a quality circle situation, and the experiment will seem a success when the quality circles achieve maximum interaction among these volunteer participants. But reporting this success to management may result in an employee public relations disaster as later quality circles across the entire plant bog down in a morass of squabbles by recalcitrant employees who didn't want to participate in the first place. Not only is it necessary to randomize group members in an experiment, but is often necessary to neutralize the effects of personality traits of volunteers.

Controlling for volunteerism should be a consideration when volunteer personality traits may influence the outcome of the experiment or when only a few people volunteer to participate. It is possible to neutralize the volunteer bias in a company because the firm can demand participation. But a more effective public relations tactic is to make the experiment attractive to everyone by increasing the rewards of participation, then selecting subjects in random manner and then randomizing subject assignments across all experimental and control groups.

One other aspect of experimental samples differentiates them from survey samples. Experimental groups can be relatively small. For instance, the groups for the quality circle experiment might be as small as 20 to 30 employees per group. The public relations researcher is not trying to extrapolate findings from sample to population. Instead the assumption is that behavior (or attitude change) identified in experimental groups will be similar to that found in the population from which the experimental subjects were drawn. Such conclusions can be reached with smaller groups because these groups will not be subdivided for further analysis. Outcomes will be based on the behavior patterns of the entire experimental group, and 25 to 50 subjects will provide sufficient evidence.

Pretesting

The usual experimental design will require a pretest of some groups. This is a measure of attitude prior to the experiment that can be compared with the same measure of attitude following exposure to the experimental variable. In the quality circle experiment, no pretest would be necessary if a reduction in the number of unacceptable production units per 100 were the only dependent measure. You know the company's quality control department always measures product quality and has continuing records of unacceptable units. But with the additional dependent measure of attitude toward the company (a customary public relations outcome measurement), the pretest is required. You have to measure attitude before the quality circle experiment takes place to determine if there is an improvement in attitude after the experiment.

Sensitizing

A problem with experimental pretests is that they *sensitize* subjects. Sensitizing means that subjects will be alerted to the purpose of the experiment. If subjects complete the pretest attitude measurement instrument—a questionnaire—before the experiment and then are given the same questionnaire after the experiment, they may try to replicate their answers to the pretest questionnaire. Even if they don't, the pretest questionnaire will alert them that an attitude change is expected. They may report an attitude change on the posttest because they think it is expected rather than because they actually experienced an attitude change. Figure 14.2 shows a brief example of the questionnaire that might be used to measure attitude toward the company. It is evident that using the same form in a pretest and again in a posttest of the same group will present problems for you, the public relations researcher.

There are two ways to avoid sensitizing experimental subjects. One is to *mask* the experiment's purpose. Masking means to hide the real purpose of the experiment so subjects can't figure out exactly what the researcher is trying to measure.

To some extent, all experimental purposes must be masked. For instance, you won't tell subjects until the experiment is completed that the real goal of the quality circles is to show a reduction in the number of acceptable units per 100 and an improvement in attitude toward the company. If you do, you're likely to measure the Hawthorne effect rather than actual opinion change. The Hawthorne effect is a normal result of subjects' participation in an experiment. An esprit de corps develops among participants, who then try harder to achieve satisfactory outcomes for the researcher. That's human nature—part of the ego-

Figure 14.2

Attitude toward Company Questionnaire for Experiment Pretest and Posttest

```
DON'T PUT YOUR NAME ON THIS FORM; IT IS COMPLETELY ANONYMOUS

1. How many years have you worked for Precision Industries:
        ____ less than 5 years
        ____ 5 to 10 years
        ____ 11 to 20 years
        ____ more than 20 years

2. Which is your job title level:
        ____ hourly employee
        ____ supervisor
        ____ manager
        ____ director
        ____ other


Please check the following scales in the blank that indicates whether
you strongly agree, agree, are neutral, disagree or strongly disagree
with each of the following statements about Precision Industries:
```

	Strongly Agree	Agree	Neutral	Disagree	Strongly Disagree
3. Precision is technologically superior to its competitors	/_____	/_____	/_____	/_____	/_____ /
4. The quality of Precision's products is superior	/_____	/_____	/_____	/_____	/_____ /
5. Precision uses its employees and resources wisely	/_____	/_____	/_____	/_____	/_____ /
6. Precision has capable managers and supervisors	/_____	/_____	/_____	/_____	/_____ /
7. Precision is concerned about its own employees	/_____	/_____	/_____	/_____	/_____ /
8. Precision shares information about its goals and objectives	/_____	/_____	/_____	/_____	/_____ /
9. Precision encourages input from its employees	/_____	/_____	/_____	/_____	/_____ /
10. Precision acts on suggestions from its employees	/_____	/_____	/_____	/_____	/_____ /
11. Precision is an enjoyable place to work	/_____	/_____	/_____	/_____	/_____ /

Figure 14.2 Continued

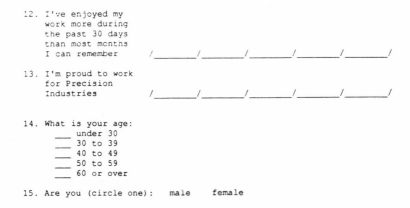

```
12. I've enjoyed my
    work more during
    the past 30 days
    than most months
    I can remember    /_____/_____/_____/_____/_____/_____/

13. I'm proud to work
    for Precision
    Industries        /_____/_____/_____/_____/_____/_____/

14. What is your age:
        ___ under 30
        ___ 30 to 39
        ___ 40 to 49
        ___ 50 to 59
        ___ 60 or over

15. Are you (circle one):   male    female
```

involvement of being selected for the experiment. If subjects know, or guess, the researcher's expectations, the experimental purpose may be ruined.

Yet research ethics require you to divulge enough about the experiment in advance so subjects who agree to participate are making that decision based on an informed judgment of what the experiment entails. You wouldn't tell subjects that they will watch video tapes and then show R-rated tapes with violent content. On the other hand, if you tell them beforehand that the tapes contain violence and you want to know if they enjoy it, those who agree to participate are likely to be people who have a high tolerance for visual violence. So some middle ground must be reached on providing enough explanation of the true experimental topic to let subjects make an informed participation choice, but not enough to divulge the intent of the experiment's outcomes.

Control Groups

The other way to avoid sensitizing subjects is through the experimental design. Figure 14.2 shows two control groups. A control group is used to take pretest and/or posttest measurements of subjects who are not exposed to the experimental variable. This may seem like an unnecessary procedure, but it is the best way to avoid sensitizing subjects and control contamination by any external variables.

Control Group 1 will receive the pretest questionnaire but will not be used as a quality circle group. After receiving the pretest, this group will continue work in the usual manner. Group 1's participation in the experiment is complete when it has completed the pretest questionnaire. Group 2 will not begin the experiment until the end of the month. At that time, Group 2 will be given the posttest— the same questionnaire given to the two experimental groups, but Group 2 will not have participated in the quality circles either. The objective is to measure attitudes in Control Group 1 before the experiment and to assume that, if all four groups had been given this questionnaire at that time, all four would have reported the same attitude toward the company.

The assumption should be valid if the subjects have been randomly assigned across all four groups. An attitude measured in one of the groups should be the same attitude that would have been measured in any of the other groups if all subjects were randomly assigned across the four groups. Hence, the attitude measure in the pretest for Control Group 1 can be assumed to be the same measurement that would have been found had any of the other groups been given the pretest.

The purpose of Control Group 2 is different. This group has not participated in quality circles either, but the attitude of its members toward the company will be measured after the experimental one-month time period just as the attitudes of both experimental groups will be measured. Control Group 2 "controls" extraneous intervening variables that may have taken place outside the experimental design during the same time period. For example, if the company happens to announce unanticipated high salary increases during the experimental month, employees' attitude toward the company is likely to improve across the entire firm. The salary raises will affect both experimental groups' attitudes toward the company, and attitude posttests for those two groups will be higher than the pretest scores given by Control Group 1. The researcher will assume the quality circles resulted in improved attitude toward the company; raises may be forgotten. But an extraneous change occurring during the experimental period will be discovered in Control Group 2's posttest. This control group will score a more favorable attitude toward the company than did Control Group 1's pretest. Such a result cannot be explained by the quality circles because Control Group 2 didn't participate. An intervening variable must have occurred outside the experimental condition that caused Control Group 2 to score significantly higher than Control Group 1.

Experimental Groups

Most public relations experiments require only one experimental group. That simplifies the typical experiment considerably. But the present example requires the four-group design because two elements must be tested simultaneously: the quality circles organized by QCM and those organized by your public relations department. It isn't necessary to describe the experiment here. Suffice it to say the QCM people will perform their job properly during the month and your public relations staff will use its information and expertise to organize the best quality circles it can. At the end of the month, all four groups will be measured for product quality (unacceptable units per 100 produced) and the two experimental groups will take the posttest questionnaire on attitude toward the company.

When the posttests have been completed, an exit interview session will be held for both experimental groups. This session will contain full disclosure about the experiment's purpose and outcomes, and there should be plenty of time available for discussion among participants and a question-answer period with the public relations staff. An exit session with full disclosure is considered an ethical requirement in experiments.

You must decide at this point if the experiment has been a success. Success is not measured by whether the hypotheses have been supported or rejected. The experiment wasn't designed to improve employee attitude toward the company or reduce the number of unacceptable units. It wasn't even designed to demonstrate that your public relations department can do an equal or better job than the QCM firm. The experiment was designed to find out if quality circles should be organized across the company and if so should QCM be hired to do the organizing. A public relations professional directs formal research projects to provide management with the information it needs for correct decision making. Nothing is lost if QCM "wins" in the experiment. On the country, if QCM proves it can do the best job (a job worth $1 million to the organization), hiring QCM is the right decision. Whether QCM is worth $1 million to the organization is your CEO's decision, once the experimental data are in.

But you, the public relations vice-president, must determine if the experiment was successful.

1. Did it control all extraneous variables?
2. Are you certain that the quality circles alone were responsible for the outcomes measured at the experiment's conclusion?
3. Were the outcomes significant, or might the differences measured by the experiment have occurred by chance?
4. Are you reasonably sure that the outcomes would be the same if the procedures employed for the experimental condition were duplicated and applied to the entire company?

If you can answer yes to all these questions, make your report to the CEO and sleep comfortably. A successful experiment is one of the surest research tools public relations possesses.

Outcomes

How might the quality circle experiment outcomes be analyzed? In most experimental research projects hypothesis statements are so precise and control of variables so rigorous that the researcher has a clear idea of exactly how the data will be interpreted. Table 14.1 shows fictional data of some findings from the quality circle experiment. It doesn't show comparisons on the demographics

Table 14.1
Quality Circle Experimental Outcome Means

	Control Group #1	Control Group #2	Experimental QCM Group	Experimental PR Group	dif.
Quality of products is superior	3.2	3.3	2.3	2.4	.1
Wise use of employees and resources	3.7	3.9	2.8	2.8	--
Concerned about employees	4.0	4.1	1.9	2.3	.4*
Enjoyed past 30 days most	2.9	3.0	1.6	1.8	.2
Proud to work here	3.1	3.1	2.2	2.4	.2
Unacceptable Units per 100	4.7	4.9	1.6	2.0	.4*

* $p < .05$

such as age and sex, and we will assume this means there were no significant differences discovered in attributes of the subjects for the four randomized groups. Finding no significant differences rules out intervening variables that might be associated with the kinds of subjects selected for the different groups.

Table 14.1 provides only five of the key questionnaire items with averages from those rating scales and the unacceptable product unit average per 100. The "strongly agree" to "strongly disagree" blanks on the questionnaire have been converted to numbers with "1" being a strongly agree and "5" strongly disagree. These six means are given in columns for the pretest control group (1) and the post-test control group (2). All of the means on the rating scales are near the neutral level or below. The control group subjects don't have a very favorable attitude toward the company and, more important for purposes of the experiment, the two groups generally have the same negative attitude toward the company. Because the pretest and post-test ratings show no significant differences, you can conclude there was no attitude change in these control groups over the course of the experiment. That rules out extraneous variables beyond the scope of the experiment. In short, the comparisons that are left should be related specifically to the effects of the experimental variable, the quality circles.

You find that both experimental groups—the QCM and Precision's PR group— have ratings higher than either of the control groups' ratings. In both QCM and PR groups, subjects rated the company higher on all attitude points by agreeing more with the item statements. The differences between either experimental group's means and means of the control groups are about one-and-one-half points on the five-point scale. Additionally, unacceptable units per 100 drops from about 4.8 units in the control groups to about 2 units in the experimental groups. The impact of this decrease in unacceptable units has to be significant because the control groups had two-and-one-half times as many unacceptable units as the experimental groups. Although statistical tests (t-tests of means) would be performed on these data to determine the probability that such differences might occur by chance, it is quite evident that these are not chance findings. You can conclude definitely that the quality circles improved employees' attitudes toward the company and reduced the number of unacceptable units. The experiment's first hypothesis is supported.

The last column in the table shows differences between means of the QCM group and the PR group. The table shows that a difference of 0.4 or more on a five-point scale (with these sample sizes) is a difference great enough to occur fewer than five times out of 100 such experiments. There are two such differences noted. Employees in the QCM group thought Precision Industries is more concerned about its employees than did those in the PR group. This might be explained by the firm's having brought in an outside commercial firm to organize that quality circle. Employees may have believed Precision went to special lengths in expending resources for QCM; those employees in the PR group may have though Precision's use of its own public relations staff was nothing special. But this is just speculation. QCM may have done a better job in organizing the quality circles.

Further evidence of QCM's superiority is found in the other significant difference noted. QCM's group reduced unacceptable units per 100 by a significantly lower number than those of the PR group.

Your analysis of the comparison of means between the two experimental groups is that two of six ratings were significantly better for the QCM group; four ratings were the same. Your CEO will be told both quality circle experimental groups had positive results for employee attitudes and production quality improvements, but that the QCM-organized quality circles reduced unacceptable units per 100 by significantly more than did the PR-organized group. Whether the difference is worth $1 million to the company depends on the projected dollar value of the 0.4 difference in unacceptable units between the two procedures. That, again, is a decision for the CEO or the company's board.

SUMMARY

Surveys are usually the information-gathering tool of choice for public relations research, but they aren't always the best strategy. Experiments should be used more frequently than they are now being employed in formal research for a variety of reasons listed in the chapter. The range of experimental applications for public relations is suggested and the two research methods are compared. An example focusing on quality circles provides a framework for describing the steps appropriate in experimental design. The chapter identifies advantages and pitfalls in using experiments.

ADDITIONAL READING

Babbie, Earl R. *The Practice of Social Research*. Belmont, CA: Wadsworth, 1979, pp. 267–89.

Bowers, John Waite, and John A. Courtright. *Communication Research Methods*. Glenview, IL: Scott, Foresman, 1984, pp. 29–51.

Diebold, John. *Making the Future Work: Unleashing Our Powers of Innovation for the Decades Ahead*. New York: Simon & Schuster, 1984.

Drucker, Peter F. *The Frontiers of Management*. New York: Dutton, 1986.

The Eastman Kodak Co. *The Quality Image*. Rochester, NY: Eastman Kodak Co, 1987, pp. 28–31. Annual Report.

Hsia, H. J. *Mass Communication Research Methods: A Step-by-Step Approach*. Hillsdale, NJ: Lawrence Erlbaum Associates, 1988.

Naisbitt, John, and Patricia Aburdene. *Reinventing the Corporation*. New York: Warner Books, 1985.

Pace, R. Wayne, Robert R. Boren, and Brent D. Peterson. *Communication Behavior and Experiments: A Scientific Approach*. Belmont, CA: Wadsworth, 1975.

Peters, Thomas J., and Robert H. Waterman. *In Search of Excellence: Lessons from America's Best-Run Companies* New York: Harper & Row, 1982.

Tucker, Raymond K., Richard L. Weaver II, and Cynthia Berryman-Fink. *Research in Speech Communication*. Englewood Cliffs, NJ: Prentice Hall, 1981, pp. 123–54.

Walizer, Michael H., and Paul L. Wienir. *Research Methods and Analysis: Searching for Relationships*. New York: Harper & Row, 1978.

Wimmer, Roger D., and Joseph R. Dominick. *Mass Media Research: An Introduction*, 2d ed. Belmont, CA: Wadsworth, 1987, pp. 89–99.

15 Content Analysis

Content analysis is another formal quantitative research methodology that should be a mainstay for public relations practitioners. It actually is the formal dimension of the customary, continuing monitoring task all public relations professionals engage in. As this text has stressed throughout its discussion of informal and formal research; there is no public relations substitute for a program of scanning and tracking to keep tabs on changing social trends that might affect the practitioner's organization. Such a monitoring program—through newspapers, trade publications, and public relations journals—is the foundation of any later research effort. Content analysis takes the idea of monitoring a step further.

DEFINITION

Content analysis has been defined as the objective, systematic, and quantitative description of the manifest content of communication. Dissecting the definition into its component parts reveals that the words "objective, systematic, quantitative" relate to a rigorous scientific approach. Rather than merely adopting a program of reading, a practitioner using content analysis will be engaging in a formal procedure involving numbers, according to certain established guidelines, in a manner that excludes opinion. "Manifest content of communication" means that which is actually printed, broadcast, photographed, cabled—the message portion that can be listened to, held in the hands, or viewed. "Description," the last element of the definition, suggests that the purpose of content analysis is to describe media content. That is true, but it only touches the surface of what content analysis can do.

PUBLIC RELATIONS PURPOSES

The range of possible uses for content analysis by public relations practitioners is so varied that it defies easy description. What is sad is there are so many potential benefits of this formal research strategy, and it is used so infrequently by practitioners. Consider the following brief list of applications:

1. determining if your firm's pricing is in line by systematically monitoring the price lists of competitors
2. learning what innovations competitors have made in the field, or learning what innovations have occurred in the field in distant parts of the country or in other countries
3. identifying the major themes the mass media use when referring to your organization or its industry area: Are they favorable themes? Can these themes be altered or used to the organization's advantage?
4. monitoring the legal trends associated with your industry or field; keeping ahead of the changes in legislation as a proactive industry leader rather than a reactive follower
5. anticipating social trends that will influence the organization's work force or its image in the community
6. cataloging the social responsibility themes other organizations use to meet their community obligations; determining which causes your organization might support
7. assessing the local image of your company through analysis of news and feature stories in the local press
8. analyzing your own public relations department's releases to the mass media as a way of knowing which organization goals are being communicated
9. predicting new trends in your industry that your competitors are likely to employ
10. tapping the pulse of employee sentiment toward the organization by monitoring the themes appearing in employee communications such as posters, notices, and fliers

These are only some of the more practical applications for content analysis. A more generic approach to focusing on public relations content analysis strategies is to consider its three primary purposes.

Comparisons

How does one thing compare with another? Content analysis usually can be employed to find out if there is any "paper trail" involved. A public relations practitioner heads media relations for a Fortune 500 corporation in the petrochemical industry. Company officials complain that one of the major television networks, let's say ABC, spends more time covering oil spills than the other networks and persistently harps on problems in the petrochemical industry. If this is true, the media relations director might devote some special attention to changing ABC's views, or at least be cognizant of the problem as it might affect his or her job. But is it true?

The media relations director purchases video tapes of the three major networks' early evening news for the past six months and supervises a content analysis of all broadcast segments (news and comment) mentioning the petrochemical industry. This content analysis could show that ABC is more friendly to the industry than NBC, and it could show that all three network newscasts are likely to contain three times as many adverse portrayals of the petrochemical industry than positive stories.

Additionally, the media relations director may discover that all three networks do a poor job of covering petrochemical research and development issues. The content analysis results might suggest an increase in research and development news releases or a company-sponsored workshop on the topic for network reporters. The only aspect of this content analysis project that may exceed the budget of a media relations departments is purchasing video tapes of the newscasts. That expense can be avoided by video taping the national evening news with in-house equipment.

Fortune 500 corporations aren't the only organizations that can benefit from making comparisons through content analysis. A local agency or company could use the same strategy to analyze its media coverage on local stations or in area newspapers.

Another example of comparative content analysis is when a chamber of commerce compares its brochures with those put out by other chambers of commerce in similar communities across the country. Chambers of commerce compete with one another to locate businesses in their cities. What do similar sized communities offer prospective businesses in the way of (1) tax incentives; (2) industrial parks; (3) reduced utility rates; (4) housing for workers; (5) relocation packages; or (6) interest-free loans? Making such comparisons should be an integral part of every chamber of commerce's information needs. A public relations practitioner for the chamber would be derelict in duty if such statistics were not collected in a systematic, quantitative, and objective manner at regular intervals.

Trends

The second most common public relations use of content analysis is charting trends over time. Analyzing messages to determine changes in content keeps public relations professionals abreast of developments that may affect their organizations. An example given in this text's first chapter was the automobile manufacturers' computerized monitoring of newspaper articles on gas prices and compact cars in the mid–1970s. This content analysis project is far more massive than most practical applications require.

Consider a public relations agency whose client is a national chain of rock concert theaters. The chain plans renovations to existing facilities and construction of more theaters in the next few years. Before committing several million dollars to these projects, the client wants to know what the national trends are in its industry. It can provide attendance figures for its theaters, but it really wants to know if large-stadium rock concerts are a passing fad yielding to 5,000-seat concert halls. The public relations agency can attack the problem by doing a content analysis of rock music magazines. A sample of leading popular and trade publications during the past ten years might show the average attendance at concerts, whether they were sold out, the size of halls, names of featured groups, etc. Specifically, such a content analysis should provide the client's answer by showing trends over time: Are rock concerts still packing the house? Can the firm expect the trend to continue?

Obviously, a well-designed content analysis of national rock music magazines will produce extensive valuable information for the client including audience trends by: (1) regions; (2) type of music; (3) performer groups; (4) seasons of the year; (5) ticket prices; (6) theater size; (7) size of city; etc. The client should know some of this information already—rock concerts are the client's business. But the objective, systematic, and quantitative content analysis will confirm the client's impressions and provide additional information for the specific question at hand and for future public relations needs a rock music theater chain will have.

To avoid giving the impression that content analysis is a cure-all for public relations needs, consider a similar request by another client: a cooperative group representing minor emergency clinics in one city. This client wants to be able to predict any adverse change in public sentiment toward emergency clinics. After all, there were no independent clinics ten years ago; they developed because the public thought hospital emergency room rates were exorbitant and treatment procedures were dangerously slow. Hospitals reacted to the emergency clinics by reducing costs and improving procedures, and the hospitals have aggressively advertised their full-service emergency room facilities. The client wonders if this city's residents still view clinics as a viable health care alternative to hospital emergency rooms.

Content analysis is not the research method of choice for this project. The manifest content of communication—mass media stories, brochures published by hospitals and clinics, medical association journals, articles in health care trade publications, broadcast media news reports or commercials–will not answer the research question. These sources will certainly provide background information on which to do a research project, but to assess local residents' attitudes toward minor emergency clinics, a public opinion survey is the methodology of choice. Content analysis should be attempted only when a public relations practitioner believes the information needed can be obtained from the manifest content of communication. However, ''paper trails'' frequently do exist and can be used effectively to chart trends relevant to public relations projects.

Intent of the Message

The most specialized use of content analysis is to discover the intent of those who construct messages. Here the purpose of content analysis is to determine from the message what the messenger was thinking. Although the concept initially may seem oblique, it stands to reason that every message has a purpose. If the message is analyzed properly, the messenger's purpose will become clear.

Consider the airlines, an extremely competitive industry with each company desperately trying to maintain and gain a larger share of the traveler's dollar. There are a variety of messages each airline might use to increase its share: (1) its safety rating; (2) its comfort; (3) its on-time record; (4) its availability in the number of cities served; (5) its baggage loss record; (6) the size of its planes; (7) the quality of its flight personnel, etc. Each airline may be expected to promote those attributes in which it excels and to ignore those in which its ratings are low. To monitor an airline's record, do a content analysis of its promotional material, including its advertising. Would you rather fly with the firm that handles baggage well or with the one that boasts the highest safety record? The content of the message suggests the messenger's intent: "We'd really like to say our company has the best safety record, but we can't." That's an example of deriving meaning from the manifest content of communication.

Another example more pertinent to public relations is that of an information officer who heads a public relations department at a large military training base. Rumors—normal operating procedure in the military—have spread again that the training base may be closed. This time the base commander is concerned and asks the information officer if there is any subtle way to determine the truth.

The officer uses a direct link computer to a military and government database to scan every mention of the base during the past three months. Some 70 mentions are found and the stories or reports are down-loaded to the officer's staff. Through careful content analysis, the public information staff counts the number of positive and negative mentions about the base. Specific instances that suggest possible base closing also are recorded along with the name and rank of the legislator or military officer making the statement. If there is an intent to close the facility, messages concerning the base should reflect that intent. If the base is to be closed, it is unlikely that the Washington command will be earmarking next year's payroll or making other statements that would commit resources or personnel to the base.

While the procedure is certainly not infallible, the information officer may be able to identify an intent to close the base, if there is one, or relieve the base commander's worries if there isn't. Deriving the thinking behind messages is the most difficult content analysis procedure, but it can be one of the most worthwhile public relations research strategies. Knowledge of human nature readily allows us to expect that insights about a person's thinking will be evident in what the person says or writes.

PROJECT EXAMPLE

A straightforward public relations problem will be used to illustrate content analysis. The newly appointed head of a state's Bureau of Environmental Affairs hires a public information director whose first assignment is to provide a report—due the first date of next month—listing the state's most important environmental issues.

The public information director has just moved from a job as publications editor for the Arizona Consumer Protection Agency. In Arizona, people discussed water resource management and atomic waste, but she knows little about environmental issues, particularly in the Great Lakes region. Unfortunately, the new governor swept house, so no one in Environmental Affairs knows much more than she, including the agency head who hired her, and who now has an urgent need for accurate information.

Possibilities for a quick study include the library, governmental data bases she can access, discussions with media contacts and former department officials, and reading the bureau's published reports and brochures. While these informal research procedures will provide the foundation on which the new director can build an expertise, she is skeptical that any of these information sources actually has the range of environmental issues. Even if she can devise a list, there is no way of knowing if it would identify which issues are the most critical in this state. A public issues survey is unsatisfactory for two reasons: (1) It's unlikely that citizens will know enough about environmental issues to name more than a couple, and (2) there isn't enough time for a survey.

But there is a way to provide a report of the state's major environmental issues and to be reasonably sure the list of issues is accurately ordered. A content analysis is the answer.

CONTENT ANALYSIS PROCEDURES

As in surveys and experiments, there are established procedures that must be followed in a content analysis project. The first, as always, is the general research problem. While identifying the problem has been previously discussed the important point to remember in content analysis is that it must be possible to answer the problem by a systematic scanning of the manifest content of communication. If the records don't contain the answers, or if the records aren't available, content analysis is not the right approach.

For the environmental issues problem, there are "records" that will identify the state's important environment issues: the recent editions of the state's daily newspapers. It is reasonable to expect that the frequency of news stories on environmental issues reported in state dailies will match the general concern state residents (and public officials) have about these issues. Using the daily newspapers as a record source will avoid biases that might be present in governmental department brochures and reports. Furthermore, the state's daily newspapers are current sources and they should contain environmental issue articles from across the entire state.

Hypotheses

Stating formal hypotheses for content analysis is absolutely critical. A statement must be more than, "I'm going to count mentions of environmental issues in the state's newspapers." The statement has to say why: "I'm going to determine the order of environmental issue importance by counting the number of stories on environmental concerns in this state's daily newspapers."

The example has a single, easily identifiable purpose. This is not usually the case in content analysis. For instance, more information could be gained through this study. While the hypothesis above should be the major hypothesis of the project, subordinate hypotheses could be:

1. Environmental issue importance will be different in each of the state's four geographic areas.

2. Environmental issue importance will be different in major metropolitan areas than in less populated areas of the state.

3. Issues involving chemicals will supersede non-chemical issues.

4. Major environmental issues will be associated with identifiable special interest groups named in articles that mention these issues.

The list could continue, depending on available time and resources for the study, and the amount of information needed. If the study were to include a trend analysis—to determine which environmental concerns have changed over time—editions of the newspapers during several years would have to be included. However worthwhile such information might be, it is beyond the scope of this example.

Selecting a Sample of Messages

Sample selection is the most critical and difficult aspect of a content analysis project. It involves several distinct features, all designed to contribute to the systematic aspect of the research.

The first stage is to identify the relevant population of messages to be analyzed. At the population selection point, the primary consideration is which population of messages will best answer the research question. Part of that decision has already occurred at the hypothesis stage in which the researcher generally identifies what is to be counted. In the environmental issues example, a decision was made to count environmental issues mentioned in the state's daily newspapers. Other types of messages might have been included in the project, determined through the following kind of decision-making process. For instance, weekly newspapers might have been included or the state might have half a dozen monthly magazines that could contain environmental issue stories.

Or the public information director might have decided to include content in daily papers and news stories aired by local network-affiliated television stations.

She might have decided that the most important environmental concerns—although they would be in the newspapers—would certainly be covered by local television news in the state. In fact, newspapers might be too difficult to collect or too cumbersome to handle. Television news would emphasize the most important environmental issues (while newspapers may contain a much wider variety of more trivial issues), and there would be perhaps only one or two stories per week on each television newscast (while newspapers might have 20 stories per week). Finally, she might correctly assume that the agenda of environmental issues mentioned in the state's dailies and on the state's local newscasts will be approximately the same. That conclusion suggests counting either newspaper or television stories, but not both.

In the example, the most efficient definition of a population of messages to include will be daily newspapers. The newspapers will have a wide range of stories, and it can be assumed any significant environmental story in a weekly paper, magazine, or on television will also be covered in a daily newspaper. If for no other reason, the decision to use newspapers will be purely practical. It would be difficult to secure tapes of local news on network-affiliate stations for the past week let alone for six months. The logistics of that task make the project unmanageable. Content analysis logistics are troublesome enough without complications associated with securing the needed messages. On the other hand, the state's daily newspapers will be found in any large library, either loose on the shelves or on microfilm. A bureau staff member could be assigned to scan selected issues of two or three papers without devoting more than a day or two to the task. So, although there are alternatives, a variety of reasons make daily newspapers the right message population choice for this project.

Next, a specific sampling design must be established. Sampling of content messages depends on the amount of relevant content there is likely to be. For instance, in considering television newscasts, it was said there might only be two environmental issues stories on a newscast per week. If there are 15 towns in the state with network-affiliate stations and each town has three such stations, there are 45 stations. At two environmental stories per station per week, one week's content would be about 90 stories, so six months' content could be as many as 2,160 relevant stories. To find the 2,160 stories, coders would have to watch a half-hour news show for each of the 45 stations for the entire six months or about 7,560 half-hour newscasts. That is 157 days of watching—far beyond the toleration limits of even the most avid news viewer, and far beyond the limits of the project. So a sampling plan would have to be established to reduce the amount of time required but still represent the range of environmental issues aired during the six months.

Daily newspapers present almost as much of a sampling problem, expect there will be more stories per paper than two per week, so the incidence of relevant content is higher. As there would be far more stories in six months than the 2,160 estimated on television, a sampling plan is needed for newspapers too. The rules follow the same rules for survey sampling. Every relevant message in the population of messages to be analyzed must have an equal chance of being selected for the sample.

Let's assume there are 20 daily newspapers in the state. The public information director could begin by sampling among the 20 newspapers. If each newspaper is considered one unit, there's a potential of excluding the largest two newspapers in the state, which might account for one-third of the entire daily circulation. So a better method might be to select newspapers by circulation levels in the same multi-stage design manner of survey sampling from cities of varying populations. This might work, or the researcher might place the 20 papers into four circulation categories and sample two papers from each. That might work also, but it might exclude portions of the state that should be represented. Some reasonable sampling plan should be developed to reduce the 20 dailies to a manageable number such as 10 or 12 chosen in a random manner but which still are representative of the population of state dailies.

Another sampling step might be to exclude all portions of the papers except the first section. There's some logic in doing this, although the researcher runs the risk of missing some relevant environmental stories that might be in a lifestyle or special hunting section. Perhaps a better plan is to use only the section of a daily paper that contains the most state news. In some papers that will be the first section; in others it may be the second section. Is it justifiable to take the first section of one paper and the second section of another? Yes, because the study seeks relevant messages wherever they are found. If there are six monthly magazines in the state but only five might contain environmental stories, the sixth can be omitted from the population of relevant material.

The public information director is now down to only one section of 12 sampled daily newspapers. Even so, six months of content would produce an unnecessarily large number of environmental stories. The editions of sampled papers must be sampled. This requires some consideration for the time element. For instance, it would be possible to sample by months: to randomly select one of the six months and assign it to paper 1. But such a procedure might result in a final sample of content that excludes some major time segments.

A better method is forming a composite week of content for each newspaper. Using a calendar, select a Monday from the six-month period for paper 1, then a Tuesday, etc. Seven random draws from the six-month period produce a random week of editions for paper 1. The same procedure can be used for each of the 12 newspapers selected. Although it isn't as precise a sample of relevant content as taking all six months, the method should produce some editions for each week of the time period, and the random method of selecting composite weeks for each paper gives each edition during the six months an equal opportunity of being selected for the sample.

The public information director has spent a few hours constructing her sample of relevant messages, but she has a sample that includes a variety of daily newspapers representing different circulation levels and different parts of the state. The sample also represents the six-month time frame (in microcosm), and it has the distinct advantage of being a manageable number of newspaper sections. In fact, there are 12 papers with seven editions each or 84 sections to be scanned for relevant articles on environment. If there is an average of two environmental issue stories per section sampled, the 168 stories found should provide enough variety to answer the hypotheses. Her staff would be able to cope with the logistics of this project without too much eye strain.

Units of Analysis

The next step is defining units of analysis. *Units* are the materials that will actually be counted. While the project thus far has been considering newspaper stories, that's a rather vague concept requiring further definition. For instance, should all stories be counted or perhaps only those more than six column inches in length. For purposes of the project, a very short article may not contain the necessary details about chemicals or special interest groups to provide the information needed. What about pictures? Is a picture considered a story for purposes of this investigation? Also, as the study deals only with this state's environmental issues, it shouldn't include wire service stories about environmental concerns in other parts of the country.

The definition of units must be very specific so coders reading the newspapers can easily identify what should be included as relevant messages. Perhaps the definition of a story—the unit of analysis for this project—should be newspaper articles longer than six column inches that mention environmental issues relating to an area of this state. Notice that the definition of units could be extended to include more stories and pictures or it could be more narrowly defined to include only articles with a two-column or longer headline. What is important is that the definition of units relates to the study's purposes and that all coders can identify what constitutes a unit to be included in the study.

Categories of Analysis

The next step is to decide categories of content to be counted. *Categories* in content analysis means what will be used to answer the hypotheses. We will deal here only with the five listed hypotheses, although the newspaper articles will contain other aspects worthy of study. In brief: (1) What are the major environment issues? (2) Are they different in the state's four geographic areas? (3) Are metro area issues different from more rural areas? (4) Do chemical issues supersede non-chemical issues? and (5) Are identifiable groups named? The categories for study are these five points, all of which can be identified in the newspaper stories. But to identify them objectively will require a definition of each and a coding scheme for coders to follow in making decisions. Figure 15.1 provides a coding sheet for the study.

Each coding sheet is designed to be used for an entire week of newspaper stories, although this is only for convenience. All of the hypotheses can be

Figure 15.1
Content Analysis Coding Sheet

Paper name:_____   Section:___   Coder's Name:_____

Date of Paper	Headline's First 3 Words	Environmental Issue	State Area	Metro or Non-Metro	Group Named

Environmental Issue Codes:
1) Atomic waste
2) Other hazardous waste
3) Underground chemical dumps
4) Chemical water dumping
5) Garbage disposals/land fills
6) Strip mining/coal or shale
7) Erosion
8) Litter
9) Acid rain
10) Air pollution
11) Insecticides and crop dusting
12) Wildlife protection
13) Combination of two or more
14) Other environmental issue

Group Named:
1) Sierra Club
2) Greenpeace
3) _____
4) _____
5) _____
6) _____
7) _____
8) 2 or more
9) other
0) none named

State Areas:
1) Northeast
2) Northwest
3) Southeast
4) Southwest

Metro: 1) Over 50,000
2) 5,000 to 50,000
3) Under 5,000

257

answered through the categories that appear on the sheet as column headings. Each story will be entered on a horizontal line beginning with the date of the paper in which the article appeared. Then the coder will write the first three words of the article's headline. That is done so every story can be identified, in case there are questions about the coding. The environmental issue column will receive one of the 14 numbered values for this category; state area will get one of four values; metro or non-metro will get one of three values; and group named will get one of the values this category will have. More explanation will identify areas of concern with the form.

The critical category dealing with the kind of environmental issue is a common example of some of the difficulty with content analysis coding. An attempt has been made—we may assume after the public information director has done her reading—to include all of the likely environmental issues that may be found related to this state. However, category values in content analysis must be all-inclusive and mutually exclusive, just as they must be in survey research. That can present problems for content analysis coders, particularly when the values aren't well defined.

For example, when does an issue cease being acid rain and become air pollution or crop dusting? We think the difference should be easily identified by a coder: Acid raid will be mentioned in the story and if it isn't the coder should write '10'' in the blank for air pollution, unless the story is about crops. So, obviously, there are problems with the exclusivity of the values in this category. The same kinds of problems pertain to underground chemical dumps and land fills, erosion and strip mining. Most content analysis projects begin with a coding scheme the researcher believes will be easy for coders to follow, and in most instances the codes will have to be changed for clarity.

In the state area category, there is room for overlap if a part of the state is on one of the borderlines, in the coder's opinion. This problem can be solved easily enough. The public information director should provide coders with a state map with the four divisions marked. Mistakes will drop nearly to zero. The same approach will work in the metro versus non-metro category if coders are provided with a list of the state's city sizes. A one-page list can be found in census documents in the library.

The group named category indicates another kind of problem. A couple of likely groups may be known, but the variety of local groups that may appear in stories will not be known until coders begin reading the newspapers. This kind of problem is similar to determining variable values for a survey. The values are identified on the survey pretest. In this case, the groups named most frequently in newspaper stories will be included on the coding sheet.

CODING PROCEDURES

Content analysis requires that agreement among coders be at an acceptable level. This is called *intercoder reliability* and it means that if one coder writes that an environmental issue story took place in the northeast section of the state, another coder would have made the same decision. If coders don't agree, the entire study is pointless because the findings will be based on apples-and-oranges comparisons. The public information director can't possibly say that chemical water dumping is the most important issue if two coders reading the same story can't agree that it concerns chemical water dumping. In fact, coders must be able to reach agreement in all of the categories.

An acceptable level of intercoder reliability is 80 percent. The level is calculated by dividing the number of agreement decisions by the total number of decisions to be made in a category. Consider the state area category. If ten stories are coded on this sheet, there are ten decisions to be made under the state area category. If two coders agree in that category nine out of ten times, their intercoder reliability level is 90 percent. The 80 percent level is considered a minimum, although it is a level that often cannot be achieved in one or more of the critical hypothesis categories. For instance, with maps and lists, the 80 percent level should be reached for state area, metro, and even group named. But it is unlikely that coders will reach the 80 percent level in the major hypothesis area of environmental issues. What can be done to improve intercoder reliability?

There are several methods used to increase coder agreement:

1. *Define the values in as much detail as possible.* This removes coder doubt because very specific instructions will be provided about how to handle all of the stories that might be found. Unfortunately, this project defies very specific instructions because the variety of possible environmental issues—and the possible overlap—is so great that a page of instructions would have to be developed for each value in the category. While detailed instructions will succeed in many cases, that probably isn't a viable alternative here.

2. *Hold coding trials with coders.* Part of the usual content analysis procedure is to have one or more trials with the coding sheets using actual content that will be coded. This is the step in which an intercoder reliability percentage is established. It is also the step in which researchers discover coders can't reach agreement because the category values are so vague. Sometimes, discussions with coders after the first attempt solve enough problems to achieve an acceptable level of intercoder reliability on the next trial. These discussions involve input from the group and instructions by the researcher that result in greater understanding of how the content is to be coded. Then another attempt is made on a different set of stories. If the discussion reveals there is too much variation in the values for consensus to be reached, the trials should be discontinued until the researcher can improve the category values.

3. *Change the category values to make them more mutually exclusive.* This is often the only way to improve intercoder reliability. For instance, it might be possible to change the environmental issue values from the 14 categories to only three or four, such as environmental concerns with land surfaces, those with water, those with air, and those with underground areas. Even these broader categories may not solve the intercoder agreement problem and prevent collecting the detailed kind of information this study seeks to obtain. There is a trade-off between specificity and the coders' ability to reach agreement. In most cases, a suitable compromise can be reached.

4. *Dismiss coders who consistently do not agree with the majority*. Some people simply don't see things the way the rest of the group does. While they are certainly entitled to their individualism, they can't be coders for content analysis projects. Release them from the coding duty and let them help tabulate the results.

A coder is ready to begin coding alone when he or she has achieved an acceptable level of intercoder reliability on a sample of messages actually to be analyzed in the project. An additional check at the halfway point may be to sample a portion of the coder's finished work and have another coder do the same stories. This procedure tests that coders haven't become lax in their duty over time, and it retains confidence in the study's results. Another check should be made on a sample of every coder's content at the end of the project. Coders should be told—as a method of keeping them alert and honest—that this final check will take place.

One aspect of content analysis procedures must be stressed, although it has been implied through the four steps listed. The researcher should not do the coding. In fact, no one who knows the exact hypotheses of a content analysis project should do the actual coding of messages. If a person knows what the study's anticipated outcomes are, objectivity is compromised. The caution here is that it is too easy for coders to "find" support for the hypotheses, if they know what outcomes are anticipated. Without meaning to bias the findings, subtle decisions will be made during the counting process that result in supporting the research assumptions.

Suppose coders knew the researcher expected to find that chemical issues would supersede all other environmental concerns. Reading a newspaper article on acid rain that happened to mention a specific chemical, the coders might improperly code the article as a chemical story rather than an acid rain story. If this happened frequently, the chemical issues count would be much higher than it actually should be, erroneously supporting the hypothesis. Such a biased outcome will be prevented if coders aren't told the project's actual hypotheses.

The entire content analysis project to this point will probably have involved no more than a week of time, including the study's design, fine-tuning the coding sheet, going through one or two trials with coders, and the actual coding of the newspapers by coders. When all of the coding is complete, the analysis of results begins.

ANALYSIS OF RESULTS

By this time it should be evident that the numbers on the coding sheets will be translated into a computer program with each of the category elements (and the paper name) as a variable.

It was stated earlier that the sheets contained all of the information necessary to answer the five hypotheses of the study. How is this possible if there are only four category columns—issue, state area, metro, and group named—related to

Table 15.1
Environmental Issues Order by Percentages

	Number of Mentions	Percent of Mentions
Underground chemical dumps	31	17%
Chemical water dumping	28	14
Garbage disposals/land fills	18	9
Other hazardous waste	17	9
Insecticides and crop dusting	15	8
Wildlife protection	12	6
Acid rain	7	4
Erosion	7	4
Air pollution	5	3
Atomic waste	3	2
Strip mining/coal or shale	3	2
Litter	1	1
Combination of two or more	33	17
Other environmental issue	14	7
	194	103%*

*all percentages rounded

the five hypotheses? The explanation is that one category column answers two hypotheses. Environmental issue provides an ordering of issue importance and will show if chemical issues are more important than other issues.

Knowing the state's environmental issue order of importance is the bureau's primary need. The public information officer will have performed her assigned task admirably if she can provide a list, and she'll be able to do this by counting the mention percentage for each issue and arranging them in an order similar to that shown in Table 15.1.

Further presentation of the issue outcomes is suggested in Table 15.2. A table similar to this could be shown for findings related to metro versus non-metro areas of the state, group named, and whether chemicals as a group is a more important issue than others.

The findings shown in Table 15.2 go beyond what the bureau chief ordered, but this information was not much more difficult to obtain than the primary order of environmental issues. And Table 15.2's findings begin to describe subtle differences about the state's geographic regions that can be addressed in the

Table 15.2
Environmental Issues Rank by State Area

	Rank by Entire	North- east	North- west	South- east	South- west
Underground chemical dumps	1	1	2	6	7.5
Chemical water dumping	2	2	1	7	6
Garbage disposals/land fills	3	4	3	8	7.5
Other hazardous waste	4	3	6	5	5
Insecticides and crop dusting	5	9	10	4	1
Wildlife protection	6	12	11	2	3
Acid rain	7.5	5	4	10	9
Erosion	7.5	10	12	3	2
Air pollution	9	6.5	5	11	11
Atomic waste	10.5	8	7	9	10
Strip mining/coal or shale	10.5	11	9	1	4
Litter	12	6.5	8	12	12

public information director's report to her bureau chief. For instance, the southern area of the state is more agrarian while the northern area is more industrial. Of course, anyone who has looked at a state map would know that information, yet the implications of urban versus rural regions' concerns about environmental issues might not be as clear, even to career veterans of the Bureau of Environmental Affairs. The differentiation of issue importance derived from content analysis is important, basic information all bureau personnel should know. There is no doubt such a report will become required reading for everyone in the department.

VALUE OF THE STUDY

This content analysis project has documented which environmental issues are of primary concern in the state. It also shows which concerns are of interest in the state's several geographic regions and in the more concentrated population areas. Additionally, it links special interest groups with the issues they support, thus identifying opinion leaders who should be excellent contacts for the bureau in its future public relations activities.

The project took some thought and required some time and personnel resources of the department. But, regardless of which day-to-day activities of the public information department may have been delayed to complete this project, its value to the bureau is evident. Public relations staff members who read the newspapers and coded the stories have just been through a one-week advanced training course in environmental issue concerns. They will be able to speak and write knowledgeably about current events related to the bureau's mission, and they will possess information that makes them more expert in their daily public relations activities. Had the bureau sponsored a week-long retreat in which the entire department heard presentations by the state's environmental leaders, the staff's knowledge gain would probably not have been greater than what this content analysis provided.

SUMMARY

Content analysis is another form of quantitative research a public relations practitioner should frequently consider as an information-gathering tool. It is defined as the objective, systematic, and quantitative description of the manifest content of communication. The parts of this definition are discussed along with the range of uses for content analysis in answering public relations questions: comparisons, trends, and message/messenger's intent. A case study dealing with environmental issues provides a framework for discussing the steps in a content analysis study including sampling, units and categories of analysis, coding procedures, and analysis of results. The chapter notes benefits of involving a public relations staff in a content analysis project.

ADDITIONAL READING

Budd, Richard W., Robert K. Thorp, and Lewis Donohew. *Content Analysis of Communications*. New York: Macmillian, 1967.

Chadwick, Bruce A., Howard M. Bahr, and Stan L. Albrecht. *Social Science Research Methods*. Englewood Cliffs, NJ: Prentice Hall, 1984.

Holsti, Ole R. "Content Analysis." In *The Handbook of Social Psychology: Research Methods*, Vol. 2, ed. G. Linzeyf and E. Aronson. Cambridge, MA: Addison-Wesley, 1968, pp. 596–692.

Krippendorff, Klaus. *Content Analysis: An Introduction to Its Methodology*. Sage CommText Series, Vol. 5. Beverly Hills, CA: Sage, 1980.

Krippendorff, Klaus, and Michael F. Eleey. "Monitoring a Group's Symbolic Environment." *Public Relations Review* 12:1 (Spring 1986): 13–36.

Stempel, Guido H. III. "Content Analysis." In *Research Methods in Mass Communication*, ed. Guido H. Stempel and Bruce H. Westley. Englewood Cliffs, NJ: Prentice Hall, 1981, pp. 119–131.

Wimmer, Roger D., and Joseph R. Dominick. *Mass Media Research: An Introduction*, 2d ed. Belmont, CA: Wadsworth, 1987, pp. 165–187.

16 Quasi-Quantitative Procedures

Three other formal research methods for public relations deserve mention because they have become popular information-gathering tools during the past decade. They are focus groups, Delphi studies, and communication audits. Of the three, only Delphi studies represent a distinct form of research. Focus groups and communications audits are formal research procedures associated with strategies previously discussed.

FOCUS GROUPS

The first mention of focus groups in the text was in conjunction with survey research. In that context, a focus group was suggested as a means of gathering insights from a small group of people taken from the larger population that would later be surveyed. The intent was to learn if the researcher's impressions of what the population might be thinking are on target. It is possible that even extensive informal information-gathering will omit significant concerns of the current population be studied. A focus group was used in the Cumberland Presbyterian Church survey so the researchers could determine what church members actually thought about the two church publications under study. Comments provided by the focus group were used to formulate items for the survey questionnaire form. Although use of focus groups is still recommended as a prelude for survey research, public relations researchers also rely on focus groups as the only formal information-gathering method in some projects.

A focus group consists of about six to 12 subjects selected from the population to be studied. If a company is interested in knowing about employees' views on plant safety, the public relations department might arrange to have ten subjects from the plant convene in a semistructured discussion group led by a public relations staff member or a paid consultant. The rationale is that subjects selected from the population will have opinions that would be found if a more formal sampling of the entire plant's employee work force were surveyed on the topic. If a dozen employees are brought in to discuss safety problems, perhaps most of the concerns of all plant employees will be reflected during the discussion.

The advantage is evident. A focus group is a relatively quick and inexpensive method of finding out the population's general attitude on a given topic. In fact, the efficiency of focus groups would seem to make them the research method of choice for most studies. Unfortunately, that is not the case because there are several drawbacks that prevent focus groups from achieving their potential as a formal research strategy.

The first drawback is that focus groups are not representative samples of a population. Using only six to 12 subjects does not provide enough representation on which to base valid conclusions. And focus group subjects aren't selected in a random manner. Because the researcher is attempting to discover the range of opinion in a population, focus group subjects are selected to represent the range of people in the population. A diversity of demographics—age, sex, occupational level, length of employment with the firm, etc.—is sought in choosing subjects for focus groups. However, there is no possibility of selecting subjects whose composite demographics actually do match the population. So a focus group is never really representative of the entire population

Second, and perhaps the most important drawback of focus groups, is that the groups don't reflect the proportion of opinion that might be found in a random sample of the population. Management and clients tend to forget this limitation. They assume that if two of 10 focus group subjects hold a similar viewpoint, that viewpoint will be found in about 20 percent of the entire population under study. This is a false assumption that can result in erroneous conclusions drawn from the focus group findings.

Third, while a focus group's discussion may reflect the entire range of opinion in the population, it also may not. The subjects have not been selected in a random manner, so their membership may exclude an important segment of the population that holds significantly different opinions.

A fourth drawback, related to focus groups' inability to provide the range of opinion, is that discussion sessions involve group dynamics which often prevent the range of opinion from being aired. For instance, it is likely that one or more members of the group will be too shy (or too uncomfortable in a group setting) to express their opinion, particularly if they perceive their views to be different from those already given at the table. Also, one or more members of the group may try to dominate the discussion, and the range of opinion won't be tapped in such situations either. So all the problems associated with interpersonal communication in groups is present in focus groups, and this group dynamic can prevent the researcher from gathering a sufficient range of viewpoints.

Yet with all of these noted limitations, effective focus groups can provide valuable information for public relations research. Some of the drawbacks can be overcome by using multiple focus group sessions. Using several focus groups increases input—more opinions, and probably more diverse opinions will be expressed. Multiple groups don't make the opinions representative of the population, but using several groups does increase the likelihood that the range of opinion will be tapped. Also, if a problem occurs in one group (a subject dominates the discussion), researchers can adjust their procedures to prevent that problem from recurring in successive group sessions.

The real benefit of focus group research is that it allows the greatest individual comment by subjects. Answers will be couched in the subjects' own words; the frame of reference will be that of the subjects rather than one structured by the researcher on a questionnaire form. This lack of structure has the disadvantage of being difficult to "code." Comments are often diverse and highly individualized. Synthesizing the results to identify common threads of opinion requires painstaking care and extensive time commitment during the data analysis stage. But management or the client will require that the focus group's comments be synthesized. Otherwise, it will be impossible to act on the information gathered.

A variety of excellent, recent publications (some of which are listed in the suggested readings at the end of this chapter) offer step-by-step guidelines for doing focus groups. In brief, these are the general procedures:

1. A research problem is identified that might be answered using the focus group procedure. Hypotheses should be stated clearly to direct the discussion along topic lines that are likely to provide the information needed.

2. Public relations staff members (or a firm specializing in focus group research) should hold several working conferences to design a script for the focus group session. Scripts consist of a series of questions or discussion statements that perform these functions: They put focus group members at ease; define the topic area of discussion; encourage participation by all subjects; seek specific answers for the research questions; and urge respondents to provide information the researcher may not have anticipated.

3. A date, time, and place are set for the focus group session. Date and time should be convenient for subjects. The place should be accessible, and travel directions should be given. The focus group meeting room should be chosen with care. It should be comfortable, large enough to accommodate a dozen people around a table, and well lighted. The room might require technical equipment, such as video taping facilities or other means of recording the session, and two-way mirrors.

4. Subjects should be carefully chosen to include the widest possible variety of representatives of the population under study. Actually, the focus group literature suggests care in selecting demographic ranges. In fact, the classic focus group would be an extremely homogeneous segment of the population. The argument for homogeneity is that it promotes freedom in group discussion. For instance, if a group is composed of six line workers and two supervisors, the line workers are likely to withhold any true feelings critical of their supervisors and management generally. Also, the supervisors may dominate group discussion or the line workers may defer to their supervisors' opinion. A researcher would be ill advised to include a wealthy middle-aged

women in a general population focus group on women's fashion if the remaining members were all in their teens or early twenties. So homogeneity is recommended to improve group performance. But a goal of focus groups is to tap the intended population's opinion as widely as possible. Demographic variability among subjects is necessary. How can the two approaches be combined? The answer is multiple focus groups, with members of each group selected for their homogeneity. If there are several key variables—years on the job, male versus female, job level, union versus non-union membership—a focus group should be held for each. Of course, the more focus groups required, the greater the time required and the more expense. Holding ten focus group sessions might be self-defeating if saving time and money is a research priority.

5. Subjects may be paid a stipend for participating in the session, or they may be compensated for their time and effort in some other manner.

6. A group moderator—usually the public relations director, a member of the staff, or a paid consultant—should be well prepared before attempting to lead the focus group. This moderator will begin the session by asking questions from the script.

7. The discussion should be flexible enough to allow subjects to deviate from questions in the script, if that seems beneficial. However, the moderator should remain in control of the session and should ensure that the primary research concerns are discussed.

8. Following the focus group session, tapes should be reviewed and discussed among the public relations staff members. The data, which will be in the form of general discussion, should be analyzed for recurrent themes and deviant viewpoints.

9. A report should be written that includes the procedures used, the script, the findings, and recommendations.

If it is clear that the first few focus group sessions have not answered the research questions sufficiently, more sessions should be arranged. When the public relations researcher is satisfied that little new information can be gained, the focus group sessions should be concluded. At this point, a random survey of the population may be indicated, or the public relations professional may be confident that the needed information has been obtained through focus group research.

DELPHI STUDIES

Delphi studies were begun in the early 1970s as a method of forecasting. Forecasting is an attempt to predict the future: how things might be one year, five years, ten years, or 50 years from today. Futurist societies were the first to use the research tactic on a broad scale by asking scientists to predict the effects that technological changes might have on society in the year 2025.

In public relations, the strategy might be to forecast the future of an organization, its relationship to its community or society, its products or policies, or to make predictions about any matter that might be critical to an organization's future. If this sounds like science fiction, consider that most research is designed to be predictive. Being better prepared to grapple with future decisions is a primary organizational concern. The data-gathering mechanism on which future decisions will be based is properly the domain of public relations.

Delphi studies are highly qualitative in nature. Researchers directing such studies identify a panel of experts. These individuals usually include some experts who will be using the information (company management) and some highly qualified experts both inside and outside the organization who have specialized knowledge on the subject being forecast. Such individuals might include product development managers, college professors with specialties in the interest area, community and regional business leaders, politicians, writers, and others with widely diverse backgrounds who can be identified as possessing knowledge worth obtaining. The idea is to arrive at a polled judgment from these experts on which to make the forecast.

Staff members directing the Delphi study design an initial questionnaire. It might be very open-ended, merely stating the topic and asking the experts for a written narrative, or it might be more structured with a series of questions directing short, essay-type responses. Each subject is sent the questionnaire form, usually through the mail or through lines linked to home or office computers. Answers from the initial questionnaire are compiled and synthesized, and these form the basis of a second questionnaire that solicits more focused and more detailed responses from the same panel of experts. Several more waves may be used as the Delphi project continues, seeking replies to even more specific probes. Finally, the research directors analyze and synthesize the results, and the completed responses are sent back to the experts to rank or rate the outcomes provided by all panelists. The staff prepares a summary report based on the expert group's consensus of opinion.

Delphi studies have been extensively used in recent years to identify public concerns or to estimate future conditions. For instance, a planning commission might wish to estimate the kinds of budgetary needs a city could face in the next two decades. There is no assurance that past conditions will continue to prevail, or even that today's budget expenditures will reflect future needs. A Delphi study may be the best approach to long-range planning. Recently, a city's cable television licensee wanted to know what kind of special programming should be aired to best meet the needs of citizens. This is the type of question that is not easily answered through a random survey of citizens, half of whom do not subscribe to cable service and many of whom watch only sports or movie channels if they do subscribe. Again, a Delphi study that relies on a panel of carefully selected community leaders—in education, business, medical, public service, the arts, etc.—might be the best research method to estimate the community's future cable programming needs.

COMMUNICATION AUDITS

This form of quasi-quantitative research is not really a distinct research method type. Communication audits embody the full range of formal and informal strategies, and they have become a frequently discussed tactic for public relations practice. The objective of a communication audit is to assess an organization's communication, primarily its internal communication networks, including the print and electronic messages it produces.

Theoretically, an "audit" is performed when management perceives some problem with the organization's communication. The goal is to identify what problems exist, determine why the problems exist, and decide what should be done to correct them. However, from a practical standpoint, communication audits are performed when the organization experiences management changes (as a method of assessing the state of communications), in a crisis situation, and as a periodic check on the organization's information flow. Ideally, auditing should be an on-going process to ensure effective communication flow.

A communication audit consists of a variety of formal and informal research tactics. Typically, employees and other target audiences of organization messages are queried about their satisfaction with the flow of information. The public relations department's print and electronic messages such as video tapes, newsletters, and brochures are audited to determine if their content is reaching the intended audience and having its intended effect. This is usually done through formal surveys and readership studies of the publications. Additionally, content analysis procedures might be used to determine what communication messages are being disseminated. Focus groups are often scheduled to discuss the publications and to assess the more general attitude of employees about flow of information in the organization.

One other tactic for information-gathering is usually employed in a communications audit: one-on-one interviews between target audience members and the researcher. Although the tactic is considered informal research, these interviews are approached in a more formal manner with a structured question form. The replies to open-ended questions and the additional comments offered by interviewees are compiled and analyzed by the researcher. A synthesis of findings from these individual interview sessions forms the report researchers will make to management.

Two aspects of communication audits have been extensively discussed in the public relations literature recently. One is whether a communication audit should be directed by the organization's public relations staff or an outside consulting firm. The current advice is to have an audit done by paid consultants from outside the company. This approach removes any bias that might be present if the audit is performed by those whose duties are being audited. Allowing the organization's public relations staff to do the audit is tantamount to having a bank teller audit his or her own cash receipt statements. It should be evident from the term "audit" that deficiencies may be identified in the public relations department's procedures. Results of an audit can include personnel changes and alterations in the print and electronic messages produced. Doing audits periodically—as a regular assessment of organizational communication—reduces fears that the firm's expectation is to find deficiencies and make drastic changes.

The other aspect of a communication audit that has received considerable attention involves the historic distinction between quantitative and qualitative research methods. Some leading authorities on communication audits insist that procedures should be quantitative because they involve survey and content analysis methodology. The assumed greater objectivity of quantifying data is thought to result in unbiased, numerical documentation of findings. For instance, employees' attitude toward information flow in the company may have been 3.6 measured on a five-point scale three years ago. Today it is 4.1. A "documented" attitude improvement has occurred. Such quantification is supposed to remove subjective judgment from the assessment process. However, other authorities insist that quantification eliminates the more subtle and richer lode of information that would be gained through open discussions between researchers and audience members. These authorities claim a quantitative increase from 3.6 to 4.1 may show improvement, but it tells little about the target audience's attitude on which to make management recommendations. Qualitative methods, such as one-on-one discussions, provide directions for correcting communication deficiencies.

The dilemma of quantitative versus qualitative research cannot be solved here. Both methods can provide objective findings and sufficient information on which to base decisions. In fact, most authorities recommend a blend of quantitative and qualitative procedures for communication audits. The strategy embodies the overriding principle offered in this text: Use the research procedure that will answer information needs in the most efficient manner.

SUMMARY

Three quasi-quantitative research methods are described and discussed as they apply to public relations information needs: focus groups, Delphi studies, and communication audits.

General procedures are given for each of these research strategies, as well as their advantages and limitations. Focus groups, while they have some distinct drawbacks as methods to assess attitude in any population, do offer a quick and relatively inexpensive way of gathering information that suggests the range of audience opinion. Delphi studies are relatively recent research designs that have gained popularity in public relations. Communication audits are described as a combination of more traditional research methods—a blend of quantitative and qualitative procedures used to assess an organization's information flow.

ADDITIONAL READING

Ayres, Robert U. *Uncertain Futures: Challenges for Decision-Makers.* New York: John Wiley, 1978.

Calder, Bobby J., "Focus Groups and the Nature of Qualitative Marketing Research." *Journal of Marketing Research* (August 1977): 14, 353–64.

Delbecq, Andre L. *Group Techniques for Program Planning: A Guide to Nominal Group and Delphi Processes.* Glenview, IL: Scott, Foresman, 1975.

Finn, Peter, and Mary-Kay Harrity. "Research." In Bill Cantor, *Experts in Action: Inside Public Relations*. New York: Longman, 1984, pp. 273–87.

Goldhaber, Gerald M. *Organizational Communication*. 4th ed. Dubuque, IA: Wm. C. Brown, 1986.

Hamilton, Seymour. *A Communication Audit Handbook: Helping Organizations Communicate*. New York: Longman, 1987.

Kreps, Gary. *Organizational Communication*. New York: Longman, 1986.

Krueger, Richard A. *Focus Groups: A Practical Guide for Applied Research*. Newbury Park, CA: Sage, 1988.

Linstone, Harold A., and Murray Turoff. *The Delphi Method: Techniques and Applications*. Reading, MA: Addison-Wesley Publishing Co., 1975.

Lorz, F. Michael. "Focus Group Research in a Winning Campaign." *Public Relations Review* 10:2 (Summer 1984):28–38.

Morgan, David L. *Focus Groups as Qualitative Research*. Newbury Park, CA: Sage, 1988.

Moriampolski, Hy. "The Resurgence of Qualitative Research." *Public Relations Journal* 40:7 (July 1984): 21–23.

Reynolds, Fred D., and Deborah K. Johnson. "Validity of Focus Group Findings." *Journal of Advertising Research* 18:3 (1978): 21–4.

Rothman, Jack. *Using Research in Organizations: A Guide to Successful Application*. Beverly Hills, CA: Sage, 1980.

Turk, Judy VanSlyke. "Forecasting Tomorrow's Public Relations." *Public Relations Review* 12:3 (Fall 1986): 12–21.

Wimmer, Roger D., and Joseph R. Dominick. *Mass Media Research: An Introduction*. 2d ed. Belmont, CA: Wadsworth, 1987, pp. 151–55, 485–92.

Bibliography

Andrews, Patricia Hayes, and John E. Baird, Jr. *Communication for Business and the Professions*. 3d ed. Dubuque, IA: Wm. C. Brown, 1986.

Beck, Arthur C., and Ellis D. Hillman. *Positive Management Practices*. San Francisco: Jossey-Bass, 1986.

Bivens, Thomas. *Handbook for Public Relations Writing*. Chicago: National Textbook Co., 1988.

Breen, George, and A. B. Blankenship. *Do-It-Yourself Marketing Research*. 2d ed. New York: McGraw-Hill, 1982.

Burton, Paul. *Corporate Public Relations*. New York: Reinhold, 1966.

Center, Allen H., ed. *Public Relations Ideas in Action*. New York: McGraw-Hill, 1957.

Chase, W. Howard. *Issue Management: Origins of the Future*. Stamford, CT: Issue Action Publications, 1984.

Coates, Joseph F. *Issues Management: How You Can Plan, Organize & Manage for the Future*. Mt. Airy, MD: Lomond Publications, 1986.

Daniels, Tom D., and Barry K. Spiker. *Perspectives on Organizational Communication*. Dubuque, IA: Wm. C. Brown, 1987.

Ehrenkranz, Lois B., and Gilbert R. Kahn. *Public Relations/Publicity: A Key Link in Communications*. New York: Fairchild, 1983.

Goldman, Jordan. *Public Relations in the Marketing Mix: Introducing Vulnerability Relations*. Chicago: Crain, 1984.

Haberman, David A., and Harry A. Dolphin. *Public Relations: The Necessary Art*. Ames, IA: Iowa State University Press, 1988.

Heath, Robert L., and Richard A. Nelson. *Issues Management: Corporate Public Policymaking in an Information Society*. Beverly Hills, CA: Sage, 1986.

Hendrix, Jerry A. *Public Relations Cases*. Belmont, CA: Wadsworth, 1988.

Kastens, Merritt L. *Long Range Planning for Your Business: An Operating Manual*. New York: AMACOM, 1976.

Lesley, Philip. *The People Factor: Managing the Human Climate*. Homewood, IL: Dow Jones-Irwin, 1974.

Londgren, Richard E. *Communication by Objectives: A Guide to Productive & Cost-Effective Public Relations & Marketing.* Englewood Cliffs, NJ: Prentice Hall, 1983.

McDonald, James O. *Management without Tears: A Guide to Coping with Everyday Organizational Problems.* Chicago: Crain, 1981.

McGregor, Georgette F., and Joseph A. Robinson. *The Communication Matrix: Ways of Winning with Words.* New York: AMACOM, 1981.

Meyer, John W., and W. Richard Scott. *Organizational Environments: Ritual and Rationality.* Beverly Hills, CA: Sage, 1983.

Munter, Mary. *Guide to Managerial Communication.* 2d ed. Englewood Cliffs, NJ: Prentice Hall, 1987.

Nagelschmidt, Joseph S., ed. *The Public Affairs Handbook.* New York: AMACOM, 1982.

Nolte, Lawrence W. *Fundamentals of Public Relations; Professional Guidelines, Concepts and Integrations.* 2d ed. New York: Pergamon, 1979.

Olasky, Marvin N. *Corporation Public Relations: A New Historical Perspective.* Hillsdale, NJ: Lawrence Erlbaum Associates, 1987.

Pavlik, John V. *Public Relations: What Research Tells Us.* Beverly Hills, CA: Sage, 1987.

Peake, Jacquelyn. *Public Relations in Business.* New York: Harper & Row, 1980.

Pope, Jeffrey L. *Practical Marketing Research.* New York: AMACOM, 1981.

Rice, Ronald E., and William J. Paisley, eds. *Public Communications Campaigns.* Beverly Hills, CA: Sage, 1981.

Roalman, A. R. *Profitable Public Relations.* Homewood, IL: Dow Jones-Irwin, 1968.

Robinson, Edward J. *Communication and Public Relations.* Columbus, OH: Charles E. Merrill, 1966.

Schiller, Herbert I. *Information and the Crisis Economy.* New York: Oxford University Press, 1986.

Schoenfeld, Clarence A. *Publicity Media and Methods: Their Role in Modern Public Relations.* New York: Macmillan, 1963.

Schramm, Wilbur, and William E. Porter. *Men, Women, Messages, and Media: Understanding Human Communication.* 2d ed. New York: Harper & Row, 1982.

Seitel, Fraser P. *The Practice of Public Relations.* 3d ed. Columbus, OH: Merrill, 1987.

Soderberg, Norman R. *Public Relations for the Entrepeneur and the Growing Business.* Chicago: Probus, 1986.

Steinberg, Charles S. *The Creation of Consent: Public Relations in Practice.* New York: Hastings House, 1975.

Walsh, Frank. *Public Relations Writer in a Computer Age.* Englewood Cliffs, NJ: Prentice Hall, 1986.

Weilbacher, William M. *Auditing Productivity: Advertiser-Agency Relationships Can Be Improved.* New York: Association of National Advertisers, 1981.

Williams, Frederick. *The Communications Revolution.* Beverly Hills, CA: Sage, 1982.

Wimmer, Roger D., and Joseph R. Dominick. *Mass Media Research: An Introduction.* 2d ed. Belmont, CA: Wadsworth, 1987.

Index

ABOUT THE AUTHORS

E. W. BRODY teaches public relations in the Department of Journalism at Memphis State University in Tennessee and maintains a public relations consulting practice in Memphis.

Public Relations Research is his fourth book. *Public Relations Programming and Production* was published by Praeger in 1988, while *Communicating for Survival: Coping with Diminishing Human Resources* and *The Business of Public Relations* were published in 1987.

Dr. Brody's articles on public relations have appeared in *Public Relations Journal, Public Relations Quarterly, Public Relations Review, Journalism Quarterly, Legal Economics, Health Care Management Review,* the *Journal of the Medical Group Management Association, Modern Healthcare, Hospital Public Relations,* and other publications. He serves on the editorial boards of *Public Relations Quarterly* and *PR Strategies USA.*

GERALD C. STONE is professor and coordinator of the Graduate Program in Journalism at Memphis State University. He is accredited by the Public Relations Society of America and is immediate past chairman of PRSA'S Midwest District. He teaches classes in journalistic writing and reporting, theories of communication, and research methods.

Dr. Stone is the author of *Examining Newspapers: What Research Reveals about America's Newspapers,* and is coauthor with Michael Singletary of *Communication Theory and Research Applications.* He is author or coauthor of more than 50 scholarly and professional journal articles in such publications as *Public*

Relations Review, Newspaper Research Journal, Journalism Quarterly, ANPA News Research Bulletin, Journalism Educator, Research in Higher Education, FEEDBACK, The Quill, Computer Publisher, and *Publishers' Auxiliary.* He also has authored several book chapters and monographs. He was founding editor of *Newspaper Research Journal.*

Dr. Stone earned his B.A.J. and M.A. degrees at Louisiana State University, where he is a member of the Manship School of Journalism Hall of Fame, and his Ph.D. degree in mass communication research at the Newhouse School of Public Communications at Syracuse University.